An Executive's Guide to Forecasting

AN EXECUTIVE'S
GUIDE TO FORECASTING

JOHN C. CHAMBERS · Xerox Corporation

SATINDER K. MULLICK · Corning Glass Works

DONALD D. SMITH · Corning Glass Works

A WILEY-INTERSCIENCE PUBLICATION

JOHN WILEY & SONS, New York · London · Sydney · Toronto

Library of Congress Cataloging in Publication Data:

Chambers, John Carlton, 1928-
   An executive's guide to forecasting.

   "A Wiley-Interscience publication."
   Bibliography: p.
   1. Sales forecasting. 2. Business forecasting.
3. Decision-making. I. Mullick, Satinder K., joint
author. II. Smith, Donald D., joint author.
III. Title.

HF5415.2.C38   658.4'03   74-2433
ISBN 0-471-14335-9

Printed in the United States of America

10 9 8 7 6 5 4

To
SHARON, MOHINI, and PEG

Preface

Although a lot has been written about forecasting, most of it has been directed toward a few specific areas or techniques, such as technological forecasting, time series analysis, or forecasting for production and inventory control. Only a few books have attempted to discuss the general subject of forecasting, and never have all of the major techniques and important considerations in forecasting been put together under a single cover. We have written this book not only to accomplish that objective but also to present the material so that it can be understood by managers, analysts, and other personnel who have had little previous exposure to forecasting techniques.

We first discuss the basic principles of forecasting and the major techniques that are used. Since the purpose of forecasting is to provide information for decision making, we then describe how the various techniques can be applied to the typical decisions made during the different phases of the product life cycle. We conclude by considering how one can manage and evaluate a forecasting activity and what further advances in forecasting methodology and techniques can be expected in the future.

Of the many sources of help and encouragement, we particularly want to give thanks to Corning Glass Works and many of its executives where we have had numerous opportunities to extend and apply our forecasting knowledge and where the seed of this book was germinated. We extend special acknowledgment to Walter MacBeth, senior editor for the *Harvard Business Review,* who assisted us in the preparation of the HBR article that served as the impetus and catalyst for this book, and to G. Scott Hutchison, executive editor of the *Harvard Business Review,* who helped considerably by editing the entire manuscript. Finally, we thank Kathryn Schmidt for her typing of the final manuscript.

JOHN C. CHAMBERS
SATINDER K. MULLICK
DONALD D. SMITH

Rochester, New York
Corning, New York
January 1974

Contents

Introduction

Each individual and most areas of business have always been interested in the future. As Charles F. Kettering has succinctly put it, "We should all be concerned about the future, because that's where we'll have to spend the rest of our lives." Looking ahead gives more perspective to the present than looking at the present alone.

Thus, in virtually all areas of decision making, some form of forecast is either explicitly or implicitly used. If it is a formal forecast, the decision maker should know how the forecast was derived—that is, the basic assumptions, the input data, and the possible forecast error or range within which the forecast is considered accurate. If no forecast has been given to the decision maker, he will either derive his own, or—by not preparing a formal forecast—he will infer one in arriving at a decision. (For example, he might say that there will be no change from the current level, or growth will continue at its historical rate.)

Since forecasting is so vital in decision making, it is critical that the manager have sufficient knowledge about forecasting techniques and methodology so that he can assign some degree of credibility to the forecast and question the analyst concerning assumptions, type of method used, relevance of historical information, and effects of various events on the forecast.

This book is for the decision maker who wants to be aware of available forecasting techniques, their accuracy, strengths, and limitations and his own role in the forecasting process. It does not contain detailed mathematical descriptions of these techniques; rather, it is concerned with how they can be used and the basic concepts behind them, with numerous examples of industrial and business applications. The manager needs only a nodding acquaintance with quantitative methods. Our objective is to assist him in becoming a more qualified user of forecasts derived from the techniques described and to help him understand how he can incorporate the forecasts and estimates of errors into his decision-making process.

The book is also for the analyst who must make occasional forecasts and wants to have a general knowledge of the available techniques. He will then be in a position to benefit from further instruction, either formally or through the literature, in the mathematical bases of the techniques or to utilize the consultation services of an experienced forecaster. (A bibliography of the various forecasting techniques that we discuss is given in Appendix A.)

Throughout this book, the emphasis is on the use of forecasting in the decision-making process. Therefore, we have organized the material so that the techniques appropriate for each type of decision are considered together. Although some duplication in the discussion of the various techniques can scarcely be avoided, it should prove helpful in understanding their applications. All of the commonly used techinques will be covered: qualitative techniques, causal models, time-series analysis, and other statistical techniques.

Numerous examples are included to show how the techniques have been applied in various business and industrial situations. They cover such areas of applications as manufacturing, marketing, financial, and new business and facilities planning. These examples are drawn primarily from our combined experience at Corning Glass Works, where most of the techniques have been successfully applied, but also include applications from previous employment positions and knowledge of work done by others. The effects of the forecasts on the related decisions are usually described; however, because of their confidential nature, we have understandably disguised the source of some of our illustrative examples.

Before our discussion of the various aspects of forecasting in Chapter 1, however, let us first define such terms as *forecasting, prediction, manager,* and *analyst*. These words are used interchangeably by some persons, while having different connotations to others.

Forecasting is generally defined as looking at what has happened in the past and attempting to project this historical experience into the future. Primarily based on analytical techniques, forecasting also considers various events and qualitative factors, where past fluctuations due to special events are evaluated and appropriately included in the forecast.

Prediction is an attempt to anticipate what will happen in the future with respect to various events, such as strikes, competitive actions, price promotions, and so on, and using these judgments, to make estimates for the future. Primarily based on how one perceives that future events will affect sales (or whatever is being predicted), prediction also takes into account current performance and trends. Obviously, prediction can be more effective if it considers what has occurred in the past, in order that there might be a basis for estimating the impact of future events and for knowing what the current sales rate is.

The term forecasting will refer to techniques that include both forecasting and prediction—that is, techniques in which analysis of historical information, establishment of relationships, projection of trends and relationships, and prediction of various events and their impact on "statititcal forecasts" are all coordinated in deriving an accurate forecast.

Most of the references and illustrations given relate to sales forecasts. However, virtually all estimates included in planning can be called forecasts, whether they are estimates of sales (units and price), production costs, capital expenditures, tax rates, or personnel requirements. Unless otherwise noted, the approaches and techniques presented apply to all types of estimates. A notable exception is in the estimation of production costs, where the use of the learning or experience curve has extensive applications, as we shall discuss later.

The examples given are primarily related to durable goods. We recognize that there are significant differences in the market characteristics of durable and nondurable goods, and distinctions are made where appropriate. These differences will often cause different approaches to be taken and techniques to be used. Services are becoming an increasingly larger segment of our economy, and some discussion or suggestions on how services should be treated are given.

While *manager* is the word we use for the decision maker, decision maker refers actually to the person who ultimately makes the decision, whether or not he is specifically in a management position. He is the consumer of the forecast, incorporating it into his decision.

The term *analyst* indicates the person or persons preparing the forecast, ignoring his organizational position, which could be staff or line (and possibly management).

Chapter I

Strategic Importance
of Forecasting
in Decision Making

One of the best known and most publicized failures in American business has been Ford's Edsel automobile, which made its public appearance in 1957. Many reasons have been given for the Edsel's failure; the reason mentioned most frequently is incorrectly forecasting the potential market. But other factors, such as bad timing, poor quality, and the name itself, appear to have contributed to the Edsel's poor market performance. However, since these other factors might have been considered either explicitly or implicitly in the decision-making process, they also relate indirectly to forecasting.

An analysis of why the forecasting error for the Edsel was so large reveals that the car industry's market forecasts in the mid-1950s did not consider what the customer wanted, rather, only what the manufacturers in Detroit had concluded the customer wanted. At that time, according to Harvard's Theodore A. Levitt, the carmakers did not conduct research on customer wants but on customer preferences among the kinds of things the manufacturers had already decided to offer.[1] Thus the industry's market research of the mid-1950s was oriented toward validating its own preconceived ideas rather than toward learning more about the buyer-users.

The fact that the new lines of compact cars subsequently introduced into the market sold so well in their very first year indicates that

[1] See "Marketing Myopia," *Harvard Business Review*, July-August 1960, p. 45.

Detroit's vast market research activities for a long time failed to reveal what the car buyer wanted and that the buyer wanted something different from what he was being offered. A related shortcoming in the car industry's market research approach was that design polls were not utilized. Instead, the final design was based on consensus hunches of sundry corporate committees.

The decision by Ford to market a medium-priced car was founded upon analyses that appear, from what was happening in the 1950s, to have been correct. Trends of automobile purchases showed that the consumers were increasingly upgrading their car purchases from low-priced to medium-priced cars as soon as their individual economical situation would permit. However, the findings and related assumptions in the trend extrapolations were seemingly not closely tracked. Otherwise, it would have become clear that (a) the price-upgrading trends had changed, (b) the market segment definitions had also changed, and (c) the medium-price market was no longer growing.

Furthermore, the projections for total automobile sales, which were based on extrapolations of the significant growth and sales of 1955, did not give adequate consideration to important economic factors (such as why sales had grown so rapidly in 1955, or what the impact would be on the various price segments should a recession occur when a new product was being introduced). There is some indication that the industry's market forecasts were not unbiased, in the sense that efforts were made to have them conform to management's hopes.

The extent to which the forecasts and their underlying assumptions were understood by management and used in the decision process is somewhat vague. According to John Brooks, the Edsel was supposed to be advertised and promoted on the basis of consumer preference polls, but some intuitive, old-fashioned snake-oil selling methods crept in.[2] Thus there was some joint use of analysis and intuition, with intuition perhaps getting a heavier weight than analysis. Brooks also cited the problems or bad effects of timing and production location (within plants making competitive models to the Edsel) on product quality and subsequent sales, which were not adequately considered in the planning.[3]

While we could devote more discussion to this subject, most observers are agreed that the sales forecasts of the Edsel were very poor and contributed to the ill-fated decision to introduce the Edsel in 1957.

In contrast, a good forecast has four characteristics. (1) It objectively takes into consideration all relevant factors and reflects the best under-

[2] *Business Adventures* (New York: Weybright and Talley, Inc., 1969), p. 27.
[3] *Ibid.*, p. 60.

standing of the system to which the forecast relates. (2) It includes an estimate of the accuracy or range of possible outcomes. (3) Management understands the way in which the forecast has been derived and its implied assumptions. (4) It is recognized by the decision maker as a good forecast and is therefore used (i.e., both the forecast and its range of possible error) in the decision-making process for which it has been prepared. A review of the Edsel situation shows that most of these characteristics did not exist.

Let us make one final point before we shift our discussion. Forecasting involves more than just the skillful utilization of existing mathematical and statistical data to project the future. It also involves an understanding of the market dynamics, using market research when necessary, and incorporating into the forecast special information such as potential competitive actions, potential changes in economic factors, and effects of other events on timing and sales.

FORECASTS AND DECISIONS

Although the processes by which managers arrive at decisions vary with their background and style, certain basic elements are common to all decision making. The manager must take into account his knowledge of the existing situation or system to which his decision applies and of the ways in which he believes this system and its components (e.g., sales) will change over time. This necessarily implies some type of forecast of what changes will take place and how the factors the manager is considering will be affected.

If the manager has neither good knowledge about the present situation nor how it will change over time, his decision will be based primarily on some set of assumptions and degree of uncertainty about present and future conditions. When he believes it is virtually impossible to make an accurate forecast, he may make a decision that assumes a continuation of current conditions, thereby implicitly assuming there are no forces that will significantly change the present situation.

For example, let us say that the decision at hand relates to the introduction of a new dinnerware product, and that the historical trends and conditions for the dinnerware market are projected statistically. In this case, two of the implied assumptions are that the consumer preferences and buying habits will not change and that there will be no new products introduced by the competition.

As his understanding of how things operate and the accuracy of forecasts improve, the manager will be able to do a better job of planning and decision making, both for short- and long-term situations. The more uncertain the manager is about the future, the more flexible and adaptive his organization must be to cope with deviations from his assumptions and estimates for the future.

In general, flexible organizations are more costly or less efficient than those that are set up to follow a specific strategy based upon reasonably accurate forecasts. Therefore, values are associated with varying levels of forecasting accuracy, and the decision maker is continually seeking better forecasts.

Manager-Analyst Considerations

The manager, on the one hand, frequently faces the problem of being given several significantly different forecasts of the same factor. This occurs even when the forecasters involved are "experts"—most notably, perhaps, in economic forecasting, where it is not uncommon for well-respected economists to disagree on the direction of the economy.

Since the analysts submitting the forecasts may have used either the same or different techniques, the manager must choose which, if any, of the forecasts are to be used in his decision. In order to make this choice, he should be familiar with the basic concepts or principles incorporated in the techniques; the underlying assumptions; and the data used to establish relationships, trends, and so forth.

Thus it is important for the manager to have sufficient understanding of forecasting techniques—for example, where they can be used, the accuracy which can be obtained, the implied assumptions—so that he can confidently evaluate several different forecasts in his decision-making process.

The analyst, on the other hand, has different but not unrelated problems. His objective is to obtain the most accurate forecast he can, taking into consideration the effects of various levels or degrees of accuracy on the decision process and the related costs of a management decision that may prove to be nonoptimal (i.e., not the best or most profitable decision that could have been made if the exact conditions relating to the decision were known).

The ability of the analyst to make an accurate forecast will depend on how well he understands the current situation and how good his projections or assumptions are about future changes and trends. In deriving a forecast, the analyst frequently will have to identify relationships or obtain knowledge about how the current system functions. This will not only enable him to prepare an accurate forecast but will also be of value to the manager in making decisions relating to that system.

It is apparent that the analyst should have the active participation of the manager in preparation of the forecast for several reasons. One of the most important is that the manager can add to the analyst's understanding of how the system currently functions. The manager can also help the analyst to establish a realistic set of assumptions and to determine the reliability or accuracy of the historical information available. Furthermore, the credibility of the forecast, from the manager's viewpoint, will be based on how well the analyst has been able to incorporate into the forecast the manager's understanding of how things operate and of how the forecast was derived.

Hence the manager and analyst both have important roles in the preparation of the forecast and must work closely together if the forecast is to be accurate and useful in the decision-making process. Otherwise, the manager will at best use the forecast only as a reference point, incorporating his own judgments, assumptions, and estimates for the future.

An illustrative example of a situation in which forecasts are frequently ignored occurs in the production control function. All too often, production planners consider the forecasts supplied by marketing personnel only as a guideline; they use their own forecasts as the primary basis for production scheduling.

USE OF FORECASTS

The way decisions are made differs considerably among managers. Although it is outside the scope of this book to discuss the decision-making process in detail, some general observations about decision making are necessary. For a forecast to be of value to the manager, it must serve as an input to his decision process and therefore have an effect on the decision itself. The way a manager actually makes a decision may be quite different from how he thinks he arrives at a decision or how, given sufficient time, he would approach the decision.

For example, if there is a preconceived idea that one alternative is better than other alternative solutions, the manager may apply different weights to the critical factors used in evaluating the alternatives. Therefore, he may give more weight to the factors having high values when evaluating the favored alternative and assign less weight to the same factors when evaluating other alternatives.

Peter F. Drucker, who has devoted much time to analyzing the decision process, describes how effective executives do not make a great many decisions, but try to concentrate on what is important.[4] Accordingly, they first classify problems as either generic or unique. A rule, policy, or principle is applied to the generic problem, while the truly unique problem requires special analysis.

Most of our discussion pertains to the unique problem, although the same forecasting methodology applies to the generic problem. This is true whether the forecast is first needed in identifying the rule, policy, or procedure that will provide the solution to that class of problems, or whether the forecast is used to ascertain that conditions will not change sufficiently so that the generic solution is no longer applicable.

The other components or steps that Drucker includes in the effective decision are described in more detail in Chapter 2. These involve the correct definition or formulation of the problem, the determination of the specifications or constraints, the decision of what is "right" rather than acceptable, the building of the action commitment into the decision, and the feedback for testing the validity of the decision.

According to C. West Churchman's teleological theory of information, a decision is a conclusion drawn from data and interpreted through a *Weltanschauung* or world view—set of warrants, or underlying assumptions about how things operate and are related to each other.[5]

The world view one holds about the larger system serves to interpret the data of his experience in deriving conclusions on plans of strategy. Thus the decision maker first collects all meaningful information pertaining to the system for which a decision is to be made, interprets this information according to his understanding of how the various factors are related (i.e., how each affects the decision criterion, such as profit), and then chooses from various alternatives the one that he believes to be the best.

While it is not our objective here to expand upon this concept of decision making, a similar conceptual approach was taken by George W. F. Hegel in his theory relating to counterplanning. He held that for every plan (thesis) a supporting world view is imputed to it, and then a credible or plausible counterplan (antithesis) is found together with its supporting world view. These opposing views are presented to the decision maker via structured debate, where a third view (synthesis) is derived.

Thus it becomes apparent that there is always a need for more knowledge and a better understanding of the system under study. The forecasting analysis should take into account existing knowledge of the system,

---

[4] "The Effective Decision," *Harvard Business Review*, January-February 1967, p. 92.
[5] *Prediction and Optimal Decision* (Englewood Cliffs, N.J.: Prentice-Hall, Inc., 1961), p. 70.

challenging questionable aspects, and hopefully improving the knowledge when possible.

Derivation of the Forecast

Based on information the manager supplies the forecaster concerning how he believes the system functions, and from information that must be collected or is readily available, the forecaster performs analyses to establish past trends and relationships of various factors to the factor or factors being forecast (e.g., the relationship of sales to economic factors, the effects of promotions and price changes, and so forth). Frequently, some areas need further analysis, and market research programs and other designed experiments must be conducted to improve understanding of the existing situation so that an accurate forecast can be made.

In one sense, forecasting is a learning process, where the analyses and research programs add to management understanding of the business being studied. Hence there will generally be valuable "side effects" to these analyses, since the manager's knowledge of the system can improve during the forecasting process.

Reasonable and Consistent Assumptions. The manager, with assistance from the analyst, states the assumptions, including the special events (e.g., strikes, competitive market strategies) that should be incorporated into the forecast. The importance of assumptions in the derivation of a forecast cannot be overemphasized, since incorrect assumptions are the major cause of forecasting errors. Assumptions should be examined for reasonableness and consistency, if possible.

In many instances, market research will be necessary to check assumptions, and should be done concurrent with the other analyses concerned with establishing relationships. Assumptions are usually optimistic in the sense that many possible constraints are overlooked and customer preferences misunderstood.

In a study in the health field, for example, relatively high sales had been forecast by the business planners on the basis of incidence of the disease for which a therapeutic device had been developed. When this sales forecast was included in a "profit" model, it was estimated that the business would exceed minimum financial criteria (return on investment, earnings as a percentage of sales, and so on).

However, profit was quite sensitive to sales volume, and it was agreed that the assumptions relating to sales should be examined more closely.

Discussions with representatives of major insurance companies indicated that because of priorities established by labor unions and industry, it did not appear likely that funds would be allocated to permit the insurance companies to increase their payment schedule so that the disease being considered would be covered for an extended period of time. Also, government priorities precluded the setting up of centers for training patients for self-treatment.

Because treatment of the disease was very expensive and historical information revealed that only a small portion of the people having the disease availed themselves of treatment, the sales forecasts were lowered significantly and the profit picture changed to the extent that the product was not marketed.

In another health-product situation, sales estimates suggested that the product would be sufficiently profitable to warrant introduction, and the product was subsequently marketed. It had been assumed that hospitals would readily convert to this product because of its overall economic and health advantages, but insufficient consideration had been given to the ways in which buying decisions were made and to what the buyers' objectives and criteria were. Subsequent investigation led to the product being withdrawn from the market.

Resources and Timing. Inconsistencies in assumptions arise primarily because of failure (a) to ascertain properly the availability of resources and (b) to give adequate consideration to timing. In a study concerned with the overall business strategy for a product to be sold to an original equipment manufacturer (OEM), sales projections included the introduction of five new products in a four-year period. Subsequent investigation revealed that the product development resources would not be available in time to achieve this objective.

By means of a simplified Critical Path Method—whereby major activities, their sequence, and resource and time requirements are incorporated in a flow diagram—it is often possible to determine whether the necessary tasks can be performed on time as well as to compute the likelihood of delays in timing and their effects on sales. Such analyses, together with the underlying assumptions, provide not only a forecast, but also a measure of the accuracy of the forecast.

Deviations and Errors. The forecast and its range of possible error are used to estimate the payoff or other implications of the alternative strategies or tactics. Where the decision is a repetitive one, such as in production scheduling and inventory control, the use of statistical averages is meaningful. (By statistical average, we mean expected values, which are obtained by multiplying each possible outcome by its probability or likelihood of occurring, and summing these products.) The objective in a repetitive-decision situation is to minimize cost or maximize profit over many decisions, recognizing that any one decision may be nonoptimal but that the decision rule for several decisions will be optimal.

This type of expected cost or profit calculation is not applicable where the decision is a major one and is not likely to be repeated; or where, at most, only a few similar decisions are to be made (e.g., how many factories to build, should a given product be introduced). However, since the forecasts have ranges due to uncertainty, the effects of deviations or errors in estimates should be considered. One approach is the use of sensitivity analysis or risk analysis.

In *sensitivity* analysis, the implications of the set of best estimates are first determined; then deviations from these estimates, as given by the estimated errors, are computed by systematically changing one or more of the factor values each time a computation is performed.

In *risk* analysis, the variability of all factors is simultaneously considered in a "Monte Carlo" way—that is, values of each factor are randomly selected, according to the probability of occurrence, and computations repeatedly performed for each set of those values until a probability distribution of the payoff criterion is obtained.

The results are frequently presented in a decision-tree diagram, where the implications of different alternatives and sets of estimates, along with their probabilities, are displayed. A formal model is normally used to perform the computations, although the manager may perform mental calculations by an informal model that exists in his mind.

The inclusion of the forecasting error in the decision-making process can often lead to a different conclusion from the one reached when only best estimates are considered. In a facilities planning situation, where a new tableware product was being introduced, the best estimates led to the conclusion that a new plant should be built. However, when uncertainties due to research and process developments were considered, the alternative of using an existing plant was chosen. Subsequent events proved this alternative decision to be definitely better than building a new facility.

Other Important Factors. In arriving at a decision, the manager considers qualitative factors that cannot be quantified (such as "political" elements), as well as quantitative factors. The manager attempts to quantify as many factors as possible, but usually some cannot be quantified, such as local community reaction due to a plant shutdown or OEM customer reaction to a price increase, although even here some "bounding" of profit implications is possible. The decision process should first be directed to determine the implications of no restrictions or compromises due to qualitative factors, and then to determine the implications when restrictions are considered.

Another important factor in forecasting-and-decision-making processes is that of a feedback system designed to obtain information to track the most important factors and assumptions; thus new estimates can be generated whenever significant changes occur. Since such changes usually have an impact on the payoff "model," the tracking of assumptions will enable the manager to make new decisions when economically desirable.

For example, in a glass forecasting model for color television, assumptions or best estimates were made for glass losses, market share, and inventory buildups. These were based on judgment and experience for similar glass products. When sales exceeded initial estimates, considerable investigation revealed an inventory buildup at a point that had not been anticipated. Failure to do such tracking would have led to an incorrect upward revision in later sales, rather than a correct downward revision for the immediate future, which later proved to be accurate.

As we have previously noted, the decision maker will consider not only data and assumptions about the present situation, but also what changes will take place over time. In essence, confidence in the validity of the data, assumptions and probable changes will depend on how well both the manager and forecaster understand the system—that is, their knowledge about the dynamics and relationships of the most important factors in the system. The way the forecast is used in the decision-making process is shown in Figure 1.1.

While each of the "boxes" might suggest that such a step is formally taken, these considerations could be informal or even subconscious. Also, not all of the elements in the diagram are included in every decision, because of time or resource restrictions.

In the diagram and the preceding discussion of the "use of forecasts," we assume that there is sufficient time to make a "good" decision. The use of the forecast in the various phases or steps of the decision process will be further demonstrated in the later examples.

PRINCIPLES OF FORECASTING

There are several principles that can aid the manager in understanding his role in the forecasting process, in knowing how the forecaster can

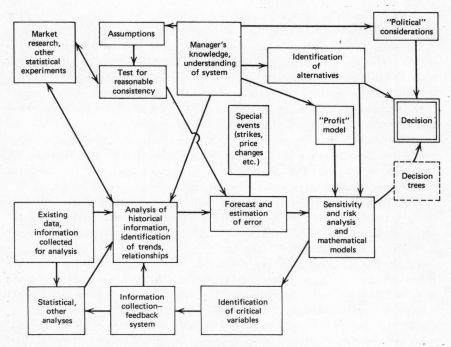

Figure 1.1. The role of the forecast in the decision process.

derive accurate forecasts, and in evaluating the forecasts that are presented to him. We shall describe these specific principles briefly in the remainder of this chapter and then consider each of them in more detail in subsequent chapters. But, first, let us make some general observations.

The manager who is involved in the forecasting process should always be aware that, despite recent progress, forecasting is still an art rather than a science. Although many useful techniques and "rules of thumb" are available to the analyst the accuracy of the forecasts will ultimately depend on the skill of the forecaster in using all of the resources available to him.

This is immediately apparent when one observes that several experts, all actively involved in deriving a specific forecast, may produce quite different estimates. The choice of which, if any, of these forecasts is to be used depends on the manager's confidence (or lack of it) in the forecaster (primarily from previous experience), and on how well the manager believes his own knowledge of the system and assumptions have been incorporated into the forecast. Thus the manager's first reaction to such a situation should be to challenge the assumptions used by each analyst.

Consider this example. When Corning Ware®* was about to be introduced into the housewares market by Corning Glass Works, the persons responsible for estimating the market potential did not come up with forecasts that suggested this product would be very profitable, because of their relatively small sales estimates. The forecasters had considerable market information available to them about consumer buying habits, the total housewares market, sales of competitive products, and so forth. However, they assumed that (a) Corning Ware would not be so well-accepted by the housewife that she would change her preferences, and (b) the total housewares expenditures would also change.

Fortunately, the division manager, who was responsible for introducing the product and who had extensive housewares experience, did not feel the forecasters had sufficiently understood the market dynamics. Therefore, he rejected their sales forecasts.

While the division manager could not estimate the ultimate market penetration of Corning Ware, he knew it would be substantially greater than the forecasts supplied to him. Thus, on the basis of some additional economic analyses and his "intuition" about a lower limit on sales, he decided to introduce the product. His judgment proved to be correct, with sales eventually being even greater than the division manager had anticipated.

A similar situation occurred in color television, where the insight of the RCA chairman of the board proved to be more accurate than the "analytical" methods. Likewise, the potential of xerography was foreseen by the top management at Haloid (later to become Xerox), even though the existing copier market at that time was relatively small and there was no sound basis for estimating future sales.

These examples emphasize both the value of human judgment, as contrasted to analytical techniques, and the necessity of the analyst to work closely with the manager so that this judgment can be incorporated into the forecast to the greatest extent possible.

Since forecasting is an art rather than a science, there is no method for assuring that mistakes will not be made in the derivation of a forecast. However, by applying the principles we shall give here, it should be possible at least to avoid blunders or large-scale mistakes that lead to disastrous results. Also, we shall offer guidelines and checkpoints for determining how much confidence the manager should place in a forecast and how he should use it in his decision making.

---

* Hereafter, the registered trade name, Corning Ware®, will be cited as Corning Ware.

Any good analyst will follow the first principle. It is based on the adage, "A problem well-formulated is half-solved." Since good forecasting requires the incorporation of all available information and as many relevant factors as possible, formulation is an integral part of forecasting.

Formulation of the Problem

If the forecasting problem is to be properly formulated, four important sets of questions must be answered.

1. *How is the forecast to be used? What decision will be based on the forecast and when must this decision be made?*

For some decision making, on the one hand, a forecasting error of greater than 5 or 10% may not be acceptable, as is the case for many tactical decisions such as market strategies (promotions, price changes, or overall sales budget), production scheduling (plant loading, purchasing of critical items), and financial planning (hedging, securing loans due to cash flows). On the other hand, the decision may only require a forecasting accuracy of 20 or 30%, or even only an indication of the direction (increase or decrease) a factor will take.

Many companies, in their strategic planning of how to allocate resources among businesses, are following the approach developed by the Boston Consulting Group, where businesses are categorized according to (a) the market growth rate, and (b) the ratio of a company's market share versus the major competitor's market share. If the market is a low-growth one and the competitor's market share is significantly larger, the business should either be phased out as soon as possible or a "milking" strategy should be followed. If it is a high-growth market and the company's market share is equal to or larger than the biggest competitor, it is a "star" business to which major resources should be allocated.

A similar approach has been taken by General Electric in its highly publicized "strategic business planning," which was developed in the late 1960s.

2. *What are the important factors in the system and how are they related to each other?*

The first step in answering this question is to develop a flow chart of how the system operates. This forces an understanding of the overall system, since information flows and relationships of various factors are included in the chart.

3. *What is the value of historical information? Has the system changed to such an extent that the historical information is irrelevant or will an analysis of past data aid in understanding the system better? Have there been related products that will give some insight into what might happen to a new product? Is good historical information available or will it be costly to obtain?*

While there was no information available for color television in its early stages that could be used as an accurate projection of the ultimate market penetration and when sales would start to accelerate at a rapid pace, the information on black-and-white television provided valuable data for projecting the sales of color TV. Similarly, it was found that reasonably accurate forecasts of design changes for new aircraft models could be obtained by comparing the new design characteristics with those of previous aircraft models and their histories of design changes.

4. *To what extent should the information be disaggregated?*

Frequently, it is valuable to break down the information into as many parts as possible so that estimates can be made for each of the segments. In the case of sales projections, for example, it is advisable to disaggregate the market into segments so that these can be analyzed separately. This includes looking at established versus developing businesses, the sales to large versus small customers, and so on.

The importance of timing should be considered at length in the formulation stage. The events that must happen in order for different forecasts or potential sales to be realized should be identified, and the probabilities that these events will happen should then be estimated. In the case of color television, it was apparent that color programming would have to increase for color sales to accelerate rapidly. Conversely, color programming would not increase until the sales of color sets had increased. This presented a circular situation, and the sequence of events had to be determined.

The proprietary position of a product versus the timing will also significantly affect the forecast. For example, suppose a new product using xerography is to be introduced and that there are likely to be delays in product development. In this case, the sales forecast still may not change because of the proprietary nature of both the product and process.

However, suppose it is difficult to get patent protection for the new product and therefore possible for the competition to duplicate it rapidly. Here it is important that the manufacturing process be fully debugged and that the marketing system be already developed if the sales potential of the nonproprietary product is to be realized.

As in any problem-solving situation, the formulation stage is very important. This is equally true in forecasting. Therefore, our second principle—the formulation as well as the derivation of the forecast—should take into account the active participation of the decision maker.

Involvement of Management

Experience has shown that, in virtually all staff activities in which there is quantitative analysis, the consumer of the research must be involved in the analytical process when the results are to be used in his decision-making process.

This is certainly true in forecasting. Unless the manager participates actively in the forecasting process, there is not only a relatively small likelihood that he will use the forecast with any degree of confidence, but also that he will perhaps consider it only superficially in his decision. To have confidence in the forecast, there must be an understanding of the implicit and explicit assumptions; the manager wants to be certain that his knowledge of the system is reflected in the forecast, as well as having at least some conceptual understanding of what the analyst did. Very few managers will use inputs without some knowledge of how they were derived.

From the other point of view, the analyst, to do a good job of forecasting, needs information that can best (and perhaps only) be provided by the decision maker. Accordingly, unless the manager intends to spend time with the analyst, he should not expect the forecast provided to him to be of much value in his decision making.

In the forecasting process, there are some things the analyst does best, some the manager does best, and other tasks that are most effectively done by a joint effort. One of the things the analyst does best is, on the basis of information obtained from the managers and others in the formulation of the forecasting problem, choose the appropriate technique.

Choice of Techniques

For a particular forecasting situation, the choice of techniques is strongly influenced by the stage of the product life cycle for which a decision is being made. The value of the decision, or the amount of profit that will be influenced by the decision, is also often a function of the stage of the product life cycle.

In the beginning, relatively small expenditures are made for research and market investigation. During the first phase of product introduction, these expenditures start to increase. In the rapid penetration stage, considerable amounts of money are involved in the decisions; therefore a high level of accuracy is desirable. After the product has hit a steady-state situation, the decisions are more of a routine nature, involving marketing and manufacturing strategies.

The number and quality of assumptions are likewise affected by the stage of the product life cycle, since knowledge about the market increases over time. Tracking helps to update and verify assumptions, thus reducing the range of error in the forecast.

The type of life cycle, the market factors, and the value of decisions may be quite different for the product dichotomies of durables, nondurables, and services. Numerous articles have been written showing how marketing approaches, market research, and product planning must differ for durable goods, as contrasted to nondurable goods and services, while a distinct type of product can usually be handled as either a durable or nondurable product.

Services such as appliance and automobile repairs, entertainment, banks, and public utilities have characteristics quite similar to those for nondurable goods. Insurance and certain medical services are quite similar to durable goods, with the techniques applicable to durable goods also being applicable to such services. Considerable market research is now taking place to learn more about consumer attitudes and buying patterns relating to services.

Certain techniques or forecasting methods may be very helpful in identifying or estimating the ultimate penetration level or what will inevitably happen to a product. However, these techniques may not prove to be particularly helpful in determining how long the product will take to reach the steady-state or ultimate penetration level. This leads us to the next important principle.

Combinations of Methods

More than one technique is frequently used for a particular forecasting problem. The ability to identify which techniques to use and how to combine them depends on the skill of the forecaster, who should be problem-oriented rather than technique-oriented. This means that during the problem-formulation phase he will have to determine the important ingredients of the system and to identify the features or characteristics of the technique or techniques that will be needed. The forecaster may find that he has to modify a particular technique or, more frequently, that he has to employ several techniques in deriving a single forecast.

In production planning, for example, a prime requirement of the forecasting technique is that the cost of a forecast for each item be held to an allowable low expenditure of perhaps only a few cents per forecast. However, for the total business or product class, it might be economically feasible to allow significantly more expenditure per item forecast in determining the basic direction of the business or product class and in incorporating that trend with the single forecast.

Technological forecasting usually involves both a sound historical analysis of patterns, trends, and reasons why things have occurred in the past, and then relies on expert opinions for projection of the future. A technique such as the Delphi Method can be utilized for obtaining the unbiased opinions of several experts concerning what might happen and when in the future. Historical analysis can be of value in several areas of forecasting; a very important aspect is to determine the present state—what is now happening, and how are things changing.

Know Where You Are

In order to estimate the future position of a boat or an automobile at a particular point in time, it is necessary to know the current speed of the vehicle, the rate at which its speed is changing, and its direction. This may sound trivial and not applicable to business forecasting. However, experience shows that unless a thorough analysis of historical data is made, the current sales rate or other factors being considered may not be accurately known. There are sound statistical methods for determining the current rate and how this rate is changing. No matter how significant the recent changes in the system have been, experience also shows that previous trends should not be discarded immediately. These trends actually undergo a more gradual change.

Perhaps the best illustration of this is in our national economy, where long-term trends in the public sector are only gradually changed, and it frequently takes from one to four quarters to see the impact of a recent change in fiscal policy. In the private sector, new market strategies obviously cause trends to change but at a more gradual rate than is normally supposed.

As we show later, incorrect conclusions can be drawn when a simple comparison is made of sales for one year with those for a similar time period of the previous year. To illustrate, although sales may currently be 20% higher than a year ago, the major growth or change in the sales rate could have occurred last year, with a no-growth situation now existing.

The analysis of historical information helps to determine how much of the variation from one time period to another can be accounted for by analytical techniques. This provides the basis for determining the accuracy of a forecast.

Measure of Accuracy

Unless an analytical approach is used, it is very difficult to obtain a measure of the forecasting error or the accuracy of the forecast. Accuracy is expressed in terms of a range and the likelihood that the true value will fall within this range. If the manager is not supplied with a measure of the forecast accuracy, he will impute some degree of accuracy, depending on his confidence in the way the forecast was derived. (Earlier in this chapter we described the way in which the manager uses the forecasting error in his decision-making process.)

While the forecasting error may sometimes be unacceptable to the manager, it at least lets him know the minimum error that can be obtained with the information available. This may lead to the decision to conduct market experiments or to generate the required information that will lead to a reduction in the forecasting error.

Because a forecast is never certain, an effort should always be made to compare what is currently happening with what was forecast and to update the forecast as necessary.

Tracking the Forecast

Unless a formal system is set up for collecting information and tracking a forecast, it is unlikely that revising and updating will be done. Many published examples indicate that although the initial forecast may have been reasonable on the basis of information available at that time, sufficient effort was not expended in tracking what was actually happening in contrast to what was forecast to determine whether the earlier decision should be revised.

Consider the Edsel automobile. Without attempting to question the initial market research, it appears that a major problem arose in failing to track and verify at very early stages the initial assumptions about customer acceptance and market penetration.

It is important that the decision maker have an information collection system not only for tracking numbers to see if they are in line with what was forecast, but also for tracking the underlying assumptions. This might involve the use of a critical path-type tracking system, since assumptions are usually based on the occurrence of certain events and such events should be tracked regularly. Previous sensitivity analyses will indicate when changes in the earlier decision should be considered.

IN SUMMARY

Although many new forecasting techniques have been developed and the expertise of analysts has improved, forecasting must still be considered more an art than a science. No manager should religiously accept a forecast because the analyst has used relatively sophisticated techniques or because the forecast has been generated by an electronic computer. If the forecast is to be acceptable, there must be a man-machine and manager-analyst interaction.

All decision making involves the use of some forecast and assumptions. For this reason, every effort should be made to ascertain (a) that the assumptions are the most reasonable that can be made, and (b) that the best understanding of the system or the best knowledge of the relevant factors have been incorporated into the forecast.

Chapter II

Manager-Analyst Roles
in Forecasting

When a manager asks a forecaster to prepare a specific projection, he often assumes that the request itself, and whatever brief statement of the problem it contains, provides sufficient information for the forecaster to go to work and do his job. This is almost never true. If the forecaster proceeds on this basis alone, there is little likelihood that his forecast will have much bearing on the manager's ultimate decision.

On the one hand, the effective manager has learned how to utilize his staff services properly and understands to what extent he is to participate actively in the analysis he has requested. Whether he has requested help in planning, forecasting, or any other activity requiring analytical assistance, he knows that in most instances he must work closely with the analyst to use the results effectively. He also knows the capabilities and limitations of the analyst, such as the latter's experience and knowledge relating to the system to be studied, his understanding of the decision process, and his ability to identify relationships and incorporate special information into the forecast.

On the other hand, in formulating the forecasting problem, the analyst must understand the important factors in the system and their relationships, the way in which the forecast will aid in the decision making, the timing and value of the decision, the way in which the system is changing, the most reasonable assumptions that can be made, and the relevance of historical information. He might obtain much of this information from persons other than the manager, such as those reporting to the manager.

24

However, since questions will probably be raised by the manager with respect to some of this information, especially the assumptions and system dynamics, it is more efficient for the analyst to have that information supplied by the manager or derived jointly with the manager. From the analyst's viewpoint, the most important contribution the manager gives to the forecasting process is how the latter intends to use the forecast and the estimated range of accuracy in his decision making.

USE AND VALUE OF THE FORECAST

Much of the thinking and analysis that a manager goes through in his decision making are relevant in the various aspects of the preparation of a forecast. Of the six steps listed by Peter Drucker[6] as essential to effective decision making, the first three—classification, definition, and specification of the boundary conditions of the problem—contain the information that tell the analyst how the forecast will be used in the decision.

The effective decision maker classifies the type of a problem he is dealing with. To ascertain this, he investigates the system dynamics to see what is common and different from other problems. This classification reveals whether he should apply a rule or policy applicable to the generic problem or whether he should derive a unique solution.

The definition of the problem involves the determination of what the decision is all about, the underlying realities, and what is pertinent and key to the situation. The manager's intent in this step is to obtain a plausible (theoretical) but incomplete definition. (The system will subsequently be redefined whenever inconsistencies are identified or newly established facts cause the "theory" to be revised.)

The specification concerning what the decision has to accomplish—that is, what the boundary conditions are—affects the manager's choice of alternative solutions. The compatibility of the boundary conditions indicates the risks or likelihood of success of a particular decision.

The completion of these three steps not only describes how the forecast is to be used and its value to the decision, but also provides valuable information about the system dynamics that can be incorporated into the forecast. The manager's analysis of how the forecast will be used helps him to establish the level of effort that can be justified in deriving the forecast.

Thus, if the decision is a major one, such as whether to introduce a new product or how many plants to build, the consequences involve

---

[6] "The Effective Decision."

large amounts of money; therefore, a relatively major effort by the analyst in preparing the forecast is justified. By contrast, a production-planning decision normally entails significantly less profit; therefore, not much money or effort can justifiably be committed to the preparation of the forecast.

For example, since the decision to introduce the Edsel automobile involved a commitment of well over 100 million dollars, it presented a value situation in which forecasting expenditures of hundreds of thousands of dollars could be justified. Similarly, the potential market for computer time sharing as compared to rental or sale is extremely important to companies participating in the computer market. Thus large expenditures can justifiably be spent on market research in the preparation of a sound forecast.

Conversely, the determination of production quantities and safety stocks for thousands of items, while obviously important to both production and sales personnel, affects relatively small amounts of profit. Hence only a small expenditure can be justified in obtaining a forecast for a single item.

Important Considerations

Many factors must be taken into account in considering the ways in which the forecast will be used in the decision-making process. These include the time at which the decision will be made, the influence of forecasting errors on the decision, whether the forecast is to be a standard for evaluating performance, the effects of delays or special events on the decision, and whether the decision can be changed as new information subsequently becomes available. In this section, we shall take a brief look at each of these considerations.

The Timing. When the decision will be made is important in the analyst's choice of techniques. If only a few weeks are available for him to prepare the forecast, he is restricted in what techniques he can use, since some of them may require several months for data collection and analysis.

Forecasting Error. Instead of obtaining an estimate of the most likely sales level, the primary concern may be in determining the likelihood that sales will exceed a level of minimum acceptable profit. Hence, while the most likely figure is of interest, the possible deviations from it are more important.

This situation exists when a new product is being developed, and the decision at hand is whether or not to build a new factory. Another example is when a new production process to reduce manufacturing costs is being introduced, and a decision about product selling price must be made.

In the case of a new product, it may be virtually impossible to predict the ultimate penetration or sales level. This was true for Corning Ware. While the analyst (in this case, the manager) could not determine whether annual sales might be $25 million or $100 million, he forecast that the sales volume would be sufficient to assure an acceptable minimum profit level. Xerox could not predict the exact demand for copiers, or Kodak the demand for instamatic cameras, but in each case minimum sales levels were estimated to be well worth the development efforts. The decision for a new product is thus frequently a go or no-go one, and forecast errors of 25 or 50% may not be critical, so long as sales are above a specified lower limit.

The main point here is that the analyst must have some idea of how accurate his forecast has to be and what the consequences are of various errors. This becomes more meaningful when illustrated in the form of a flow chart. As Figure 2.1 shows, cost and accuracy increase with sophistication in comparison with the corresponding cost of forecasting errors, given some general assumptions. The most sophisticated forecasting technique that the analyst can economically justify falls in the region where the sum of the cost of preparing the forecast and the error implications are minimal. As illustrated, techniques vary in cost, scope, and accuracy (we shall discuss forecasting techniques in detail in the next chapter).

The analyst, with help from the manager, will fix the level of inaccuracy that can be tolerated. This allows the forecaster to trade off cost against the value of accuracy in choosing a technique.

Evaluation Standard. Another consideration is whether the forecast is to set a standard against which to evaluate performance or to include all possible factors. If it is to be a *standard,* the forecasting method should not take into account special actions, such as promotions and other marketing devices. These are meant to change historical patterns and relationships; hence they form part of the *performance* to be evaluated.

Generally, a statistical forecast is primarily made to show what will happen if nothing out of the ordinary is done and business continues "as usual." If this "forecast" is unacceptable, strategies will be formulated to change the future and to make the forecast wrong. This is frequently the first step in long-range planning: to determine what will happen if

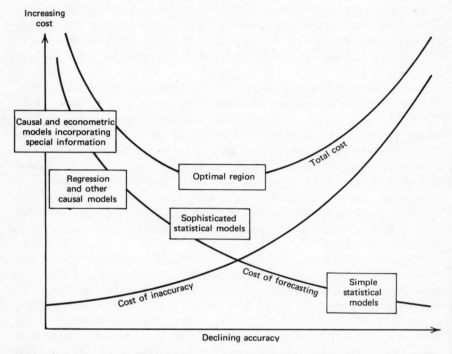

Figure 2.1. Cost of forecasting versus cost of inaccuracy for a medium-range forecast, given data availability

no drastic changes are made (or the current plan is adhered to) and to consider other opportunities if goals and objectives are not forecasted to be met.

Delays or Special Events. If the forecast is for a proprietary (patented) item, then the occurrence of special events or delays in introduction are not particularly critical. By comparison, for a nonproprietary item, which will be duplicated quickly by the competition, delays in introduction or special events will significantly affect sales.

Special events, as we use the term here, may be subsequent events that must occur in the market. For example, these events might be an increase in color-television programming, more communication channels for time sharing or picture phones, breakthroughs in R&D or manufacturing, and development of a nationwide distribution system.

For a proprietary item, the effect of timing is less critical than for a nonproprietary item. The eventual penetration level will not change (unless the competition catches up), even though it may take longer than anticipated to reach the peak sales level. (Cash flows and discounted return-on-investment, however, will be lowered as delays occur.) In a similar way, forecast errors for a proprietary item are not too critical, since the major drawback, if sales are underestimated, is just a delay in reaching the peak.

From the foregoing discussion, we can see that forecasts for proprietary items consist of two virtually independent elements: (1) the ultimate penetration level; and (2) the time to reach the ultimate penetration level, with forecasting errors being derived for each part of the forecast.

When an item is nonproprietary, or when the competition can "get around" a patent, timing is so important that delays will significantly lower sales penetration. An example of a nonproprietary item is the automobile emissions-control device, where if delays occur, the design might change or even the engine characteristics, which could cause a more radical design change), so that the market share for an OEM supplier could change significantly. In the case of medical instruments, technology can be duplicated very rapidly. Thus the company that first introduces a new instrument must have the manufacturing capability and distribution channels to effect wide-scale penetration before the competition can duplicate the product.

For nonproprietary items, the forecaster must first obtain estimates of timing, based on the critical events that have to occur, and then forecast the sales for different timing estimates. Since there will be errors—in both timing and sales for each specific timing estimate, the overall forecasting error will be a combination of the two.

The timing analysis considers events such as customer acceptance, research breakthrough, process development, establishment of a distribution system, training of personnel, and design and implementation of marketing programs. Estimates are made of the most likely times for each event, the range of these times, the likelihood of achieving complete or partial success in accomplishing each event, and the variations in these estimates for different levels of resources.

If there are several critical events, it is difficult to perform the computations of overall timing by hand, and a computer is generally utilized to do this. For handling large-scale project scheduling there are specially designed computer routines that can be applied to this problem. Among them are Program Evaluation Review Technique (PERT), Project Control System (PCS), and Critical Path Method (CPM). However, CPM does not include variability, and neither CPM nor PERT include resources but give attention to timing only.

The *Critical Path Method* (CPM) was one of the first computerized project scheduling techniques. It takes into account the best estimates of the time required to complete each activity (event) and the dependence of one task upon another (i.e., which events are preceded by which other events). As the name implies, the technique identifies the critical path—the events that control or determine the minimum total elapsed time.

The *Program Evaluation Review Technique* (PERT) has the same features as CPM; in addition, it considers variability in the time estimates. The best estimate and possible variation in this estimate is specified for each event, and the technique derives the best estimate for total elapsed time and the possible variation in that estimate.

The *Project Control System* (PCS) a software package developed by IBM, has the features of CPM and PERT, and also permits the incorporation of resource requirements. It shows the total resources required over time for the project as well as for each event.

Decision Flexibility. Finally, in considering how the forecast will be used in the decision making, the ability to change either the decision or the action that could be taken as new information becomes available will help determine the forecasting accuracy required. If the decision is irreversible (no change in strategy at a later time is possible after the decision has been made), much greater accuracy is needed than if changes can be made later. The cost of making a change is obviously important, and the forecasting accuracy must be greater as the cost of changing the decision increases.

Use of a decision tree, which shows the sequence of decisions and subsequent effects on cost, profits, and so on, helps to identify what alternative changes in strategy can be made and what the payoff implications are for each strategy. The design of a tracking system and the total amount spent on the initial forecast versus tracking will be determined by the ability to change or modify the decision.

SYSTEM DYNAMICS AND COMPONENTS

The degree to which the analyst determines and expands the corporate knowledge of the system dynamics will have a major effect not only on the forecast itself, but also on subsequent decisions relating to the system and on the ability to track forecasts and decisions.

The Flow Chart

The first step in understanding the overall system, or in determining how well the system is understood, is to develop a flow chart of the system for which the forecast is to be made. This helps to clarify the possible relationships of the interacting variables and to provide a definite guide for the forecaster's subsequent analyses. Unless the forecaster has been actively involved in the area he is analyzing, he will not have personal knowledge about how the system functions and will need the help of others in learning this. Since the manager needs such information at his disposal in his decision making, he can be a primary source in identifying the relevant factors and how they are related.

In any event, by the manager and the analyst jointly working on the flow chart, they will be able to clarify how well they understand the system, what parts of it are subject to the company's control, what analyses have been performed in the past, and what additional information or analysis is needed to better establish the relationships. The flow chart shows the relative positions of the different elements of the distribution system, sales system, production system, or whatever is being studied.

Figure 2.2 displays these elements for the system through which Corning Glass Works' major component for color-television sets—the bulb— flows to the consumer. Note the points where inventories are required or maintained in this manufacturing and distribution system. These are the *pipeline elements,* which exert important effects throughout the flow system and hence are of critical interest to the forecaster.

All the elements outlined in solid black directly affect forecasting procedure to some extent (the data key suggests the nature of CGW's data at each point), again a prime determinant of technique selection since different techniques require different kinds of inputs. Where data are unavailable or costly to obtain, the range of forecasting choices is limited.

The flow chart should also show which parts of the system are under the control of the company doing the forecasting. As illustrated in Figure 2.2, this is the volume of glass panels and funnels supplied by CGW to the tube manufacturers.

In the part of the system where the company has total control, management is tuned in to the various cause-and-effect relationships. Hence the forecaster can frequently use techniques that take causal factors explicitly into account.

The flow chart has a special value where causal prediction methods are called for because it enables the forecaster not only to conjecture the possible variations in sales level caused by inventories and the like, but

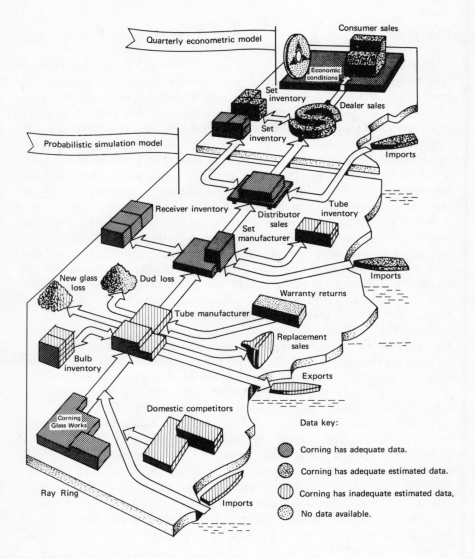

Figure 2.2. Flow chart of TV distribution system.

to also determine which factors must be considered by the technique to provide the manager with a forecast of acceptable accuracy. Experience reveals that the further back a company is in the product-line system, the harder it is to forecast product sales. In some causal models, primarily where forecasts are for points far back in the distribution system, as little as 30% of the variation in sales could be explained by analytical methods, partly because of data availability.

The flow chart might be expanded to show what competitive products are available to the consumer. If there is evidence that consumers are shifting from one product to another, it might be necessary to include the competing products in the analysis.

For example, in forecasting the total beer demand for the United States in the early 1960s, analysis revealed that for more than five years beer had been losing its market share of total alcohol consumption to liquor and wine. While some leveling off of the trend was beginning to show, the forecasting accuracy was considerably improved by taking into account total alcohol consumption and projecting the beer market share of it.

One of the major benefits in forecasting is the preliminary indication it gives the manager of (a) how well the system is understood, and therefore the accuracy that can be expected, and (b) what the results will be so that they do not surprise him. Another major benefit in forecasting is that it also provides the foundation for making assumptions.

EVALUATION OF ASSUMPTIONS

As is true of long-range planning, the identification and evaluation of assumptions are very important in the forecasting process. Unfortunately, the assumptions are frequently not spelled out, limiting the ability to track the forecast after the decision has been made. If assumptions are not explicitly stated when the system dynamics are identified, the analyst should develop a comprehensive list of the implied assumptions, and then review these with the manager. At the very least, the manager should review and agree to the assumptions. Better still, he should participate in the initial listing of the assumptions. And, certainly, all assumptions should be checked for internal consistency.

Incorrect Assumptions

One common error is the assumption that resources either are, or can be made, available. The use of PERT, CPM, PCS, and other specially designed computer routines, as we cited earlier, will assist in estimating total resource requirements. These can then be compared with what will be available.

Another assumption frequently in error is the extent to which the product being introduced is superior to existing products, and those that that can be developed by the competition. This assumption is usually based on just one or two factors, instead of all of the factors the consumer takes into account in making his product choice. Also, incorrect weights are frequently assigned to the factors affecting consumer choice, biased toward the best features of the new product. Our discussions with persons in different industries indicate this is a common problem, and that some form of rating system to reduce bias is needed.

An allied problem is incorrect assumptions based on too little or incorrect market research. In the automotive industry, the major United States manufacturers—on the basis of market research that only gave the consumer choices according to what they thought he or she wanted—assumed that the consumer did not want a small economy car, thereby permitting Volkswagen to secure a significant portion of the market. Because of such preconceived ideas or attempts to force a particular strategy, the market research efforts often turn out to be biased.

Also, it is frequently assumed that there will be a steady growth in market penetration; thus the innovator-imitator situation is not considered. For most consumer products, there is a small group of innovators who will try most new products, and the imitators will not follow until it is clear that the product is acceptable to the innovators. This can cause an initial surge in sales, followed by a decline or plateau period, and then either a sharp increase or virtual phasing out of sales.

The analyst should attempt to verify assumptions, whether through market research or expert opinion. This may include conducting a small, supplementary sample of interviews with consumers and manufacturers. In several instances where we have done this, the assumptions have been changed and the forecasts revised.

AVAILABILITY AND RELEVANCE OF DATA

No analysis can be better than the data used in it. The flow chart aids in the identification of the type of information required for analysis, its availability, and hopefully the effect that information might have on the accuracy of the forecast. The cost of getting the various types of information must be determined and included in estimating the cost of getting various levels of accuracy, so that the value trade-offs of accuracy vis à vis cost can be considered.

Relevance of data is another key factor. Significant changes in the system—for example, new products and new competitive strategies—diminish the similarity of the past and the future. Over the short term, recent changes are unlikely to cause overall patterns to alter, but over the long term their effects are likely to increase. The manager and the forecaster should discuss these fully, and come to a mutual understanding. For example, even though the analyst may be convinced that past information is relevant, he must minimize the use of it when the manager firmly believes the past must be discarded because of the dynamic nature of the business. Otherwise, the manager is unlikely to place much credence in the forecast.

An alternative is for the analyst to demonstrate how the past has been relevant when previous changes have occurred so that the manager is willing to accept the incorporation of historical analysis in the forecast. Our own experience has been that, no matter how dynamic is the system or how extensive is a change, there is still some continuation of historical trends for a minimum of three to six months into the future.

Nonhomogeneous Aggregates

In many instances, forecasts are either inaccurate or misleading because the element being forecasted consists of subelements that are nonhomogeneous, experiencing different trends, or undergoing different changes. Sales for established and developing businesses are sometimes aggregated, so that any analysis of the totals could lead to incorrect interpretation of trends of the overall business. As we mentioned earlier, if sales to innovators are distinguished from sales to imitators, it should be possible to forecast and track sales more accurately.

Another type of disaggregation occurs in the forecasting of design changes in the aircraft industry. Design changes can take place for several reasons, such as lack of engineering coordination, problems discovered in flight test, tooling problems, problems arising from field operation, and general product improvement or economy changes at later stages of aircraft production. The overall number of design changes may be relatively constant or changing over time, depending on the number of changes due to each type of problem. Thus the proper data base should be utilized—for example, the data broken down into as many parts as *feasible* to increase the forecast accuracy. We hasten to point out here that there is the danger of excessive disaggregation, to the extent that the parts have greater variability than the total.

Disaggregation is an art, wherein the analyst must determine the extent to which disaggregation is advantageous. Thus breaking sales down by customer may decrease forecasting accuracy, because of the customer's randomly shifting purchases from one supplier to another. Also, sales to a customer may fluctuate irregularly according to the customer's production schedule. The flow chart we described earlier is of considerable help in determining the level of disaggregation.

Disaggregation at the proper level may make it easier to estimate the effects of changes in the assumptions or deviations from expected competitive strategies. For example, an ophthalmic forecasting model, which includes estimates of percent eyeglass wearers, multiple pairs, and type of lenses, for example, permits the evaluation of the effects of new government programs directed toward specific age groups, such as special school programs for the young or eyeglasses for the aged. Further detail at the level of the wholesaler and lens manufacturer, such as factors for inventory fluctuation by lens type, make it possible to estimate the effects of the economy and subsequent inventory cutbacks or buildups for new products.

The techniques of forecasting, especially time-series analysis, can also be incorporated into management information systems and short-term business analyses to identify changes in trends in specific business segments.

Illustrative Examples.   The problem of dealing with nonhomogeneous aggregates and poor data bases (e.g., because of cost allocation) can be best illustrated by concrete examples. These examples are primarily for tracking profit, not sales, but the principles described are applicable to short- and long-term forecasting.

The misallocation of marketing effort in industry is a problem encountered by many companies, as illustrated by William J. Baumol and Charles H. Sevin in their article on marketing costs and marketing expenditure allocation, where they indicate that the use of average cost data is the major reason for misallocation.[7] Richard H. Hillman also stresses the need for proper disaggregation in his article on redeploying assets.[8]

---

[7] See "Marketing Costs and Mathematical Programming," in Edward C. Bursk and John F. Chapman, editors, *New Decision Making Tools for Managers* (Cambridge, Mass.: *Harvard University Press,* 1963), p. 247.

[8] "How to Redeploy Assets," *Harvard Business Review,* November-December 1971, p. 95.

For example, if unit costs are computed by including both the direct cost and overhead, the average cost approach can lead to various types of errors. Thus when the overhead costs are allocated among several products according to sales volume or some similar method, the unit cost for one product can change significantly because of a variation in the sales volume of another product involved in the overhead allocation. This creates problems in both tracking and forecasting, since the data for the various products are not independent.

Consider the data in Table 2.1, where Products A, B, and C are made in different plants but sold by the same sales department. The unit manufacturing cost for Product A has remained constant over the two-year period shown, while it has increased for Product C and decreased for Product B.

Table 2.1   Effects of Overhead Allocations on Unit Costs: S&A Costs: $60,000 in 1971; $64,000 in 1972

Year		Product A Selling Price = $2.00	Product B Selling Price = $4.00	Product C Selling Price = $1.00
1971	Units sold	50,000	25,000	100,000
	Sales	$100,000	$100,000	$100,000
	Prorated S & A	$ 20,000	$ 20,000	$ 20,000
	Unit manufacturing cost	$ 1.00	$ 2.00	$ 0.50
	Total manufacturing cost	$ 50,000	$ 50,000	$ 50,000
	Total cost	$ 70,000	$ 70,000	$ 70,000
	Unit cost	$ 1.40	$ 2.80	$ 0.70
1972	Units sold	62,500	50,000	75,000
	Sales	$125,000	$200,000	$ 75,000
	Prorated S & A	$ 20,000	$ 32,000	$ 12,000
	Unit manufacturing cost	$ 1.00	$ 1.90	$ 0.53
	Total manufacturing cost	$ 62,500	$ 95,000	$ 39,750
	Total cost	$ 82,500	$127,000	$ 51,750
	Unit cost	$ 1.32	$ 2.54	$ 0.69

However, because the sales volume for Product B has gone up significantly, so that Product B now absorbs one-half of the overhead costs instead of one-third as in the prior year, it appears that the unit costs for both Products A and C have decreased. If the sales volumes for Products A and C decrease while sales for Product B increase, the total unit cost for Product B may actually increase even when the unit manufacturing cost has decreased.

The solution to the problem involving overhead allocation is either to present to the decision maker the direct costs as well as the total cost, or to allocate the S&A expenses to the products according to actual utilization of the resources.

The aggregation of sales for new and established products can lead to an incorrect interpretation of what is happening and consequently to ineffective marketing strategy.

For example, it often happens that sales for a new product increase significantly while sales for older established products decrease. Unless sales for the total business are broken down, the decision maker might assume that sales for the established products are remaining constant or increasing, while the new product either is not meeting expectations or is rapidly penetrating the market.

Experience shows that disaggregation of sales data in this way can result in a better understanding of how product sales are doing in the marketplace. Another form of disaggregation is by marketing sector or geographical grouping, where there may be different marketing dynamics (e.g., various levels of advertising and competitor actions) for the various areas.

A similar situation exists when looking at inventory turns for a business that includes both a new product and established products. Since there is generally an inventory buildup for a new product, the overall inventory turns for the total business may be going down, whereas the actual inventory situation could appear to be constant. Hence inventory turns should also be computed separately for new and established businesses.

Another type of problem relating to market disaggregation occurs when market share is under consideration. If market share is declining, this means either that company sales are not increasing at as fast a rate as the total market or that market share is falling off in a constant or declining market. Initially, reaction to declining market share is that the marketing strategy is not effective and some action, such as an increased marketing expenditure or a price change or promotion, is required.

However, consider a situation where sales for Product A are declining, while sales for Product B are increasing. Product A could be part of a market segment that is also decreasing and the market share for Product

Table 2.2 Cigarette Sales, Industry and for American Tobacco, 1950-1959

| | Total Industry Cigarette Sales[a] | American Tobacco Cigarette Sales | American Tobacco Company | |
| | | | Share of the Market | Net Change in Share of the Market |
	(in billions of cigarettes)			(percent)
1950	361.4	113.0	31.27	
1951	377.4	121.0	32.06	+0.79
1952	391.7	128.5	32.81	+0.75
1953	391.0	127.8	32.69	−0.12
1954	367.1	123.0	33.51	+0.82
1955	377.8	124.0	32.82	−0.69
1956	388.5	122.3	31.48	−1.34
1957	407.5	119.0	29.20	−2.28
1958	433.5	115.5	26.64	−2.56
1959	460.2	120.6	26.21	−0.43

[a] Big six manufacturers.

A might be actually increasing within that segment. In contrast, Product B could be in a rapidly growing market but losing market share. Hence, even though the overall market is increasing, the strategy for Product B should be reevaluated, and possibly some of the resources should be redirected from Product A to Product B.

Robert S. Weinberg describes an excellent example of this type situation in his analysis of the competitive performance of the American Tobacco Company for the 1950 to 1959 period.[9] In looking at the total cigarette industry sales, as shown in Table 2.2, there was virtually no growth for the 1950 to 1956 period, after which sales grew rapidly. Likewise, the American Tobacco sales and market share remained relatively constant for the same period, after which sales remained constant, but the market share declined significantly.

An analysis of the American Tobacco sales by product class, as Table 2.3 illustrates, reveals that the company's regular sales declined steadily over the 10-year period, the king sales increased over the first five years and remained constant thereafter, and filter sales showed a relatively steady increase from 1954 to 1959. Management concluded that its marketing strategy for regular cigarettes was ineffective and more money

[9] "Top Management Planning and the Computer," presented at the Chemical Marketing Research Association, November 16-17, 1965, Cleveland, Ohio.

Table 2.3   American Tobacco Company Cigarette Sales by Product Class, 1950-1959 (in billions of cigarettes)

	Regular	King	Filter	Mentholated	Total
1950	82.5	30.5	—	—	113.0
1951	79.0	42.0	—	—	121.0
1952	73.5	55.0	—	—	128.5
1953	66.3	61.5	—	—	127.8
1954	58.5	63.0	1.5	—	123.0
1955	57.5	63.0	3.5	—	124.0
1956	55.5	61.4	5.4	—	122.3
1957	51.5	59.4	8.1	—	119.0
1958	47.2	61.5	6.8	—	115.5
1959	44.5	66.2	9.7	0.2	120.6

should be spent in that area, as well as in the king market, where there was no growth from 1954 to 1959.

However, in the "Industry Sales by Product Class," as shown in Table 2.4, American Tobacco observed there were significant shifts in the market structure and that the company was participating primarily in market segments that were declining in absolute sales and in their share of the total cigarette industry.

The major problem was not that the company was losing market share in the segments in which it was competing (Table 2.5), but that filter and mentholated cigarette sales were growing rapidly, and American had very

Table 2.4   Industry Cigarette Sales by Product Class, 1950-1959 (in billions of cigarettes)

	Regular	King	Filter	Mentholated	Total
1950	314.7	35.3	2.2	9.2	361.4
1951	315.7	48.0	3.2	10.5	377.4
1952	305.0	70.3	4.9	11.5	391.7
1953	264.8	102.4	12.3	11.5	391.0
1954	215.8	102.0	37.2	12.1	367.1
1955	193.4	97.7	74.0	12.7	377.8
1956	172.4	91.2	108.6	16.3	388.5
1957	154.5	84.3	142.3	26.4	407.5
1958	142.7	86.2	167.5	37.1	433.5
1959	136.8	86.4	185.3	51.7	460.2

Table 2.5 American Tobacco Company Share of the Market by Product Class, 1950-1959 (percent)

	Regular	King	Filter	Mentholated	Total
1950	26.22	86.40	—	—	31.27
1951	25.02	87.50	—	—	32.06
1952	24.10	78.23	—	—	32.81
1953	25.04	60.06	—	—	32.69
1954	27.11	61.77	4.03	—	33.51
1955	29.73	64.48	4.73	—	32.82
1956	32.19	67.32	4.97	—	31.48
1957	33.33	70.46	5.69	—	29.20
1958	33.08	71.35	4.06	—	26.64
1959	32.53	76.62	5.23	0.39	26.21

little participation in those markets. The company failed to exploit the filter-tip market, which gained increased importance from 1955 on and the mentholated market that began to grow quite rapidly in 1956. From 1955 to 1957, American Tobacco captured a significantly larger share of regular and king-size cigarettes, which were a declining submarket, and only got a moderately increasing but lower share of the expanding filter-tip submarket. The net effect was a decrease in the company's share of the total market.

IN SUMMARY

The manager has much to contribute to the forecasting process and his participation will help in minimizing the effort required to prepare the forecast. This applies not only to the formulation stage, to which much of the discussion in this chapter alludes, but throughout the time period in which the forecast is prepared.

The analyst should review with the manager what he is doing as work progresses. This is to ensure that the manager agrees with the approach and concepts and that he will effectively use the forecast and its range of accuracy in his decision making.

Detailed analysis and understanding of the system, its significant factors, and their relationships will improve the accuracy of the forecast and aid in future decision making. Also, unless the forecasting process includes a thorough analysis of the major areas, there will not be a sound basis for tracking the forecast and determining how and why it should be revised.

Chapter III

Forecasting Techniques

After the forecasting problem has been properly formulated, the analyst is in a position to choose the technique or combination of techniques that will best fit his needs. Although the manager does not participate directly in this selection, the analyst will have ascertained the types of assumptions the manager views as acceptable and will hopefully have identified the manager's philosophy or attitudes toward forecasting, all of which may place constraints on the choice of techniques.

For convenience, we have grouped the techniques into three basic categories: (1) qualitative techniques, (2) time-series analysis and projection, and (3) causal models. The first category uses qualitative data (e.g., expert opinions) and information about special events, and may or may not take the past into consideration. The second focuses entirely on patterns and pattern changes and, thus, relies entirely on historical data. The third uses highly refined and specific information about relationships between system elements. It is powerful enough to take special events formally into account, and it also uses the past as an important input.

Virtually all forecasting techniques fall into one of these three groups. However, there are many variations of each basic technique; thus for a specific application, the analyst may decide that none of the techniques precisely meets his requirements and he may combine or modify the ones given here. In our descriptions of each technique, we shall include the basic concepts and objectives, the analytical time required, the data requirements and associated costs, some typical applications, the degree of accuracy that can be expected, and the utilization of the technique to identify turning points. (The definition of turning points depends on the technique being described: short-run turning points, such as changes in the economy, apply to statistical techniques while long-run turning points, such as technological changes, apply to techniques like input-output.)

Some of these characteristics—especially the cost and time requirements—should be considered by the experienced analyst as general guidelines and "ball park" estimates only, since they are dependent on, for example, the amount of data available, the variability, and the type of computing equipment and programs available. (The cost estimates are based on our own experience, using as our machine configuration an IBM 360-40, 256K system, and a Univac 1108 Remote Batch System, together with such smaller equipment as GE and On-Line Systems Time Sharing and IBM 360-30's and 1130's.) Also, the costs of some of the techniques depend on (a) whether they are being used routinely or are set up for a single forecast, and (b) whether weightings or seasonals have to be determined anew each time a forecast is made.

The information we shall cover here is summarized in tabular form in the Appendix to this chapter. It may be used as a reference to the examples presented in subsequent chapters. We have made no attempt here to give an exhaustive list of the techniques but to have included only the ones that are more commonly used. For the reader interested in more detailed descriptions of each technique, see the comprehensive bibliography in Appendix A at the end of the book.

QUALITATIVE METHODS

These are used primarily when data are scarce, either because there is no relevant history (e.g., a new product) or good information is virtually nonexistent. As the name implies, these techniques rely primarily on qualitative or judgmental information. However, qualitative information provides a poor basis for comparison and can be interpreted differently. Therefore, it is obviously better if the qualitative information can be translated in some way to a quantitative base. The objective of the techniques is to bring together in a logical, unbiased, and systematic way all information and judgments that relate to the factors being evaluated.

Qualitative techniques are frequently used both in new technology areas and, to a large extent, in technological forecasting, where (a) development of a product idea may require several "inventions," so that R&D efforts and likelihood of success are difficult to estimate, and (b) market acceptance and penetration rates are highly uncertain. Technological forecasting will be covered in more detail in Chapter 5, which includes illustrations for utilizing qualitative techniques in that area.

Delphi Method

The objective of the Delphi method is to gain the consensus of a group of experts on an uncertain matter. This is accomplished by questioning them individually and providing them with anonymous feedback information from other people in the group until there is a convergence of the estimates or opinions of the total group. Any set of information available to some experts is passed on to all of the other experts, enabling them to have access to all of the information for forecasting. All questioning is handled impersonally by a coordinator. This technique eliminates committee activity almost entirely, thus reducing the influence of certain psychological factors, such as specious persuasion, unwillingness to abandon publicly expressed opinions, and the bandwagon effect of majority opinions.

The need for the Delphi method has arisen because of the extreme difficulty in getting unbiased opinions of experts. Generally, one person has more weight or dominates group opinion, and it often happens that each expert has different information available to him and gives a different weight to the same information. Both the inquiry into the reasons each expert gives for his opinions and the subsequent feedback of the reasons stated by others stimulate the experts to take account of information and considerations that they might otherwise inadvertently neglect. Also, feedback might cause them to give more weight to factors that they were initially inclined to dismiss as unimportant.

The results of a Delphi study reflect explicit, reasoned, self-aware opinions expressed by the experts in light of the opinions of associate experts. Such estimates or opinions should lessen the chance of surprise and provide a more sound basis for long-range decision making than those arrived at by implicit, unarticulated, intuitive judgments.

The Delphi method has been used in a variety of applications, and it has had extensive use in technological forecasting. It is more concerned with when events will occur and the likelihood of those events occurring, such as the development of a particular technology, the eventual magnitude of a market, the emergence of new consumer patterns, and political trends.

For the method itself, no historical information is required, although in technological forecasting and other similar situations it is best if some analysis of historical information has been performed to obtain a preliminary list of possibilities to be further considered by the experts. Otherwise, the experts may not be considering all of the possible alternatives or events. During the Delphi exercise, a coordinator issues a sequence of questionnaires, editing and consolidating responses as they are obtained, so that most of the data collection is performed during the Delphi exercise.

It can take from a minimum of two months to more than a year to complete a Delphi study, and any number of experts, from a few to thousands, can be involved. On the one hand, when some United States industrial corporations have performed Delphi exercises for forecasting technological developments, they have had from 25 to 200 of their scientists participating at various times throughout the study. On the other hand, a large-scale study has been performed in Japan in which approximately 4000 experts were involved over a period of approximately six months, with the study being concerned with technological, sociological, and political projections for a 10-year period.

Accuracy for the Delphi method has generally been relatively good and definitely better than other methods that neither employ the same level of detail nor give the necessary attention to obtain unbiased estimates. The method can also be used with reasonable accuracy in predicting when turning points will occur—that is, when there will be significant changes from current trends and what the magnitude of the changes will be.

The Delphi method is likewise used increasingly to obtain unbiased opinions of experts and to achieve either a consensus of these opinions or at least to reduce the range of such opinions.

Market Research

We include under this "technique" only that part of market research related directly to forecasting, which is the systematic, formal, and conscious procedure for evolving and testing hypotheses about real markets. While expert opinion could be elicited from knowledgeable marketing persons by use of the Delphi method or a similar approach, it is generally of value to obtain information directly from the market. The estimates of accuracy and other descriptions of market research forecasting techniques are based on the assumption that *good* market research is performed.

Unfortunately, most market research is biased and incomplete, even though large amounts of money may be spent in obtaining consumer opinions. This can happen especially when the market research is product-oriented instead of customer-oriented, as we described earlier in our example of United States automotive manufacturers' reaction to the introduction of foreign compact cars in the United States.

There are two aspects to market research: (1) the conducting of surveys or the use of other methods to obtain unbiased information about consumer preference under varying conditions, and (2) the analysis of the information obtained to identify the factors that have the greatest impact on consumer preferences. Major attention is often given to the first aspect, and relatively simple statistical analyses or "eyeballing" methods are utilized for the second.

Even when good research is done at the consumer level, it is very easy to misinterpret the findings and to draw wrong conclusions from the research. There are often strong interactions between market variables that are neither evident from visual examination of the data nor can be observed by simple statistical analysis.

Several powerful statistical techniques have been developed for analyzing data where relationships are obscure and difficult to establish. These are called multivariate techniques, with many employing the analysis of variance methodology. One technique that is particularly effective in determining which factors are significant is called the AID routine (Automatic Interaction Detector), developed by the University of Michigan and initially used to analyze data from sociological surveys.

When good, objective market research is performed, it is highly accurate for short-term forecasting (up to six months), reasonably accurate for intermediate forecasting (six months to two years) and then becomes less accurate for the long range (two to five years), primarily because customers are not able to accurately identify what their preferences or desires will be at later points in time. The ability of the analyst to use market research for identifying turning points depends on how far out into the future they are anticipated, with the technique enabling him to do a good job for the near future (up to one year) and a poor job beyond that.

Market research is used to obtain forecasts of long-range and new-product sales, as well as to estimate the implications of price changes and other marketing strategies over the short term. It can also be used to forecast profitability in those situations where price sensitivity and other factors are obtained by market research and then incorporated into a profit model.

With respect to market research data requirements, at the very minimum two sets of reports are required over time to identify changes in consumer preferences.

The analyst needs a considerable collection of market data from questionnaires, surveys, and time-series analyses of market variables to get good accuracy from market research. Forecasting by this method can cost $10,000 or significantly more. The cost will, to a large extent, depend on how well the market research is designed, the ability to anticipate what the decision will be for various forecasts and thus to determine the sensitivity of the decision to forecast errors, and how much previous knowledge there is so that sound hypotheses can be established.

For large-scale projects, computers are needed to analyze the results of surveys and other data collection; for smaller studies, hand calculations are feasible. In general, it is advisable to use a computer in analyzing data, not only for economical purposes but also because nonhypothesized relationships might exist that cannot be identified without powerful statistical analyses. Three months' time or more is usually needed to perform a routine market research forecasting projection. However, the time requirements increase significantly where innovator-imitator conditions exist and where estimates must be obtained for both the innovator group of buyers and the imitator group of buyers.

Panel Consensus

In this approach, as in the Delphi method, the objective is to obtain a consensus or at least some agreement between experts. The technique itself is based on the assumption that several experts, by collectively considering all relevant factors, can arrive at a better forecast than one person.

However, it is not done in an unbiased way. There is no secrecy, and communication is in fact encouraged among the panel members. Thus the forecast may not reflect a true consensus, since it is affected by the group dynamics that the Delphi method is meant to circumvent. Obviously, personalities will enter into the arriving at a consensus, because the persons are brought together for only one or a few meetings.

The cost is less than the Delphi method, generally ranging from $2000 upward, depending on the number of experts involved. Computers are not required for this technique and results can be obtained in as little time as two weeks. Little or no historical data are needed; the panel of experts are presented with and contribute information to the group meetings. Here again, as we noted with respect to the data requirements of market research, a minimum of two sets of reports or estimates should be made over time to determine changes.

The panel consensus technique is also used for forecasts of long-range and new-product sales, as well as for margin estimates. Accuracy is usually fair at best, and quite frequently poor accuracy is obtained. This technique is primarily used for expediency purposes, where the feeling is that, if the experts are brought together and given sufficient time, the panel members can arrive at a consensus.

Visionary Forecasts

Although the title of this technique is impressive, the visionary forecast is generally an unscientific method characterized by subjective guesswork and imagination. It can best be described as a prophecy that uses personal insights, judgments, and possibly facts about different scenarios of the future. It consists of one or a set of possible scenarios, prepared by one or more experts, where the alternative scenarios are considered the most likely ones that can occur, taking into account past trends and knowledge about market dynamics.

A visionary forecast is usually performed with little research, no substantial data collection or processing, and at a cost of $500 or more, depending on the number of scenarios. Since computers are not needed, this approach provides forecasts rather quickly, in as little time as one week. Overall, however, forecast accuracy is poor from short-to-long range, and the technique also does not enable the analyst to do a good job in signaling turning points. The main value of the visionary forecast approach depends to a large extent on the effort expended and the skill exerted in the preparation of the scenarios.

Historical Analogy

As the name implies, this is a comparative analysis of the introduction and growth of a new product with other products that have similar characteristics. The forecast itself is based on these similarity patterns. Efforts are made (a) to quantify the degrees of similarity by rating-ranking methods and other expert-opinion approaches, and (b) to determine what the dissimilarities will do to the basic patterns.

The accuracy of the technique obviously depends on the ability to find analogous products or situations. In some instances, the products may be quite different but have similar market characteristics.

The historical analogy is not generally accurate for short-range forecasting and for identifying turning points. However, it is a reasonably good approach for intermediate and long-range forecasting, depending on the analysts' skill in interpreting or estimating the effects of differences in product and market factors. Several years' history, preferably five to 10 years, must be available for all of the analogous products.

At least one month's time is required, and the analysis costs $1000 or more, depending on the man-effort expended. Computers are not often utilized, since many of the measures of similarity are subjective.

Major applications are for forecasts of new-product sales and profitability. In some instances, the historical analogy may be the only feasible approach for forecasting sales and profits of a new product, such as in the case of color television, where experience with black-and-white television provided a sound base for projection when the product differences were properly interpreted.

Cross-Impact Analysis

This technique is rapidly emerging as one of the more promising methods for medium and long-range forecasting of new products. It combines the use of some of the preceding techniques, such as the Delphi method, market research, or panel consensus, to provide inputs for the cross-impact analysis. It takes into account key factors that must be evaluated, in terms not only of their importance but also the probability of their occurrence, and the mutual interactions between the factors.

The need for cross-impact analysis arises from the problem of projecting complex interrelationships, because of mutual reinforcing or opposing trends in probabilistic environments, in the light of events that may or may not happen and in those cases where there are many factors belonging to one or several interacting disciplines.

Cross-impact analysis consists of assessing systematically the possible impact of every single event on every other event. Estimates are obtained for each of the possible events that can occur, and then the mutual interactions between such events are examined for inconsistencies or unexpected results. The forecaster must either be convinced of the validity of these estimates, or refer back to the inputs for their reasonableness.

Cross-impact analysis can be done as soon as the background or exploratory matrix is built. (This matrix is essentially a table containing the probabilities of events occurring under varying conditions.) The technique requires the use of a computer program to calculate the shifting value of the matrix, as events are included, excluded, or pushed to certainty. It accepts the forecasters' estimates of probabilities, whether obtained from Delphi rounds, trend extrapolation, other qualitative techniques, or intuition.

There are time-sharing programs available at a cost as low as $100 for a complete analysis (excluding the cost of the estimates for the matrices). Although it might cost a company several thousand dollars to do its own programming, a commercial vendor, Homa and Associates of Montreal, offers a program for $1500. The technique is designed to enhance the competence of intermediate and long-range forecasts for new products.

TIME-SERIES ANALYSIS AND PROJECTION

These are statistical techniques that can be used when several years' data for a product or product line are available and when relationships and trends are both clear and relatively stable.

One of the basic principles of statistical forecasting—indeed, of all forecasting when historical data are available—is that the forecaster should use the data on past performance to get a "speedometer reading" of the current rate (e.g., of sales) and of how fast this rate is increasing or decreasing. The current rate and changes in the rate—"acceleration" and "deceleration"—constitute the basis of forecasting. Once these are known, various mathematical techniques can be used to develop projections from them.

However, the matter is not so simple as it sounds. It is usually difficult to make projections from raw data. This is because the rates and trends are not immediately obvious; they may be mixed up with seasonal variations, for example, or perhaps distorted by such factors as the effects of an ambitious sales promotion campaign or some random event. Thus the projection of raw data and their use in an unadjusted form to establish current rates and trends is perhaps the major source of error in forecasting.

Dr. Herbert Stein, Chairman of President Nixon's Council of Economic Advisors, in chiding newsmen for using raw unadjusted figures to report a rise in the cost of living, said: "To look at these figures in an unadjusted way is like looking out the window at night and saying there is an eclipse."

The raw data must be massaged before they are usable, and this is frequently done by time-series analysis. A time series is a set of chronologically ordered points of raw data—for example, a division's sales of a given product, by month, or for several years. Time-series analysis helps to identify and explain:

• Any regularity or systematic variation in the series of data because of seasonality.

• Cyclical patterns that repeat—for example, every two or three years or more.

• Trends in the data.

- Growth rates of these trends.

- Inherent randomness in the data—that is, variations in the data that cannot be explained by statistical means.

(Unfortunately, most existing methods identify only seasonality, the combined effect of trends and cycles, and the irregular or chance component. In other words, most methods do not separate trends from cycles. We shall return to this point later on in this book when we discuss time-series analysis in the final stages of product maturity.)

Once the analysis is complete, the work of projecting future sales (or whatever) can begin. Although we have separated analysis from projection here for purposes of explanation, many statistical forecasting techniques actually combine both functions in a single operation.

It should be apparent from this description that all statistical techniques are based on the assumption that existing patterns will continue into the future. This assumption is more likely to be correct over the short term than it is over the long term. For this reason, the time-series techniques provide reasonably accurate forecasts for the immediate future but do quite poorly further into the future (unless the data patterns are extraordinarily stable).

Similarly, for this same reason, these analytical techniques ordinarily cannot predict accurately when the rate of growth in a trend will change significantly—for example, when a period of slow growth in sales will suddenly change to a period of rapid decay. Such changes are called turning points. They are naturally of the greatest importance to the manager. Thus, as we shall see, the forecaster must use supplementary methods to pure statistical techniques to predict when the turning points will occur.

Costs and time requirements for performing time-series analysis are generally omitted, since the cost and time will depend on the type of computing equipment available, the form and accessibility of the data, the number of analyses being made, and the experience of the analyst. Depending upon the technique used, the cost per analysis will range from less than one cent to more than $20, excluding data collection. The most expensive analysis is the Box-Jenkins method and the least expensive is the moving average technique. If data are available, all of the time-series techniques require one day or less to complete an analysis.

Moving Average

This method is probably used more frequently than any other technique, and it is the one that the most people are familiar with. Each point of a moving average of a time series is the arithmetic or weighted average (i.e., where each component or point of the average is given a specific weight, with the weights adding to 1) of several consecutive points of the series. The number of data points is chosen so that the effects of seasonality, irregularity, or both are eliminated, yet the trend-cycle is not "buried" or distorted. Virtually all time-series analysis techniques use some form of a moving average. Obviously, the weights for the different points may differ, and the length of the moving average may also vary, depending on the characteristics of the time series.

The moving average is a very simple technique to use, requiring a minimum of two years of sales history (if seasonality is present). Without "seasonals," less data are required—although, of course, the more history available, the better the projection should be. The length of the moving average must be specified or analytically determined. The moving average is an extremely low-cost technique; it can be obtained without the use of a computer. However, for large volumes of data and time series, a computer is very helpful in the analysis.

Two of the major applications of moving averages are (1) in forecasting for production planning and inventory control for low-volume items, and (2) in relatively simple marketing analyses. Although in specific instances the technique may provide good accuracy, in general the accuracy is relatively poor. In addition, the moving average is an ineffective tool for identifying turning points.

Exponential Smoothing

Essentially, this is a moving-average technique, except that the more recent data points are given more weight. The new forecast is basically equal to the old one, plus some proportion of the past forecasting error. An extension of exponential smoothing is adaptive forecasting, where the computational procedures are greatly expanded to include the determination of seasonals, which single exponential smoothing does not handle.

There are many variations of exponential smoothing, primarily focusing on the method of weighting the data points and the particular model used to fit the trend of the data. Some of the variations are more versatile than others, some are computationally more complex, and the computer requirements vary considerably.

Exponential smoothing, which was originally developed because of the high cost of storing data, permits the storing of relatively few bits of information. It is another low-cost technique—less than one cent per analysis when a large number of time series are done together. The use of a computer is generally recommended, although it is not absolutely necessary when there are a small number of computations. Adaptive forecasting, in contrast, is more costly, with more effort and more data (at least two to three years) being needed for initialization and first calculation of seasonals.

The most common applications are in production and inventory control, with forecasts of margins and other financial data being handled by this technique. It is not effective for identifying turning points. However, on short- and intermediate-range forecasting, it will do a good job, especially for stable time series. Because of frequent changes in data trends over a long period of time, it is not particularly applicable to long-range forecasting.

Census Bureau X-11

This technique is getting increasing use, although it is still too expensive to use on a repetitive basis for forecasting in such applications as production and inventory control. Developed by Julius Shiskin of the U.S. Census Bureau, it primarily decomposes time series into seasonals, trend-cycles, and irregular (or random) components.

The basic use of the X-11 technique is for detailed time-series analysis, including estimating seasonals. In our own use, we have extended the basic computational procedures by adding other analytical techniques to include applications in forecasting, tracking and warning, and budget setting and analysis.

The Census Bureau X-11 is a good tool for estimating the effects of past special events. When coupled with special knowledge or assumptions about special events for the future, it is perhaps one of the most effective techniques for intermediate-range forecasting—that is, three months to one year ahead—since it allows the analyst to predict turning points and to tie in special events with his forecast. As is true of all statistical methods, it does not enable the analyst to do a good job of long-range forecasting.

The X-11 technique was initially developed for decomposing government time series, but it is now being used extensively by business and industry. Several of its applications when the basic computations are extended include forecasting company, division, or department sales; tracking sales, profits, and inventories; analyzing profit ratios, promotions, and budgets to determine imputed patterns or assumptions; and identifying turning points (within one to two months of when they occur, although special methods can even reduce this). The Census Bureau X-11 method requires a minimum of three years' historical information to obtain statistically valid estimates of seasonals; a computer is necessary; and the entire history is used each time computations are performed.

Box-Jenkins

This is the most comprehensive time-series analysis/projection technique that has been developed thus far. All techniques in this group can be considered, in one way or another, as a special case of the Box-Jenkins method. Basically, the forecaster fits a time series with a mathematical model. This model is optimal in the sense that it has smaller errors or variability than any other model fitted to the data. The type of model must be specified, and the parameters of it are then computed.

Box-Jenkins is apparently the most accurate statistical technique available, but also one of the most costly and time-consuming computational procedures. Although it is possible to do these computations by hand, we recommend the use of computer programs that are now commercially available.

The Box-Jenkins technique determines what lengths of moving average should be used and the weights to be assigned to past history, as well as the other parameters of the specified forecasting model. (It also provides assistance in identifying, selecting, and testing the correct mathematical model.) As a minimum, it requires the same amount of data as a moving average, but much better results are obtained if several years of history are used. One or two days turn-around time is normal.

The forecasting accuracy obtainable is excellent for the short range, good for the intermediate range, and poor for the long range. However, without the special extensions, such as those included in the Census Bureau X-11 routine (e.g., variations in trading dates and irregular events), it does only a fair job of identifying the turning points.

The Box-Jenkins method is the first technique of its kind to have the versatility to merge time-series projection (i.e., purely statistical projections) with other special knowledge, such as causal relationships.

Typical applications are forecasts of demand for large-volume items in production scheduling, cash-balance forecasts, and basic analyses of time-series data to determine the types of models that will produce the greatest accuracy. Efforts are currently being made both to simplify the computational procedures and to reduce the computer costs so that there will be an increased number of applications. It is expected that there will be considerably increased use of the Box-Jenkins method in the near future.

Trend Projections

As the name implies, the objective of this technique is to fit a trend line to a mathematical equation and then to project it into the future by means of that equation. The equation can take several forms; hence there are several variations or types of trend projection. These include slope-characteristic techniques, polynomials, and logarithmic equations.

Trend projection is primarily applied to annual data where five or more data points are available, depending on the variation used. The technique will give good forecasting accuracy for short, intermediate, and long-range projections for sales or other business data that are relatively stable—that is, not subject to significant short- or long-term fluctuations. All data points are needed each time a forecast is made.

Because they are extensions of recent trends, trend projections are not effective for predicting turning points unless they occur very gradually.

Trend projections are usually not very accurate for long-term forecasts since they are too easily influenced by changes in market share and advertising, for example.

The costs and computer requirements vary with the application. Generally, however, they are less than $100 per analysis. The overall time needed to prepare a forecast depends on the analyst's skill in selecting the proper model to fit the trend, but for a specific model the analysis can be done in a day's time. Typical applications are new-product forecasts (particularly, intermediate and long-term) and business-outlook forecasts.

Learning Curves

Initial applications of this technique were in the aircraft industry several decades ago and, thus, it is frequently called the "aircraft learning curve." The approach has applications both in forecasting the rates of technological development and in estimating future production costs—and psychologists have also used the learning curve in their work.

The basic concept is that learning occurs at a consistent rate over time, or as effort is expended, so that technological progress takes place as research is performed and production costs are lowered as the number of units produced increases. It follows a logarithmic function, where for production costs each time that the cumulative number of units produced doubles, both the cumulative average cost and the unit cost are reduced by the learning percentage.

For example, if we assume an 80% learning curve, the production costs will be reduced 20% each time the cumulative number of units produced doubles. Thus, if the first 100 units cost $50 each, the average cost for 200 units will be $40, or the second 100 will cost $30 each.

Technological development in a particular field will progress in the same way, but to use the technique it must be possible to quantitatively measure the extent of that technological development.

Computations can be performed manually, or a log-log graph paper or a nomograph can be utilized to make projections. The learning curve is extremely useful for estimating production costs in the short, intermediate, and long term. Obviously, since such estimates are based on the assumption that costs are reduced or technology developed at a constant rate, the technique is ineffective in forecasting turning points.

With respect to data requirements, either the production costs for two points in time (and cumulative units produced) or for one cumulative cost point and an assumption about the learning percentage must be available to establish a learning curve from which projections can be made. In some instances, for example, the learning percentage changes at different stages of a product's life cycle. Much work has been done in determining the learning percentages for different types of work, for example, in applying historical analogies to new products provides a basis for forecasting new-product production costs. There have been relatively few learning-curve applications thus far in the prediction of technological development.

CAUSAL MODELS

When historical data are available and enough analysis can be performed to spell out explicitly the relationships between the factor to be forecast and other elements, such as related businesses, economic forces, and socioeconomic factors, the forecaster often constructs a causal model.

This is the most sophisticated kind of forecasting tool. It expresses mathematically the relevant causal relationships, and it may include pipeline considerations (i.e., inventories) and market survey information. It may also directly incorporate the results of a time-series analysis.

The causal model takes into account everything known about the dynamics of the flow system, and it utilizes predictions of related events, such as competitive actions, strikes, and promotions. If the data are available, the model will include factors for each location in the flow chart (as in Figure 2.2), and the forecaster will connect these by equations to describe the overall product flow.

If certain kinds of data are lacking, initially it may be necessary for the forecaster to make assumptions about some of the relationships and then to track what is happening to determine if those assumptions are true. Typically, a causal model is continually revised as more knowledge about the system becomes available.

In essence, the ultimate objective of a forecasting system incorporating causal models is to develop a comprehensive model of the system, which explains all of the system parameters and includes their interactions. This model can be used not only for forecasting but also for evaluating the implications of various tactics and strategies.

Regression Models

Functionally, a regression model relates sales or other factors that are to be predicted to elements of the system that explain some of their variation, such as economic, competitive, or internal variables. Regression analysis is the computational technique that estitmates the coefficients of the regression model, using the least-square technique. Relationships are primarily analyzed statistically, although any relationship should be selected for testing on a rational ground.

The approach taken by the analyst should be pragmatic. From a study of the flow chart of the system dynamics and on the basis of his experience, he hypothesizes certain relationships; then, with actual data, he determines statistically whether they are plausible. It is dangerous to perform regression analysis by merely identifying several possible variables and letting the computer routine select the ones that are most significant. Because of randomness, intercorrelations, or other peculiarities in the data, the relationships (i.e., the signs of the coefficients) obtained by this approach could possibly be opposite to what one would normally or rationally expect.

Several years of quarterly history are needed to get meaningful relationships. Mathematically, it is necessary to have at least two more observations than there are independent variables (factors used as a basis for predicting the dependent variables). Regression analysis can usually provide good to very good accuracy for short- and intermediate-range forecasting but, unless the relationships are very sound and have been proven by experimentation to be valid, it will do a poor job of long-range forecasting. Another problem with long-range forecasting is the necessity to forecast the variables to which the one under consideration is related.

Regression analysis is used for many different applications, such as forecast of sales by product classes, profit margins, or any other similar factors. Regression analysis can usually be performed for less than $100, depending on the pieces of data and the number of variables being considered. Unless there are only one or two independent variables, it is not practical to perform the computations by hand. On a short-term basis, regression models should do a good job of identifying most turning points. The overall time that the analyst requires for developing a regression model depends on his ability to identify relationships. This may take as long as several weeks, and is a function of the availability of data and the ability of others to help identify the meaningful variables.

Econometric Models

This is essentially a system of interdependent regression equations that describes some sector of economic sales or profit activity. The equations take into account all of the interdependencies of the factors in the system being modeled. Econometric models use regression analysis, where the parameters of the regression equations are usually estimated simultaneously. (This requires special computer programs.)

As a rule, the econometric models are relatively expensive to develop and can easily cost between $5000 and $10,000 for a business within a company, depending on the detail and the number of factors included in the equations. An econometric model for an entire company could easily cost between $50,000 and $100,000 or more. However, because of the system of the equations inherent in such models, it will better express the causalities involved than an ordinary regression equation; hence it will predict turning points more accurately than regression equations.

Because econometric models are similar to regression equations, the amount of data required and the applications are similar to regression analysis. Econometric models can be expected to provide good forecasting accuracy for short, intermediate, and long range. A minimum of two months' time is required for developing econometric models, and computers are necessary for their derivations.

Intentions-to-Buy Surveys

These surveys of the general public are used to determine intentions to buy certain products or to derive an index that measures general feelings about the present and the future and that estimates how these feelings will affect buying habits. These approaches to forecasting are more useful for tracking and warning than for forecasting itself. The basic problem in using them is that a turning point may be signaled incorrectly (and hence never occurs). In this case the likelihood of a turning point occurring at a specific time should be stated.

Several years of data are normally required to relate intentions-to-buy indices to company sales. This means that several surveys must be conducted over time before the indices can be meaningfully and accurately applied. The analytical time itself takes several weeks and will cost $5000 or more, with computers used to perform the analyses.

This type of technique is normally used to forecast sales by product class. It does not provide good forecasting accuracy for the long range but may be the only alternative available at the time. It should usually be considered a secondary technique to help validate the forecasts obtained from other methods.

Input-Output Models

This is a method of analysis concerned with the interindustry or interdepartmental flow of goods or services in the economy or a company and its markets. It shows what flows or inputs must occur to obtain certain outputs. Considerable effort must be expended to use these models properly. For example, if they are to be applied to specific businesses, additional detail, not normally available, must be obtained.

Corporations using input-output models have expended as much as $100,000 or more to develop useful applications. The most common input-output models are on a national scale, although some attention is now being given to regional models. Corporation input-output models are usually tied in with national models, and most national economic forecasting activities now include a tie-in of their econometric models with input-output to get longer-range economic forecasts.

Input-output models are not applicable to short-term forecasting; but, if proper relationships are obtained, one can get good-to-very good accuracy for intermediate- and long-range forecasting. For these longer-range forecasts, these models are fairly good at identifying turning points.

Considerable data are required for input-output models, usually at least 10 to 15 years of history. Considerable amounts of information on product and service flows within a corporation (or economy) for each year in which input-output analysis is desired must be obtained. Computers are required for calculations and a minimum of six months is needed to develop a corporate input-output model. Within a company, they are useful for forecasting company sales and divisional sales for industrial sectors and subsectors.

A good input-output model requires the participation of econometricians, marketing experts like Daniel Yankelovich, and technological experts. Without that, the forecasts are highly questionable. For example, Arthur D. Little's I-O model ranking of industries varies significantly from Battelle's.

Econometric Input-Output Models

As indicated in the preceding section, econometric models and input-output models are sometimes combined for forecasting. The input-output model is used to provide long-term trends for the econometric model, and it also helps to stabilize the econometric model. These I-O models cost as much as $100,000 or more to develop, require a computer, and at least six months to derive. They are good at predicting major turning points and for intermediate- and long-range forecasting.

Diffusion Indices

This is again what may be called a secondary technique, not giving very good accuracy for any length of forecast but helping to validate a forecast derived by other techniques. A diffusion index is the percentage of a group of economic indicators that are going up or down. A diffusion index is good at identifying turning points, and requires the same amount of data as intentions-to-buy surveys, where company sales and several years' data of the economic indicators are needed.

A forecast using a diffusion index will cost over $1000, it will require one month's time, and it could be derived without a computer, although it would usually be more economical to use one. This cost could be greatly reduced if one of the diffusion indices developed by the United States government is applicable to the problem at hand. The United States government employs diffusion indices to indicate the direction of the economy.

Leading Indicators

This approach is a time series of an economic activity whose movement in a given direction precedes the movement of some other time series in the same direction. This might be considered a subtechnique of regression analysis. However, because causal relationships are not necessarily established, the accuracy of this approach may not be good. Moreover, applications are limited, especially in the long range, where forecasts of the leading indicator must be made.

Nevertheless, this approach does a good job of identifying turning points, which is one of its primary functions. Five to 10 years of history are needed to perform such an analysis, at a cost of about $1000 and with at least one month of a forecaster's time normally required. Forecasts of sales by product class are one major application of the leading-indicator technique.

Life-Cycle Analysis

This technique consists of an analysis and forecast of new-product growth rates based on S-shaped curves. The life-cycle pattern for a particular family of products is determined historically. The phases of product acceptance by the various consumer groups, such as innovators, early adapters, early majority, late majority, and laggards, are central to the analysis, and help to determine the parameters of the S-shaped curves. The life-cycle technique provides limited accuracy, it is not particularly good at identifying turning points, it costs over $1500 to perform the analysis, and it requires one month or more of analytical effort.

The minimum data requirements are for the annual sales to date of the product being considered and for the entire history of a similar product or products. This technique frequently requires market surveys as well, and is used primarily for forecasting new-product sales. It is also frequently used in conjunction with trend-projection techniques, such as the slope-characteristic method.

IN SUMMARY

As we have just seen, there are many forecasting techniques available to the analyst, each having its own strengths and weaknesses. The data requirements, costs, basic principles and assumptions, accuracies, and overall effectiveness differ for each technique for various conditions. One technique may be best for a given set of data. Another technique will prove better for a set of data from the same general type of business but with a different degree of variability.

The analyst must carefully determine what is required of the forecast and examine each of the techniques to determine which is most applicable for the particular forecast being prepared. This can only effectively be done through proper formulation of the forecasting problem, because each technique has strength, weaknesses, and underlying assumptions that must be evaluated for each specific situation.

APPENDIX: SUMMARY OF TECHNIQUES

A. Qualitative Methods

Technique	1. Delphi Method	2. Market Research	3. Panel Consensus
Description	A panel of experts is interrogated by a sequence of questionnaires in which the responses to one questionnaire are used to produce the next questionnaire. Any set of information available to some experts and not others is thus passed on to the others, enabling all the experts to have access to all the information for forecasting. This technique eliminates the bandwagon effect of majority opinion and dominant personalities.	The systematic, formal, and conscious procedure for evolving and testing hypotheses about real markets. The techniques most commonly used are called multivariate statistical techniques.	This technique is based on the assumption that several experts can arrives at a better forecast than one person. There is no secrecy, and communication is encouraged. The forecasts are sometimes influenced by social factors and may not reflect a true consensus. Results greatly influenced by group dynamics.
Accuracy			
Short term (0–3 months)	Usually not applicable	Usually used as inputs to other forecasting techniques.	Poor to fair
Medium term (3 months–2 years)	Fair to very good		Poor to fair
Long term (2 years and up)	Fair to very good		Poor
Identification of turning points	Fair to good	Fair to very good	Poor to fair
Typical applications	Forecasts of long-range and new-product sales, forecasts of margins, and technological forecasting.	Forecasts of long-range and new-product sales; forecasts of margins; changes in market share, customer attitudes, and buying habits.	Forecasts of long-range and new-product sales, forecasts of margins.
Data required	A coordinator issues the sequence of questionnaires; editing and consolidating the responses.	As minimum, two set of reports over time. One needs a considerable collection of market data from questionnaires, surveys, and time-series analyses of market variables.	Information from a panel of experts is presented openly in group meetings to arrive at a consensus forecast. Again, a minimum is two sets of reports over time.
Cost of forecasting			
With a computer	$3000+	$10,000+	$2000+
Is calculation possible without a computer?	Computer often not utilized	Yes, but usually extremely difficult and often impossible.	Yes
Time required to develop an application and make a forecast	2 months to 1 year	3 months +	2 weeks +

A. Qualitative Methods

Technique	4. Visionary Forecast	5. Historical Analogy	6. Cross-Impact analysis
Description	A prophecy that uses personal insights, judgment, and, when possible, facts about different scenarios of the future. It is characterized by subjective guesswork and imagination; in general, the methods used are nonscientific.	This is a comparative analysis of the introduction and growth of similar new products, which bases the forecast on similarity patterns.	This consists of systematically assessing the possible impact of every single event on every other event. Estimates are obtained for each of the possible events that can occur, for their relative importance, and probability of occurring.
Accuracy			
Short term (0–3 months)	Poor	Poor	Not applicable
Medium term (3 months–2 years)	Poor	Good to fair	Fair to good
Long term (2 years and up)	Poor	Good to fair	Fair to good
Identification of turning points	Poor	Poor to fair	Fair to good
Typical applications	Forecasts of long-range and new-product sales, forecasts of margins.	Forecasts of long-range and new-product sales, forecasts of margins.	Forecasts of long-range and new-product sales.
Data required	A set of possible scenarios about the future prepared by a few experts in light of past events.	Several years' history of one or more similar products.	Estimates of each of the important events, their interrelationships, and probabilities of happening. Usually requires the inputs of experts.
Cost of forecasting			
With a computer	$1000 +	$1000 +	$2000 +
Is calculation possible without a computer?	Yes	Computers often not utilized.	Yes, but difficult.
Time required to develop an application and make a forecast	1 week +	1 month +	1 month +

B. Time-Series Analysis and Projections[a]

Technique	1. Moving Average	2. Exponential Smoothing	3. Box-Jenkins
Description	Each point of a moving average of a time series is the arithmetic or weighted average of several con-	This technique is a weighted moving average, except that more recent data points are given more	Exponential smoothing is a special case of the Box-Jenkins technique. The time series is fitted

secutive points of the series, where the number of data points is chosen so that the effects of seasonals or irregularity or both are eliminated.

weight. Descriptively, the new forecast is equal to the old one plus some proportion of the past forecasting error. Adaptive forecasting is somewhat the same except that seasonals are also computed. There are many variations of exponential smoothing; some are more versatile than others, some are computationally more complex, and some require more computer time.

with a mathematical model that is optimal in the sense that it assigns smaller errors to history than any other model of the class. The type of model must be identified and the parameters then estimated. This is apparently the most accurate statistical routine presently available but also one of the most costly and time-consuming ones.

Accuracy			
Short term (0–3 months)	Poor to good	Fair to very good	Very good to excellent
Medium term (3 months–2 years)	Poor	Poor to good	Poor to good
Long term (2 years and up)	Very poor	Very poor	Very poor
Identification of turning points	Poor	Poor	Fair
Typical applications	Inventory control for low-volume items.	Production and inventory control, forecasts of margins, and other financial data.	Production and inventory control for large-volume items, forecasts of cash balances.
Data required	A minimum of two years of sales history, if seasonals are present; otherwise, less data. (Of course, the more history the better.) The moving average must be specified.	The same as for a moving average.	The same as for a moving average. However, in this case more history is very advantageous in model identification and parameter estimation.
Cost of forecasting			
With a computer	$.005[b]	$.005[b]	$100 +
Is calculation possible without a computer?	Yes	Yes	No
Time required to develop an application and make a forecast	1 day or less	1 day or less	1 or 2 days

[a] These and the accompanying time-series analysis and projection estimates are based on our own experience, using this machine configuration: an IBM 360-40, 256 K system, and a Univac 1108 Time Sharing System, together with such smaller equipment as GE Time Sharing and IBM 360-30's and 1130's. Cost estimates for Group B include computer cost only, assuming that the appropriate computer program is available. Most of these programs are commercially available.

[b] Manpower costs are not included, as it is usually minimal for the routine application if it is computerized.

B. Time-Series Analysis and Projections[a]

Technique	4. X-11	5. Projections	6. Learning-Experience Curve
Description	Developed by Julius Shiskin of the Census Bureau, this technique decomposes a time series into seasonals, trend cycles, and irregular elements. Primarily used for detailed time-series analysis (including estimating seasonals), but we have extended its uses to forecasting, and tracking and warning by incorporating other analytical methods. Used with special knowledge, it is perhaps the most effective technique for medium-range forecasting—three months to one year—allowing one to predict turning points and to time special events.	This technique fits a trend line to a mathematical equation and then projects it into the future by means of this equation. There are several variations: for example, the slope-characteristic method, polynomials, and semi-log graph paper.	The original learning curve, first noticed in the manufacture of aircraft, focused primarily on the increased efficiency and decreasing manufacturing costs, which occurred as production volume was accumulated in this particular product type. The recurrence of this efficiency improvement enabled production planners to closely predict future costs. The experience curve is a generalization of the familiar learning curve. The Boston Consulting Group has expanded it to include other factors, such as cost-volume and all components of final product unit costs delivered to the customer (e.g., manufacturing costs, selling and distribution costs, and product development and administrative costs).
Accuracy			
Short term (0–3 months)	Very good to excellent	Very good	Fair
Medium term (3 months–3 years)	Good	Poor to good	Fair to good
Long term (2 years and up)	Very poor	Poor to good	Fair to good
Identification of turning points	Very good	Poor	Fair
Typical applications	Tracking and warning; forecasts of company, division, or department sales; setting and critiquing budgets.	New-product forecasts (particularly intermediate and long term).	Forecasts of a short- to long-range costs for established and new products; budgeting; forecasting manpower and capital requirements; scheduling; purchasing; pricing; and so forth.

Data required	A minimum of three years' history to start. Thereafter, the complete history.	Varies with technique used. However, a good rule of thumb is to use a minimum of five years' annual data to start. Thereafter, the complete history.	Several years' history of one or more products.
Cost of forecasting			
With a computer including manpower	$5.00	Varies with application	$100 +
Is calculation possible without a computer?	No	Yes	Yes
Time required to develop an application and make a forecast	1 day or less	1 day or less	1 day

[a] These and the accompanying time-series analysis and projection estimates are based on our own experience, using this machine configuration: an IBM 360–40, 256 K system, and a Univac 1108 Time Sharing System, together with such smaller equipment as GE Time Sharing and IBM 360–30 s and 1130 s. Cost estimates for Group B include computer cost only, assuming that the appropriate computer program is available. Most of these programs are commercially available.

67

C. Causal Methods

Technique	1. Regression Model	2. Econometric Model	3. Intention-to-Buy and Anticipations Surveys	4. Input-Output Model
Description	This functionally relates sales to other economic, competitive, or internal variables, and estimates an equation using the least-squares technique. Relationships are primarily analyzed statistically, although any relationship should be selected for testing on a rational ground.	An econometric model is a system of interdependent regression equations that describes some sector of economic sales or profit activity. The parameters of the regression equations are usually estimated simultaneously. As a rule, these models are relatively expensive to develop and can easily cost between $5000 and $10,000, depending on detail. However, because of the system of equations inherent in such models, they will better express the causalities involved than an ordinary regression equation and, hence, will predict turning points more accurately.	These surveys of the general public (a) determine intentions to buy certain products or (b) derive an index that measures general feeling about the present and the future, and estimates how this feeling will affect buying habits. These approaches are more useful for tracking and warning than forecasting. The basic problem in using them is that a turning point may be signaled incorrectly (and hence never occur).	A method of analysis concerned with the interindustry or interdepartmental flow of goods or services in the economy or a company and its markets. It shows what flows of inputs must occur to obtain certain outputs. Considerable effort must be expended to use these models properly, and additional detail not normally available must be obtained if they are to be applied to specific businesses. Corporations using input-output models have expended as much as $100,000 and more annually to develop useful applications.
Accuracy				
Short term (0–3 months)	Good to very good	Good to very good	Poor to good	Not applicable
Medium term (3 months–2 years)	Good to very good	Very good to excellent	Poor to good	Good to very good
Long term (2 years and up)	Poor to good	Good	very poor	Very poor
Identification of turning points	Very good	Excellent	Good	Fair
Typical applications	Forecasts of sales by product classes, forecasts of margins.	Forecasts of sales by product classes, forecasts of margins.	Forecasts of sales by product class.	Forecasts of company and division sales for industrial sectors and subsectors,

Data required	Several years' quarterly history to obtain good, meaningful relationships. Mathematically necessary to have two more observations than there are independent variables.	The same as for regression.	Several years' data are usually required to relate such indices to company sales.	Ten to 15 years' history. Considerable amounts of information on product and service flows with a corporation (or economy) for each year for which an input-output analysis is desired.
Cost of forecasting				
With a computer including manpower	$300 +	$5000 +	$10,000 +	$25,000 +
Is calculation possible without a computer?	Yes	Yes	Yes	No
Time required to develop an application and make a forecast	Depends on ability to identify relationships	2 months +	3 weeks +	6 months +

C. Causal Methods

Technique	5. Econometric Input-Output Model	6. Diffusion Index	7. Leading Indicator	8. Life-Cycle Analysis
Description	Econometric models and input-output models are sometimes combined for forecasting. The input-output model is used to provide long-term trends for the econometric model; it also stabilizes the econometric model.	The percentage of a group of economic indicators that are going up or down, with this percentage then becoming the index.	A time series of an economic activity whose movement in a given direction precedes the movement of some other time series in the same direction is a leading indicator.	This is an analysis and forecasting of new-product growth rates based on S-curves. The phases of product acceptance by the various groups such as innovators, early adapters, early majority, late majority and laggards are central to the analysis.
Accuracy				
Short term (0–3 months)	Not applicable	Poor to good	Poor to good	Poor
Medium term (3 months–2 years)	Good to very good	Poor to good	Poor to good	Poor to good
Long term (2 years and up)	Good to excellent	Very poor	Very poor	Poor to good
Identification of turning points	Good	Good	Good	Poor to good
Typical applications	Company sales for industrial sectors and subsectors.	Forecasts of sales by product class.	Forecasts of sales by product class.	Forecasts of new-product sales.
Data required	The same as for a moving average and X-11.	The same as intention-to-buy survey.	The same as an intention-to-buy survey +5 to 10 year's history.	As a minimum, the annual sales of the product being considered or of a similar product. It is often necessary to do market surveys.
Cost of forecasting				
With a computer	$25,000 +	$1500 +	$1500 +	$1500 +
Is calculation possible without a computer?	No	Yes	Yes	Yes
Time required to develop application and make a forecast	6 months +	1 month +	1 month +	1 month +

Chapter IV

Decision Making During
the Product Life Cycle

In the previous chapter, we gave brief descriptions of the most frequently used forecasting techniques. However, these techniques can best be understood in the context of their applications in decision making; thus in this chapter and in the following eight chapters we shall be concerned both with the types of decisions that are made at the various stages of the product life cycle and with the techniques that are most appropriate in generating forecasts for those decisions.

At each stage of the product life, from conception through steady-state sales and on to the phasing-out period, the decisions that management must make are quite different; the kinds and accuracy of information needed as a base for arriving at a decision will differ; and the understanding of the system dynamics (i.e., the relevant factors and their interactions) usually will be evolutionary over the product life cycle. In addition, the information available for obtaining the forecasts will change throughout the various stages, so that the techniques for deriving the desired inputs will differ analogously. Furthermore, different products may require different kinds of forecasting for the same stage of the product life cycle.

On the one hand, much will depend on the "control" that the company has over the sales of the product, which is influenced by the product's position or location in the distribution system. For example, Corning Glass Works produces Corning Ware cookware, a proprietary consumer-product line, over which its control of the distribution pipeline extends at least through the distributor level.

Thus the manufacturer can affect or control consumer sales directly, as well as control (at least to some extent) the pipeline elements. Many of the changes in shipment rates and in overall profitability are therefore due to actions taken by the manufacturer himself. Tactical decisions on promotions, specials, and pricing are usually left to the manufacturer's discretion as well. The technique or combination of techniques selected for projecting sales or profits should therefore permit incorporation of such "special information." The forecaster may have to start with the simple techniques and work up to more sophisticated ones that permit such possibilities, but the final goal is there.

On the other hand, where a company supplies a component to a consumer-goods manufacturer, such as the glass for a television tube or the steel for an automobile, the supplier does not have such direct influence or control over either the pipeline elements or the final consumer sales. It may be impossible for the supplier to obtain good information about what is taking place at points further along in the flow system. As a consequence, the forecaster will necessarily take a different approach to forecasting than for a consumer product.

THE LIFE-CYCLE STAGES

Normally, there are five stages in the life cycle of a successful product: product development, testing and introduction, rapid growth, steady state, and phasing out. However, to encompass another aspect of forecasting that relates indirectly to the product life cycle, we shall include another stage: the initial preproduct or technology development stage, which embraces the rapidly growing field of technological forecasting. Table 4.1 summarizes these six stages, the typical decisions made, and the main forecasting techniques suitable at each stage.

The remainder of this chapter contains a brief, introductory discussion of these six stages. Chapters 5 to 12 present further descriptions with detailed illustrations of how the various techniques have been applied in specific decision situations.

The typical decisions and shape of the life-cycle curve in Figure 4.1 are mainly representative of durable goods. While nondurable goods and services also have life-cycle curves that contain the same major phases, the shapes of the curves will differ, and the values of the decisions will change. Furthermore, the components of the curves are different: the durable goods life-cycle curve components consist of purchases represented by new orders, multiunit owners, and replacement sales; the nondurable goods

Table 4.1 Types of Decisions Made Over a Product's Life Cycle, With Related Forecasting Techniques

Stage of life cycle	Preproduct	Product Development	Market Testing and Early Introduction	Rapid Growth	Steady State	Phasing Out
Typical decisions	Allocation of R&D resources Distribution system needs Personnel needs Acquisitions	Amount of development effort Product design Business strategies	Optimum facility size Marketing strategies, including distribution and pricing	Facilities expansion Marketing strategies Production planning	Promotions specials Pricing Production planning Inventories	Transfer of facilities Marketing effort Production planning
Forecasting techniques	Delphi method Progress functions Panel consensus Trend analysis Historical analogy Tracking for signals	Delphi method Historical analysis of comparable products Priority pattern analysis Input-output analysis Panel consensus	Consumer surveys Tracking-and-warning systems Market tests Experimental designs Sales	Statistical techniques for identifying/turning points Tracking-and-warning systems Market surveys Intention-to-buy surveys	Time-series analysis and projection Causal and econometric models Market surveys for tracking and warning Life-cycle analysis	Slope characteristic Statistical tracking and market research Historical analogy and regression analysis

and most services curves consist of initial buyers and repeat buyers. The values of the decisions will frequently be less for nondurable goods than durable goods, although the ultimate costs of overstocking will be higher for nondurable goods because of the shorter phasing-out period.

Stage 1.   Preproduct Development

Before a specific new-product concept emerges, there are usually socio-logical, political, or technological developments that make the new product possible or necessary. The forecasting objective, prior to product development, is to determine when new products will be possible or required by legislation and what the characteristics of these products' will be.

Here are the major forecasting questions in the preproduct stage.

• When is a particular technology most likely to be developed to the stage that products are feasible and marketable?

• When will social and political pressures force a change in a product or require a new one?

• What are the potential sales for opportunities that will emerge from this technology or new-product requirement?

• What will the characteristics of these markets be?

• What events must occur for technological breakthroughs or for legislation to force new products or changes in existing products?

These questions should be answered for the manager to make decisions relating to (a) how much R&D effort should be expended in techno-logical development, (b) what extent the company will participate in a new or expanding industry, (c) what type of distribution system will be needed to sell the new products and when it should be available, and (d) the personnel and facility requirements associated with the business. These are some of the same questions and decisions that arise during the product development stage. But they must be considered in at least a macro way at this stage so that preliminary work can be undertaken if long lead times are necessary in preparing for product introduction (e.g., the obtaining of a research capability and the establishment of a reputation in a business).

Most of the decisions at this stage will include contingency planning, with tracking-and-warning systems used to determine whether initial fore-casts and related assumptions are correct or strategies should be changed as time passes and new information becomes available. Also, the forecasting system itself may involve tracking of signals to identify technological breakthroughs and new legislative possibilities.

Qualitative techniques, not requiring historical information, are often utilized. The primary basis for such forecasts is expert opinion, although historical analogies should be used as cross-checks when possible. This type of forecasting will cover periods up to 20 years into the future.

A common objection to much long-range forecasting is that it is virtually impossible to predict with accuracy what will happen several years into the future. We agree that uncertainty increases when a forecast is made for a period of more than two years. However, at the very least, the forecast and a measure of its accuracy enable the manager to know his risks and to choose an appropriate strategy from those available. As a minimum, it is also advisable to consider expert opinions and judgments in an objective rather than a subjective way.

Stage 2.   Product Development

In the early stages of product development, the manager wants answers to questions such as the following.

- What are the alternative growth opportunities to pursuing Product X?
- How have established products similar to Product X fared?
- Should we enter this business; if so, in what segments?
- How should we allocate R&D efforts and funds?
- How successful will different product concepts be?
- How will Product X fit into the markets five or 10 years from now?

Forecasts that help to answer these long-range questions must necessarily have long horizons themselves.

Systematic market research is, of course, a mainstay in this area. For example, priority pattern analysis can describe the consumer's preferences and the likelihood that he or she will buy a product, thus being of great value in forecasting (and updating) penetration levels and rates. But there are also other market research tools, which will be used according to the state of the market, the product concept, and whether the product will compete in a clearly defined and basically established market, or in an undefined and new market.

While there can be no direct data about a product that is still a gleam in the manufacturer's eye, information about its likely performance can be gathered in several ways, provided that the market in which it is to be sold is a known entity.

For example, the forecasts can compare a proposed product with competitive products, and rank it on quantitative scales for different factors. This is called product differences measurement. Another and more formal approach is to construct disaggregate market models by splitting out different segments of a complex market for individual study and consideration. A third method of forecasting sales or profits for a new product in a defined market is to compare it with an "ancestor" that has similar characteristics, such as color television versus black-and-white television.

Even within a defined market, it will be necessary to determine whether the total market is elastic or inelastic—that is, will it continue its historic growth rate or will the new product expand the size of the total market?

When the market for a new product is weakly defined and the product concept may still be fluid, few data are available and history is not relevant. This has been true for modular housing, pollution-measurement devices, time-shared computers, and educational learning devices. The Delphi method or other "expert opinion" techniques and market research are most applicable here, with input-output analysis in combination with other techniques occasionally being of value.

Because techniques used for new products in defined versus undefined markets vary considerably, we shall devote separate chapters to these two cases.

Stage 3.   Testing and Introduction

Before a product can enter its (hopefully) rapid-growth stage, the market potential must be tested and the product introduced—and then more market testing may be advisable. At this stage, management needs answers to these questions:

- What shall our marketing plan be—that is, which markets should we enter and with what production quantities?
- How much manufacturing capacity will the early production stages require?
- As demand grows, where should we build this capacity?
- How shall we allocate our R&D resources over time?

Significant profits depend on finding the right answers. Therefore it is economically feasible to expend large amounts of effort and money on obtaining good forecasts in the short, intermediate, and long range.

A sales forecast at this stage should provide three points of information: (1) the date when rapid sales will begin, (2) the rate of market penetration during the rapid-sales stage, and (3) the ultimate level of penetration or sales rate during the steady-state stage. The date when a product will enter the rapid-growth stage is hard to predict three or four years in advance (the usual horizon). A company's main recourse is to use statistical tracking methods to check on how successfully the product is being introduced, along with routine market studies to determine if there have been any significant changes in the market and sales rate.

Furthermore, the greatest care should be taken in analyzing the early sales data that accumulate once the product has been introduced into the market. For example, it is important to distinguish between sales to innovators, who will try anything new, and sales to imitators, who will buy a product only after it has been accepted by innovators. It is the latter group that provides demand stability. Because of purchases by innovators, many new products have initially appeared successful only to fail later.

Tracking the two groups means market research, possibly via opinion panels that contain both innovators and imitators. The innovators can sometimes teach the manufacturer a lot about how to improve a product, while the imitators provide insight into the desires and expectations of the whole market. Although statistical tracking is a useful tool during the early introduction stages, there are rarely sufficient data for statistical forecasting. Market research studies can naturally be useful, as we have indicated. But, more commonly, the forecaster tries to identify a similar, older product whose penetration pattern should be similar to that of the new product, since overall markets can and do exhibit consistent patterns.

When it is not possible to identify a similar product, a different approach must be used. For the purpose of initial introduction into the markets, it may only be necessary to determine the minimum sales rate required for a product venture to meet corporate objectives. Analyses like input-output, historical trend, and technological forecasting can provide a base for estimating this minimum. Also, the feasibility of not entering the market at all, or of continuing R&D right up to the rapid-growth stage, can best be determined by sensitivity analysis of yearly profit and loss, income, and cash-flow statements.

To estimate the date by which a product will enter the rapid-growth stage is another matter. This date is a function of many factors: for example, the existence of a distribution system, customer acceptance of or familiarity with the product concept, the need met by the product, and significant events (such as color network programming).

In addition to reviewing the behavior of similar products, the date may be estimated through Delphi exercises or through rating and ranking schemes, whereby the factors important to customer acceptance are estimated, each competitor product is rated on each factor, and an overall score is tallied for the competitor against a score for the new product.

Stage 4. Rapid Growth

When a product enters this stage, the most important decisions relate to facilities expansion. These decisions generally involve the largest expenditures in the life cycle (except major R&D decisions). Here commensurate forecasting and tracking efforts are justified.

Forecasting and tracking must provide the executive with three kinds of information at this juncture:

- Firm verification of the rapid-growth rate forecast made previously.
- A hard date when sales will level to "normal" steady-state growth.
- For component products, the deviation in the growth curve that may be caused by characteristic conditions along the pipeline—for example, inventory blockages.

Intermediate- and long-range forecasting of the market growth rate and of the attainment of steady-state sales require detailed marketing studies, intention-to-buy surveys, and product comparisons.

When a product has entered rapid growth, there are generally sufficient data available to construct statistical and possibly even causal growth models, although the latter will necessarily contain assumptions that must be verified later.

The sales of most products follow some form of an S-shaped curve, and quantitative methods can help to establish the parameters of the curve. However, while the ware-in-process demand in the pipeline may have an S-curve similar to that of retail sales, it may lead or lag retail sales by several months and thus distort the shape of the demand on the component supplier.

Simulation is an excellent tool for these circumstances because it is essentially simpler than the alternative of building a more formal, more "mathematical" model. Simulation bypasses the need for analytical-solution techniques and for mathematical duplication of a complex environment and allows experimentation. Simulation also indicates to the fore-caster how the pipeline elements will behave and interact over time—knowledge that is very useful in forecasting, especially in constructing formal causal models at a later date.

This knowledge is not absolutely "hard," of course, and pipeline dynamics must be carefully tracked to determine if the various estimates and assumptions made were indeed correct. Statistical methods provide a good short-term basis for estimating and checking the growth rate and signaling when turning points occur.

One main activity during the rapid-growth stage, then, is to check earlier estimates; if they appear incorrect, the forecaster should compute as accurately as possible the error in the forecast and obtain a revised estimate. In some instances, models developed earlier will include only "macroterms"; in such cases, market research can provide information needed to break these terms down into their components.

Stage 5. Steady State

The decisions the manager makes at this stage are quite different from his earlier decisions. Most of the facilities' planning and expansion has been completed, and trends and growth rates have become reasonably stable. It is possible that swings in demand and profit will occur because of, for example, changing economic conditions, new and competitive products, and pipeline dynamics. Thus the manager will have to main-tain his tracking activities and even introduce new ones. However, gen-erally, he will concentrate his forecasting attention on these areas:

- Long- and short-term production planning.
- Setting standards to check the effectiveness of marketing strategies.
- Projections designed to aid profit planning.

The manager will also need a good tracking-and-warning system to identify significantly declining demand for the product (but hopefully that is a long way off).

In planning production and establishing marketing strategy for the short and intermediate term, the manager's first considerations are usu-ally an accurate estimate (a) of the present sales level and (b) of the rate at which this level is changing. The forecaster thus must make two related contributions at this stage:

1. He should provide estimates of trends and seasonals, which ob-viously affect the sales level. Seasonals are particularly important for both

overall production planning and inventory control. To do this, he needs to apply time-series analysis and projection technique—that is, statistical techniques.

2. He should relate the future sales level to factors that are more easily predictable, or have a "lead" relationship with sales, or both. Therefore, he needs to build causal models.

At this point in the life cycle, sufficient time-series data are available and enough causal relationships are known or suspected from direct experience and market studies so that the forecaster can indeed apply these two powerful sets of tools.

Since historical data for at least the past several years should be available, it is well worth the forecaster's effort to do a detailed analysis of what has previously occurred and what the most recent trends are. This will provide the basis for making projections or forecasts. (Chapter 10 is devoted solely to time-series analysis because of its role in making a good forecast when data are available. The use of time-series analysis in trend projection is discussed in Chapter 11.)

During the steady-state stage, the determination of significant changes from current trends is critical, and may prove to be the signal for the final stage.

Stage 6. Phasing Out

Virtually all products go through a final phasing-out stage, whether it lasts only a few months, a few years, or extends for as long as 10 or 20 years. Most product analysis is concerned only with estimating or establishing the S-shaped curve and not in determining when the plateau or gradual growth will turn down. This can result in lost profits because of inventories that must eventually be scrapped, inability to phase in the excess capacity with new-product requirements, and excessive marketing effort for a dying product.

The most important questions to answer in this stage are: When will the decline or phasing out begin? And how long will it last? Answers will aid in decisions relating to marketing strategies (promotion efforts, pricing, and when to withdraw the product), production scheduling and inventory control, and facilities planning. Three basic approaches are normally taken to answer the foregoing questions.

1. Trend-projection techniques and primarily the slope-characteristic method can help to make good forecasts for the entire life cycle, includ-

ing prediction of the down-turn point and duration of the phasing-out stage.

2. Historical analogies can be used to determine the overall pattern of the life cycle, and regression analysis (or some similar technique) can provide estimates of the parameters of the overall curve, using product characteristics and differences as the independent variables.

3. Good tracking- and-warning tools, such as the Census Bureau X-11 (Shiskin routine), can identify turning points, and market surveys and other techniques can then be employed to determine the reason for the turning point. That is, is it temporary because of competitive moves or is it a long-term market trend? Tracking techniques can also be used in the first two approaches to determine the correctness of the assumptions and models.

Perhaps the least amount of effort in forecasting is normally expended in this area, although there are significant rewards for good forecasts here. Forecasts for phasing out products with short life cycles, such as cereals and apparel, are particularly crucial.

IN SUMMARY

The types of decisions made throughout the product life cycle vary considerably, according to payoff implications and the need for forecasting accuracy. It is therefore apparent that the types of techniques used throughout the product life cycle will change over time, and new methods should be introduced as the need for new forecasts arises. Since data availability also differs significantly over time and affects the selection of the forecasting technique, the value and effectiveness of a particular technique cannot be precisely stated without considering its specific application.

Chapter V

The Preproduct and Technology
Development Stage

There are three types of new-product opportunities that occur in the preproduct stage: (1) those for which there must be a technological breakthrough; (2) those for which the technology exists, and the need is established by sociological and political developments; and (3) those that require technological, sociological, and political developments. The methodology for forecasting the new-product opportunities for each of these types is similar, even though the types of events that must occur are quite different.

Four major approaches can be used in identifying and preparing forecasts for these new-product opportunities: (1) trend projection; (2) objective solicitation and analysis of expert opinion; (3) comprehensive environment analysis of historical trends, patterns of customer behavior, and so forth to determine the potential market demand for a product (e.g., the need for pollution measurement devices and the need for better and cheaper diagnosis techniques in health care); and (4) the tracking of what is happening in the technical, social, and political areas to obtain signals of when new products will be required or are possible. Additional approaches involve a combination of these four.

However, before elaborating on the techniques for preproduct forecasting, we shall first consider why effort should be expended in this area.

POTENTIAL BREAKTHROUGHS

The main questions at issue, and the ones that confront every corporation, are: Can forecasts with acceptable accuracy be made of new-product opportunities and their potential sales and profits? If so, what can and should the company be doing about it?

Obviously, a company cannot perform research in every area where new technology might be profitable. At the most, it must choose a few areas that will hopefully maximize the returns from R&D. During the 1960s, considerable expenditures were made on R&D, with little if any money or effort being spent on technological forecasting. The disappointing number of new products and profitability that resulted from following this strategy have led many companies to reevaluate the amount and allocation of R&D funds, and to divert some of their R&D budget to forecasting.

Peter Drucker has stated that even the largest corporations cannot afford to spend too much on basic research of questionable payoff. He says that this type of research should be government-sponsored or performed by educational institutions.

Instead of basic R&D, most corporations should direct their efforts (a) toward the extension of governmental and institutional findings that appear to have commercial value, and (b) toward the development of new products that utilize this kind of research.

Technological and Legislative Forecasting

Such a strategy requires the assignment of personnel to be specifically on the lookout for possible new technical breakthroughs and new or potential legislation and sociological trends, so that the company can take action to exploit the new-product opportunities emerging from them at the earliest possible time.

Unless tracking of "signals" occurs, it will often be too late to enter the new-product field because of the competition. Corporations cannot wait too long for someone to make an invention, and for the values of new technology and legislation to become apparent. Otherwise, they will be participating on a "me-too" basis, which necessarily reduces any ultimate profitability.

Consider the development of the automobile emissions systems. Both the pressures from the antipollution groups to clean up auto emissions and the ultimate passage of legislation relating to emissions were apparent long before the requirement of pollution devices became law. Many companies correctly read the signals and entered into research-and-product development for emission devices several years prior to legislation enactment.

However, the companies that waited until actual passage of the law before working seriously on emission devices and technology have missed out on the initial design and sales opportunities. Furthermore, they will apparently not be able to participate until new designs emerge (unless there are further delays or revisions in the enforcement date). While the technological breakthroughs had not all occurred when the legislation was passed, they were close to becoming reality and they certainly afforded sufficient confidence in their feasibility for development to take place.

The early spotting of signals will often permit entry into a competitive market, even though much of the basic research is done externally. Henry Ford II stated a few years ago that the Europeans are extremely good at developing technology and the Americans are very effective at exploiting that technology.

Another reason for technological and legislative forecasting is to avert the expenditures of large funds in expanding facilities for an established product or process, only to see the product or process become obsolete shortly thereafter. For example:

American Saint Gobain built a new glass plant in the early 1960s that was made obsolete by the Pilkington float process. The new facility produced high quality flat glass, utilizing an existing forming process and a modern twin-grinding process. It was assumed that either all forming processes would also require grinding or that costs at the new facility would be competitive with any new process.

However, the Pilkington float process, which produces quality flat glass that does not require a finishing process, was introduced shortly after the Saint Gobain plant was built. This made available on a license basis a process that could produce finished flat glass at a much lower cost than existing processes. Virtually all United States flat-glass producers are now licensees of the float process.

Another factor also seriously affected the Saint Gobain operation. There was already sufficient capacity for quality flat glass, and since the existing facilities were either already depreciated or could be considered "sunk-cost," they were vulnerable to price-cutting, which did actually occur. There were signals and available information that could have made it possible to predict both of these situations.

Sociological Forecasting

Many changes in preferences and buying habits in the past decade have significantly altered the types of products wanted by the consumer. Aspirations have changed along with living habits. About 16% of Americans (excluding babies) now relocate each year; city dwellers stay in one home an average of less than four years; and passenger miles traveled in North America are increasing at a rate six times as fast as the population. Consider the decline of the status department store and the rise of the boutique, the disappearance of the luxury streamliner and the appearance of the compact car. Many changes, such as these, were forecastable on the basis of long-term trends and other signals.

Consumerism is a relatively new force to which virtually every corporation must give attention. Although some businessmen feel that the consumerism movement is synonymous with harassment, they are being pressured to make substantial changes in manufacturing and marketing. There must now be a dialogue between the vendor and purchaser to have satisfied customers, who will provide repeat purchases. Failure to recognize the consumer changes and forces has had serious adverse effects on market share and consequently on profitability.

Thus corporations should do some type of technological, political, and sociological forecasting, whether they are participating primarily in established product lines or in new-product ventures. Primarily, the two purposes of these forecasts, with respect to decision making, are (1) to aid the process of choosing corporate objectives by placing realistic bounds on expectations and showing what is possible, and (2) to serve as inputs for accessing the value of the future.

Whether a company will do any long-range forecasting and, if so, the type or approach it will utilize depends on the philosophy of the company toward the future. R. L. Ackoff states that there are three attitudes toward the future, which ordered from the most prevalent to the least prevalent are "wait and see," "predict and prepare," and "make it happen." Preproduct forecasting is necessary for companies with the last two of these attitudes..

While technological breakthroughs frequently lead to new-product opportunities, the analyst should be reasonably certain that when a new technology, process, or product becomes available it will replace an existing one.

When integrated circuits were introduced into the electronic components market, for example, it was generally predicted that the sales of resistors, capacitors, and other discrete components would be significantly reduced within a few years. But sales of discrete components have in fact increased since the introduction of integrated circuits. Analyses of the uses of discrete components would have shown that there are many electronic applications where integrated circuits are neither practical nor economically feasible. The technology of integrated circuits has opened up new applications that have greatly expanded the total electronic components market.

A similar situation can happen for a new process; even though it may be more economical than an existing process when usual accounting procedures are used, if there is sufficient capacity and if the equipment and buildings are considered "sunk-cost," it may not be competitive with the existing process.

Although relatively new, the "futuristic" techniques described here have provided acceptable accuracy for most of the companies using them. However, because the accuracy of most of these techniques has not been fully established, any strategy based on these forecasts should include a tracking system and a contingency plan ready to implement in the event the forecast proves inaccurate.

The demand for persons trained in preproduct forecasting has led to the introduction and inclusion of "futuristics" courses at many colleges. In 1972, futuristics were being taught in more than 200 colleges and universities, including Yale and Princeton. The University of Minnesota now offers a program leading to a degree in futuristics.

Social and Political Factors

Technological forecasting must take into account sociological and political developments of the past, present, and future. The rate at which technology develops and is useful can be significantly affected by such developments, since funding can be drastically changed (increased or decreased) by legislation resulting from sociological and political actions.

Furthermore, the value of technology in the marketplace can be substantially reduced by social and political pressures, as happened with the SST. Although the SST is technically feasible, the sales potential for the immediate future appears drastically lower than initial estimates. This is because of the concern over noise pollution and after-effects of the sonic boom caused by the SST. Passage of pending legislation would further diminish this new product opportunity.

Social and political pressures affect the ultimate sales of a product, as well as the rate of technological development, and these pressures must also be taken into account in the other stages of the product life cycle. The technological developments for nuclear power generation took place approximately when anticipated, but social pressures on possible radiation leaks and the low or negative economic payoffs have delayed widespread installation of nuclear power plants.

Legislation is frequently the outcome of social and political pressures (e.g., laws and government agencies relating to consumerism). Thus the time and type of legislation can be predicted by analyzing trends and current conditions, and by using some form of trend projection. This has been done in projections of pollution legislation. The forecasting of sociological and political developments should serve as inputs for the technological forecasts. Pressures other than sociological or political might also accelerate technological developments, such as wartime needs for offensive or defensive weapons. Serious errors can arise when technological forecasting is done without consideration of these other factors.

The commitment of a company or an agency to develop a particular technology is a major factor in forecasting a breakthrough. The assignment of key personnel and public statements of commitment are critical in estimating both the likelihood of success and the completion date of research.

TREND PROJECTION

This technique involves the analysis and projection of the historical rates at which technological, sociological, and political developments have occurred in the past. Trend projection can either be used as the basis for a forecast itself or as input for expert opinion, identifying the signals of progress. An example would be the development and cost of integrated circuits, where there has been a consistent increase in the number of functions per circuit and a mathematically smooth decrease in the cost per function. Since these trends are not linear, there will obviously be a plateau in the cost per function, and probably a change in the rate of increase of functions per integrated circuit.

The use of trend projection in preproduct forecasting will frequently also require some technique for translating qualitative factors to a quantitative scale, especially when dealing with sociological and political developments. Most developments are expressed verbally as events (e.g., the invention of xerography, the passage of a law, consumer behavior, and so forth), rather than quantitatively, as when technology can be measured in terms of output or time for a major breakthrough (e.g., lumens per watt, probability of detection of a disease, cost per unit produced, or time to double output).

The translation of qualitative events to a quantitative scale can often be accomplished by an approximate measure-of-value technique, such as where the event is rated by experts on a scale of, say, one to 10 for the factors that are critical for that type of event. The factors are then weighted to get an overall score, with this score being plotted against time or some other factor with which it is correlated. Another approach is to obtain some measure of performance for events or accomplishments, such as the activity of an enzyme or the cost per piece of information processed.

Because of the difficulty of converting events to quantitative scales, trend projection has had limited use in preproduct forecasting. However, the approach is implicitly applied in an informal way, in which the time between events is considered, along with some "feeling" about the complexity of the event to be forecast.

Linear Projection

The simplest form of this trend technique is linear projection, obtained by fitting a straight line to historical data and extending this line into the future. Unfortunately, most trends are not linear, especially when projected five to 20 years out. Technological and sociological advances are being made at an increasing rate and are rarely found to be linear; the time between changes generally decreases, the relative change increases. Performance of aircraft (supersonic speed) illustrates the increasing rate at which aircraft technology is developing. Furthermore, rates can change significantly because of government funding, unexpected events, organizational changes, and so forth.

Another obvious problem with linear projection is that an extension of a linear trend indefinitely may give an absurd or impossible forecast. Consider the projection of IBM corporate sales. If IBM's growth rate of 15 to 20% annually is projected far out into the future, sales will eventually be larger than the Gross National Product, which is growing at about a 7% rate. (We recognize that some, if not most of IBM's growth, will take place in the international market. This is true of most companies that have growth objectives greater than the growth of the markets in which they are competing, and where it is obvious that they cannot increase their market share indefinitely.)

Linear trends will generally plateau or slow down because of such factors as market saturation and competitive forces. But the linear trend for a new product in the early introduction stage will turn upward sharply as it enters the rapid-growth stage.

When linear projection is used, care must be taken to choose the correct factor. Rates are more likely to be linear or constant than the factor itself. For example, the percent change in government expenditures should be graphed, rather than the absolute change in dollars or change in sales, since the percent change will be declining when the absolute change is constant. When the percent change is constant, the sales will give a linear trend when plotted on semilogarithmic graph paper. Technically, such a relationship is a trend curve, instead of a linear projection.

Trend Curves

These curves consider nonlinear changes and can be used in conjunction with similar technology or historical analogy analyses. A well-known trend curve is the S-shaped growth curve, such as shown in Table 4.1. The historical development of a particular technology may be studied to obtain its development growth curve, and this pattern can then provide the basis for the development curve of the technology being considered, with modifications made because of differences in technology. Trend curves permit the forecaster to make judgment modifications in situations where, say, he wants the curve to fit some predetermined model or to incorporate special considerations, as in a technological forecast that incorporates sociological factors.

Two special cases of trend curves are envelope curves and progress functions. Forecasting with envelope curves has been done in several areas. such as in the performance of electronic computers (the future ratio of high-speed memory capacity to add time). It involves plotting the hypothetical maximum performance available for any particular product characteristic and making the performance curve tangential to the individual performance trend. This therefore assumes a continually increasing growth of the technological development rate; thus it can be considered as a trend curve.

Progress functions are based on the assumption that learning, improvement, technological developments, and social change are exponential functions of the effort expended or prior activity. The increase in lumens per watt, computer programming efficiency, and aircraft turbojet engine development are examples of development rates to which the progress-function technique applies.

Each of the preceding types of trend projection involves the plotting and curve fitting of the factor to be forecasted versus time. Variables other than time may also be used in trend-projection forecasting, such as is done in correlation and regression analysis, which involves the identification of historical relationships between the factor to be forecast and other factors and which makes projections on the basis of the relationships.

Lead-lag relationships between the factors are included in this technique; therefore the precursor-events technique is a special case of regression analysis, where the forecaster looks for the relationship of two events, one lagging the other by a constant interval, such as the speed of transport aircraft lagging military aircraft speed. Sociological events can provide good lead indicators for technological developments, where public pressure forces a technological breakthrough. In general, however, when regression analysis is applied to preproduct forecasting, it merely transfers the problem from forecasting one factor to another, since the lead-lag relationships are seldom of sufficient length to be of value.

EXPERT OPINION

The eliciting of expert opinion is often the only approach possible to obtain technological forecasts for 10 to 20 years or more into the future. The major objectives or applications of this type of forecasting are to determine the level and allocation of basic research effort and to make "commitments" to new businesses (such as building a research capability, developing consumer confidence, developing a distribution system, or acquisition) where long lead times are required to gain a competitive position.

As we indicated earlier, there is usually sufficient lead time to enter a business by tracking and interpreting signals when the basic research is being conducted by government-sponsored groups and the technology will be made available to others. When there is a high probability of significant payoff, it can well be advantageous to do research to gain a proprietary position. However, tracking the signals of technological, social, and political changes will frequently make it possible to obtain a license or to acquire technology with sufficient lead time.

Solicitation of expert opinion is primarily concerned with when events are most likely to occur, how much effort will be required, and what the probabilities are of the events happening. Forecasts of potential profitability may also be made, but only in a very macro way, such as: Will the payoffs of technology be large or small? And what will the profit margins be as a percent of sales?

The first step, and an important one, is to obtain a comprehensive, well-defined list of possible events. This list can be compiled from trend projections or preliminary lists supplied by the experts, who will later provide estimates, or from both sources. For a technological forecast, estimates of related sociological and political developments may be needed.

Thus, for example, the market for pollution-control equipment and measurement devices could not have been forecast accurately without considering when federal legislation would require them.

In such a case, the social and political pressures are more important than current technological progress, with laws stating that technology will be available by the specified times. Conversely, adverse public reaction to potential technological breakthroughs can delay R&D efforts, as we have seen in situations where companies have cut back on R&D in product areas when consumer preferences have changed.

"Laboratory" Approach

The accuracy of expert-opinion forecasting, which has thus far been demonstrated in relatively few instances, needs more validation. To some extent, it is possible to estimate the accuracy from the range of opinions obtained, but this assumes that the true value (e.g., time to complete and probability) lies within that range. Because of the limited experience for most of the approaches, efforts have been made to measure the accuracy of the technique under "laboratory" conditions (e.g., having people give estimates for situations about which they do not have information, and comparing results with what is known). However, it is generally accepted that meetings held to obtain group opinions provide biased results, because of dominating personalities, the bandwagon effect, and so on.

A technique that helps to overcome these problems is the Delphi method, which we discussed in Chapter 3. The main feature of this expert-opinion technique, aside from the avoidance of biases due to individual personalities, is the feedback of relevant information. It is important that each person making an estimate have approximately the same information available upon which to base an opinion.

(This usually does not happen with the other two main techniques—visionary forecasts and panel consensus—for eliciting expert opinion. Visionary forecasting is based primarily on personal knowledge and insights, while panel consensus does bring out more facts but in a biased way. Since there is little documentation of visionary forecasting and panel consensus, we have omitted examples.)

One of the early applications of the Delphi method was in forecasting space technology, including when a man would land on the moon. These forecasts were made in 1962–1963, and the forecast concerning landing on the moon was accurate to within one year of its actual occurrence in 1970. There have been other government studies relating to sociological forecasting (social conditions and health care) as well as overall technological forecasts. The National Industrial Conference Board carried out a large-scale Delphi exercise in 1968 relating to social responsibilities of corporations. The largest Delphi study conducted thus far (see Chapter 3) provides inputs for the Japanese governments' planning activities.

Technological forecasts based on expert opinion have been made at many large corporations, including TRW, Smith-Kline-French (SKF), and Monsanto, for use as inputs or checks on business planning and R&D allocation. TRW performed one of the earliest Delphi studies to provide a basis for perceiving the need and feasibility of new products and service, the modification of long-range R&D planning, and the evaluation and revision of corporate plans and objectives. The first TRW "probe," completed in 1966, was made by 27 experts. They provided estimates for 401 events in a broad spectrum of technologies that could have an impact on TRW's products, processes, and services. The possible events related to categories, such as electronics and electro-optics, materials, information processing, transportation, oceans, and so forth. A second TRW probe in 1967 expanded the number of categories and events.

One major problem with the expert-opinion technique has been the failure to consider adequately the interrelationships and dependency of the events upon each other. Cross-impact analysis, which has recently been developed to take into account the interrelationships of events, has already seen considerable use. It uses inputs from the foregoing approaches and other types of forecasts. Then, by systematically considering the impact of each event on every other event, it identifies and eliminates inconsistencies in the original estimates. It also provides a vehicle for feedback and for determining how changes in estimates for one event will affect the other events.

ENVIRONMENT ANALYSIS

This approach to preproduct planning is used primarily by those companies whose attitude to planning is "make it happen." They want to determine—through analysis of trends, logic, market research, and so forth—what products will inevitably be demanded or required by the consumer. Then, they can take the necessary action to make it happen and profit from it.

Although considerable effort is required to identify the potential market demand, the rewards are usually well worth the effort, since the people who help to create the future are the ones who will benefit most from it. Even when the efforts for determining the inevitable future products or events are unsuccessful, the side benefits from the analyses, such as an improved understanding of the business, may make it worth-while.

In one sense, this approach should not be included in preproduct fore-casting, but rather should be described as understanding and modeling the environment to predict the inevitable market demand. R. L. Ackoff states that the problem of the planner is to perceive what is virtually cer-tain to occur, of determining how to exploit and possibly accelerate the inevitable, and of taking credit for doing so.[10] The analyses required to perceive the inevitable will also help provide some direction in exploit-ing it.

The approach to identifying the inevitable demand cannot be rigidly outlined, since it may vary from one situation to another, and relies on the ingenuity of the investigator. Essentially, it involves detailed analysis of the environment for the business or social sector under consideration.

The approach includes (a) trend projections of sociological, political, and technological developments (what will happen if nothing radical occurs); (b) an analysis of these trends to see if they are consistent; (c) market research (if previous studies have not been performed) to learn why consumers demand existing products—and on the basis of sociological and economic forecasts—to determine how customer preference and be-havior are likely to change; and (d) analyses of basic data and relation-ships obtained from previous work.

Illustrative Examples

The success in deducing the environment will depend on the skill of the analyst in structuring the information and studying it in a logical man-ner. Since the identification of the environment is an art, it can best be described by the following examples.

Multitesting Instruments.   As the knowledge and technology of the medi-cal profession grows, there is an increasing requirement for additional tests to determine the condition of various parts and fluids in the human body. The analysis and interpretation of the tests by physicians are diffi-cult and frequently uncertain, leading to inconclusive results or causing new samples to be taken. Additional lab personnel for analyzing the tests

[10] *A Concept of Corporate Planning* (New York: John Wiley and Sons, Inc., 1970).

are both costly and scarce. Because of the still-limited understanding of the body, doctors often make diagnosis errors in interpreting the results.

Instrument manufacturers have been making equipment for analysis of tests for many years, but these instruments generally apply to only one test. The limitation or upper limit on the number of samples that can be taken from the patient, the need for greater accuracy, automation, improved interpretation, and lower costs per test have made it inevitable that instruments of the future will do several analyses simultaneously and will be interfaced with a computer to interpret the results.

Costs of the equipment will not be prohibitive because of the emergence of outside labs servicing several hospitals, and improved transportation and conveyor systems for rapid turn around (e.g., vacuum tubes for transporting test tubes from floor stations to labs, internal and external). New systems are also being introduced for avoiding patient misidentification.

The increasing amount of information in the hospital makes automated hospital information systems a necessity, although the structures or organization of hospitals and their measures of the performance of specific functions will make the introduction of a total information system virtually impossible. The subsystems that are ultimately brought together will be the means of implementing total information systems. Technicon has identified the inevitable need for multitesting instruments, and has already marketed some of them. The interface of testing instruments and computer interpretation is progressing rapidly.

Maintenance Modularization. The expansion of the service industry because of the growing number and variety of appliances has created a shortage of experienced repairmen. More sophisticated operations have increased the number of parts, and the demand for smaller, more compact appliances has made accessibility and repair more difficult. The relatively small growth of the total appliance industry with additional competition has made the pressures greater for a way of increasing the overall sales dollar, other than by inflation.

The modularization of the repair function is therefore inevitable and corporations that design products with a modularization capability will gain a marketing advantage, as well as increased sales of replacement parts. RCA and other television manufacturers have identified this need and have announced partial modularization of their most recent color-television models, where each module is designed to concentrate on separate electronic operations. If something goes wrong, diagnosis of the problem is usually quick and simple, and more sets can be repaired in the home instead of the shop. It is not difficult to see that modularization will be extended so that some owners of appliances will be able to perform their own maintenance.

Small Urban Automobiles.   R. L. Ackoff refers to a planning study carried out in 1961, where it was found that with the increasing number of automobiles cities could not possibly add streets and highways at a rate that would maintain their then current levels of automobile traffic. It was felt that increased congestion would not be tolerable and, therefore, that one or both of two alternatives would have to be pursued: increase in mass transit or reduction in the size of the automobile. Further study of the consumer indicated that increased mass transit would not be acceptable to him because of the inconvenience and lack of comfort necessarily involved in its use.

Therefore, it was concluded that a small urban automobile was inevitable. The fact that automobiles in the city currently carry an average of only slightly more than one person led to the conclusion that a two-passenger (or at most a three-passenger) vehicle would serve most needs. It was found that by restricting the use of city streets during working hours to such vehicles, existing streets would enjoy an increase in capacity that could not be obtained by cities even if they were to spend all of their available funds on improving the current system. Add to this the growing threat of air pollution and out comes the recommendation that development of a small urban vehicle be made a planning goal. Corporations that recognized this need for small urban cars, such as Westinghouse, have gotten the jump on others, and Ford, General Motors, and Chrysler are known to be rushing the development of similar cars.

Rise of the Trucking Industry.   Railroads did not read the signals and see the inevitable demand in the 1930s for improved service that would substantially reduce delivery times. The proliferation of product lines, diversification and growth of markets, along with more geographically distributed manufacturing facilities and warehouses made it clear that corporations could not have large inventories of a variety of items at each location to provide good customer service. Furthermore, the growth of products and increased volume would only magnify the problems at switching yards, which were already a bottleneck.

Public sentiment toward monopolies and political antitrust legislation pointed toward a lessening of the umbrella of legal protection that railroads would have. Failure of the railroads to observe these trends and to take the necessary action gave the trucking industry the opportunity to capture a large part of the commodity transportation business from the railroads.

Gas Turbine Engines.   These have been technically feasible for many years, and there have been numerous forecasts that a large demand for them was imminent, with forecasts in the early 1950s indicating significant growth by the mid-1960s, and later forecasts revising that date. The main factor in making these forecasts was the fuel economy of the gas turbine engine and less maintenance cost. But the forecasters did not give consideration to the fact that the automobile buyer does not trade-off engine cost with fuel cost, as does the trucking industry, which also is concerned about maintenance. In addition, the fact that the gasoline and diesel engines are moving targets—that is, they have not yet reached the point where they can no longer be improved—was apparently not adequately considered in eveluating the potential of the gas turbine engine.

However, while there are now some who question whether the gas turbine will ever have a large overall market, the penetration of it into the trucking market is inevitable. (This is not true of the automobile market.) Noise pollution legislation is increasing and some of it is now being implemented. This, with the air-pollution requirements, will accelerate the entry of the gas turbine into trucks, although these pressures and further improvement in the diesel engine will not bring about a large market share for the gas turbine until the early 1980s. Ford Motor Company, which originally planned to manufacture diesel engines, has seen this and—along with the recognition of the strong competition in the diesel industry—has elected to concentrate on gas turbines instead.

The New Consumerism.   This can ultimately pose a serious challenge to the profit system itself. As corporations have grown in size, as communications have improved, and as more and more people realize and aspire to affluence, the economic process of making a profit necessarily has social consequences. The profit-making process has such an impact on man that full accountability to the individual citizen, for both social and economic consequences, is becoming a business necessity.

A survey in the fall of 1968 of the social involvement and attitudes of America's top industrial firms found that business is expected by the public to respond to the social challenges facing all of us.[11] It is inevitable that there will be increasing pressures for corporations to participate actively in the solution of social problems. However, since the consequences will affect the sales of a corporation's products, there will likely be special tax benefits for corporations that participate.

[11] The Conference Board, "Prospectives for the '70s and '80s," New York: 1970.

If corporations do not recognize this and take the initiative now, they will be forced to do so at a later time, with little or no benefit from a marketing and public relations vantage point. Strategies for social action should be included in corporate long-range plans. Several large corporations, such as General Motors, Xerox, and Kodak, have recognized this and have publicly declared their commitment to it.

SIGNALS OF CHANGE

This type of forecasting is not a new approach, with many companies being aware of the value of it and having established tracking systems, formally or informally, many years ago. Planning systems with the attitude of "predict and prepare" can effectively use this approach, since the rapid detection and interpretation of signals will still give ample lead time for profitably entering a business or protecting an existing one. Most companies recognize the need for tracking signals of change—with primary if not exclusive attention being given to technological change—and believe they are doing it by having researchers actively keep abreast of new developments.

But, according to James R. Bright, this role is played neither wisely nor well in many R&D departments.[12] He says that the reasons for not doing a good job of tracking signals are: (1) most R&D departments are expected to concentrate on product development and refinement and new applications and, therefore, tend to keep their eyes on the technology on the one-to-five year horizon and their company's immediate concerns; (2) R&D managers lack support from higher levels for doing long-range, broadband technological surveying; and (3) the R&D director usually lacks a systematic methodology for assessing the innovative process. (Also, because signals can occur in areas other than technology, there is little coordination.)

In tracking or monitoring the environment, Bright says, certain research findings, which provide direction in designing the tracking system, helpful in having better understanding of the process of technological innovation are:

1. Long before a radical new technological advance achieves widespread usage it is made visible to society first in written words, and then in increasingly refined, enlarged, and more effective material forms.

[12] "Evaluating Signals of Technological Change," *Harvard Business Review*, January-February 1970, p. 62.

2. Social, political, and ecological changes may alter the speed and direction of the innovation's progress.

3. Innovation may be abruptly influenced by decisions of key individuals, who control supporting resources or determine policies that affect their application.

4. Technological capabilities (e.g., power, strength, capacity) increase exponentially over time, once bottlenecks are broken, but will begin to level off when they encounter scientific, economic, or social barriers.

Monitoring includes (a) searching for signals that could be forerunners of change, (b) determining the consequences if the trends continue, (c) identifying what other events must occur for the potential development to be realized and to be of value to the company, (d) choosing the events, decisions, policies, and factors that should be followed to verify the true rate of technological change and its value, and (e) presenting the informaton at the right time to management in order to influence the relevant decisions. Monitoring may, in some instances, help identity the inevitable, when detailed analyses to determine the consequences of continuation of the trend are performed.

Types of Signals

The sources of information can be grouped by the type of change they are meant to detect: technological, sociological, and political. Ecological and economic changes are included under the sociological and political headings.

Technological Developments. Some of the indicators of such developments are recent data and trends of performance; attendance at conferences and other meetings; surveys of various types, such as computer-controlled retrieval produced by the Smithsonian Institution (e.g., government-funded projects, research performed by nonprofit institutions); publications of professional research societies and government agencies; patent applications and award listings; special Delphi exercises in which the results are made available to the public; and speeches of corporate officers to security analysts.

An analysis of the increase of the number of electrical circuits per unit of space leads to the conclusion that (a) electronic products will rapidly and continuously be made obsolete in the next decade, (b) a new product must be exploited quickly because of its probable short life, and (c) large-scale cost-and-size reductions in electronic equipment will still occur. Several manufacturers are now exploiting the signals of integrated circuit

(IC) technology and the increasing demand for portable computers by marketing electronic pocket calculators that have slide-rule portability and computerlike powers.

Scanning publications of trade journals will many times provide valuable information to the people who can benefit from the technology. The exploitation of Corning Glass' capability of stabilizing enzymes and bonding them to inorganic materials is already being pursued by several companies. IBM and Kodak both spotted the signals of Chester Carlson's patent on xerography when it was published in 1940, but did not take advantage of this knowledge. It was not until the Haloid Company introduced the first Xerox machine in 1948 that the technology was exploited.

Attendance figures at conferences may indicate where activity exists within corporations and when there is widespread interest in a particular technology. For example, if average attendance of a conference for a tech-nology is relatively stable for several years and then doubles or quadruples, it suggests either that progress is to the point where product development is imminent, or that there is a "curiosity-seeker" effect due to recent publicity. Conversations with attendees can ascertain which is true.

Some of the patents issued to IBM, and other actions taken by IBM, should have provided signals of the recently announced introduction of its 370-158 and 168 models, which will have "virtual" data storage. This can potentially change the magnetic disk market to such an extent that Telex, one of the leading manufacturers of magnetic-disk data-storage units that are direct replacements for IBM units, has filed a law suit because of the market implications. This development of virtual data storage also provides a partial solution to the high cost and availability of computer programming. Consider these facts.

- With real storage, an entire program must generally occupy space in the computer itself while the program is being executed.

- With virtual storage, only those parts of the program actually needed at any given time are stored in the computer. The rest of the program is kept on disk files, ready for use when needed.

- Each element of a program stored in a computer must have an address—that is, a location where it can be found in real storage. Each address is usually reserved for one element throughout the program.

- With virtual storage, however, program elements are brought in from disk files, placed in the computer's available storage, and transferred back to the disk files when no longer needed. Thus, during the execution of a program, the same element may occupy different addresses, and the program may refer to it as if it were at its original address.

- This is made possible by a facility called dynamic address translation, working in conjunction with one of the new IBM operating systems and with the program being executed. The entire process takes place automatically, without any need for intervention by the user.
- In general, more programs can be run concurrently under virtual storage, thereby potentially expanding the capabilities of computer installations. Individual programs, however, may require more time for execution under virtual storage.

Sociological Changes. Demographic data and trends, such as shifts in location and size of populations, may help assess the economic benefits of technological developments. The emergence of activist groups, demonstrations, speeches, publications, and shifts in product preferences may all signal future trends that can effect the rate of technological development. Measurements of such parameters as incidence of crime, poverty, changes in values, political opinions, attitudes toward abortion and birth control, decline of importance in status symbols, and consumer expectations of a corporation's performance are all signals of future legislation or the demand for a product that has not yet been conceived or identified.

Sociological changes may also make technological advances obsolete, such as the SST. No manufacturer can afford to ignore the effect a potential new product can have on the environment. For example, the government measures of productivity per man-hour, and consumption of various types of goods, when analyzed statistically, may show changes in trends that can be early warnings.

Market research and public opinion polls are often needed to predict sociological changes. Unless they are carefully designed and evaluated, they may lead to incorrect conclusions, especially if there are preconceived ideas. The design of market tests and the types of tests for analyzing and interpreting the results of surveys and questionnaires are discussed in detail in Chapter 6.

The success of previous efforts to pass legislation can indicate the type of new legislation that can be expected. The creation of government committees or agencies are also forerunners of new laws. Noise abatement laws will have an effect on the design of tires, engines, appliances, lawn mowers, aircraft, manufacturing equipment, and so forth. Availability of skills because of vocation preferences may force changes in certain types of manufacturing processes or product designs. Package design will be influenced by public reaction and legislation concerning disposability and recyclability. Depletion of natural resources may force the development of new technology. Pollution measurement devices, modularization, emissions controls, and safety features in automobiles and other consumer products have all come from changes in attitude of the consumer.

Political Pressures.   As we indicated earlier, the allocation of government funds to various types of research can accelerate or slow down technological development. Wartime pressures can force technological developments, such as radar, where—because England has a shortage of aircraft and could not adequately prepare for defending against enemy strikes at all possible locations—it was essential that there be an early warning system, so that the RAF could efficiently deploy its fighters and other defense equipment.

Formal government actions are almost always preceded by major committee reviews and recommendations, and by reports of debates about alternatives. It is important to observe not only what committees or agencies are formed, but also who is assigned to head them up (i.e., is it someone who has a good reputation and is considered a government favorite?). The type of and amount of funding and freedom given to the committee are also critical.

The political pressures and amounts spent on health care research have led many companies to enter the health care field. The emphasis on social programs for the aged has opened up new markets and brought about consumer demand for new products.

Measurement of social and political developments are often more difficult than measuring technological change. Changes in value systems are particularly difficult, and frequent polls and market research studies must be carried out to detect value changes. Nevertheless, if good technological forecasting is to be done, changes in sociological and political forces and their effect on technological developments must be considered.

IN SUMMARY

Some form of technological forecasting is essential to avoid potential obsolescence or deterioration of competitive advantages in existing products and processes and to identify and exploit new product opportunities. A variety of approaches are available, none of which can assure accurate forecasting but which, if used in concert, can be invaluable to the planning process. It is apparent that not all potential technological opportunities can be pursued. Accordingly, there must be some information for choosing from the many potentialities and for still being alert when developments enhance a particular opportunity. More money needs to be allocated to preproduct forecasting to improve the payoffs of R&D.

Chapter VI

The Product Development Stage:
An Existing Market

In the early 1960s, the alarmists were still crying about the United States population explosion when it was already turning into an echo. There were then 116 births per year for every 1000 American women of child-bearing age, so that the average mother would have 3.6 children. However, by the spring of 1972, the birthrate had dropped to 2.1 children per woman, a rate at which the parents would not quite be reproducing themselves when child mortality is considered.

While it will still take about 70 years at current rates to achieve zero population growth, the important point is that population growth in the future will continue to get smaller and smaller. This trend could have serious business and political implications.

The French demographer Alfred Sauvy states that France's social, cultural, and economic problems are the direct result of the fact that for the past century its population has been virtually stable.[13] His contention is that a growing population is a stimulus to society.

By contrast, the Japanese situation is at least partially a result of a concerted drive to cut the birthrate sharply by encouraging abortion. With her already crowded conditions, Japan might have become unlivable without such action.

Here in the United States, the President's Commission on Population Growth has concluded that the average person will be better off if we follow the two-child projection instead of the three-child projection. The

[13] *General Theory of Population*, New York: Basic Books, Inc., 1969.

ultimate answer lies in our national ability to adjust to the type of environment that results from a slowdown in population growth.

One of the economic implications is that an increasing number of Americans will have more disposable income for travel, entertainment, recreational equipment, and second homes. In the types of edibles consumed, greater emphasis will be placed on gourmet foods. Ben J. Wattenberg, a leading writer on population trends, predicts that Americans will spend in constant dollars 79% more in 1985 on food, drink, and tobacco. than in 1968; 95% more on clothing and clothing materials; 107% more on transportation; 110% more on household operations and furnishings; 172% more on housing; 185% more on personal and medical care; and 149% more on recreation, education, and the like.[14]

There has already been a considerable impact in several areas. The effects of the sharp drop in school population are well-known, with excess classrooms and teachers being the major result. The drop in the birthrate has created what Dr. Michael Sumichrast, chief economist of the National Association of Homebuilders, calls a revolution in home building, a switch from detached houses to condominiums. Such a trend is bound to have an effect on the home-furnishings and household-equipment industry, since the average condominium apartment has less than half the average floorspace of a house. The savings in housing expenditures have enabled the owners to spend more money on travel, boating, skiing, and other leisure expenditures.

The Whirlpool Corporation is one company that appears to have considered the implications of the declining birthrate. A task force, including five university professors, concluded that people are bound to demand smaller space-saving appliances, which can be stored where they will still be visible but blend into the surroundings better, and which never need repair. An executive of Westinghouse Electric Corporation stated that his company's most immediate concerns are our changing life-styles and changing social values.

The questions of how people want to run their lives, and their concerns with the environment and with the good life, are important to them since two-thirds of their activities involve power systems. Furthermore, as the population grows older, there will be government subsidies to increase health-care delivery, and to try to upgrade preventive health care.

A recent issue of *Forbes,* from which we have obtained much of the foregoing discussion, lists judgments on the long-range effects of the

[14] "The Demography of the 1970's: The Birth Death and What It Means," *Forbes,* September 1, 1972, p. 37.

"Baby Bust."[15] Those industries helped include travel, autos, jewelry, photography, restaurants, vacation homes, convenience foods, child care, big shifts in packaging and marketing, sports equipment, professional sports, and most areas of health care. Those industries probably hurt include steel, aluminum, stone, lumber, glass, many types of clothing, liquor, tobacco, children and youth-oriented operations, movie theaters, cable or pay television, and life insurance.

In a similar way, changes in consumer trends can have a significant impact on the sales of a market segment. Several companies provide measures of social trends that can be of value in forecasting sales for the market sector in which a new product is to compete.

One such service is the Yankelovich Monitor, which measures 35 social trends that can affect consumer marketing.[16] Through over 2500 personal interviews conducted annually, it estimates the size and composition of the trend, the current manifestations (i.e., how they are expressed by the consumer at the marketplace), and changes in the trend size as compared with previous measurements. The main objectives are to identify opportunities for new products, define population subgroups that can be new target markets, signal threats to the stability of an established product, determine the need for changes in product features, and detect shifting patterns in distribution.

For example, the trend toward "natural foods" is important to the food industry. Although a change in technology in the form of TV electronics caused the mass market for theater moviegoing to diminish significantly, changing sex mores and other social trends led to a massive new youth market for motion pictures in theaters. Taste trends that have been stimulated by social trends have begun to change and will have an impact on businesses such as the beer industry.

The awareness and understanding of the impact of such changes is especially important when forecasting for a new product that is to compete in an existing market. When a market is expanding, it is much easier for a new product to gain a sizable market share, as compared with when a market is declining or experiencing little growth. In the latter situation, actions such as price cutting and other vigorous marketing tactics are employed to maintain growth, which will necessarily require an increase in market share. Under such conditions, a new product must have clear advantages. However, profit erosion due to strong competitive actions should eventually be expected.

[15] *Ibid.*
[16] "Yankelovich Monitor" is a service of Daniel Yankelovich, Inc., New York.

NEW VERSUS EXISTING MARKETS

In the first part of the product development stage, the specific product to be marketed may not yet have been selected, since there may be several product concepts or alternatives from which to choose. However, both the function of the product and at least the broad market in which the product will compete will have been determined.

The market may already exist, because of established competitive products that perform the same or similar functions, or it may be where a new need is being met by the product and a new market will thus be established. If the market does exist, it can either be fixed (because the total units or dollars to be sold will not change significantly from previous levels and trends), or it can be variable (because the new product will change the size of the market). In the latter case, the market would generally increase, but the new product may have a longer life than existing products so that the total market would decrease.

In this chapter, we are concerned with new products in existing markets, while in the next chapter we shall consider new markets. The techniques used for the two situations are often quite different, because of such factors as how much is known about the customer, total market size, and data availability.

When we speak of an existing market, it may in fact be a new market to the company introducing the new product. The main distinction is in the information available for forecasting. Here, we shall assume that although the company introducing the new product may not initially have the necessary information about the market, it can obtain it from industry sources, market research, and so forth. If the data cannot be obtained, the existing market should be considered a new market and forecasts should be handled as described in Chapter 7.

Differences in Forecasting

The techniques used in the product development stage and the way in which they are applied will depend on whether the new product is a durable good, a nondurable good, or a service. The distinctions are important, since both the value of the decisions to be made and the market factors often differ significantly for the three product classes. Some of the distinguishing characteristics that require different forecasting approaches are briefly described here, with further discussion given in subsequent chapters where appropriate. While most of the illustrative examples and direct references herein are for durable products, the reader should assume that the same techniques apply to the other types of products unless otherwise noted.

Consumer Durable Goods.   These sales are primarily dependent on economic and demographic factors, with other factors also affecting total sales volume. Total sales include replacement sales due to mortality, as well as new sales due to initial consumer penetration or multiple ownership. Consumer durable goods' sales are generally regarded as a function of cumulative stock (i.e., consumer inventory). The amount that is bought is proportional to the difference between what consumers actually own and what they would like to own (saturation level). The saturation level and the proportionality constant are related to socioeconomic and demographic factors.

Most consumer durables have significant development costs and require large investments for manufacturing facilities, unless there is excess capacity for products requiring similar facilities. Development times and time spans from introduction to saturation are relatively long (e.g., compared with nondurables). Therefore, unless it is a proprietary item, it is important to penetrate the market rapidly to establish market share.

Nondurable Goods.   As the name implies, these products are usually short-lived or perishable, so that the importance of stock is minimized. However, as we shall discuss later, the ultimate penetration level will depend upon the extent of distribution. The most important marketing factors are consumer preferences (likes, dislikes), and tastes that can be influenced by selection of media (advertising and promotion).

Therefore, marketing tactics become important factors in forecasting nondurable sales. Market segmentation—that is, which groups of people buy a particular product—becomes a critical factor, since repeat sales or repeat purchase rates (influenced by brand loyalty and other factors) are a major determinant of the sales rate of a new product.

On the one hand, market research has generally not revealed what the precise factors are that affect nondurable sales, although there is strong evidence that "mental makeup" is critical and that socioeconomic and demographic factors are not as important as life-styles and psychographics. On the other hand, interproduct relationships are significant, and we shall discuss these in Chapter 8.

In general, nondurable goods require low investment costs to manufacture the volumes needed for testing. Therefore, the amount that should be spent on forecasting at this stage will depend primarily on the cost of product development. If the cost is high, the techniques used will be similar to those for durable goods, although proportionally more will be spent on market research for nondurables as contrasted to durables. If the development cost is low, relatively little expenditure on forecasting is justifiable at this stage, with the first major effort in forecasting occurring at the product introduction and testing stage. (While pilot-run costs may be low, a major capital investment is usually required to have a large-volume capacity.)

Nondurable goods include such items as grocery products, apparel, batteries, and drugs. As the reader can see from even this abbreviated list, there can be extreme differences in devlopment costs for nondurable goods, with grocery products and apparel requiring very little investment in the first stages of the product life cycle, while large expenditures are required to develop and test a drug prior to introduction. Proprietary position and development time will influence the length of time that market research is feasible.

Services. These are defined as intangible products that are consumed immediately, usually at the time of production. The interrelation of production and consumption is a differentiating characteristic of services, since goods are produced, sold, and consumed, while services are sold and then produced and consumed simultaneously. In fact, no services are produced unless they are consumed. Services therefore cannot be stockpiled or carried in inventory. Since there is no transfer of ownership in the sale of a service, relationships between buyer and seller and control over the use of the product are indeterminant.

Consumers tend to buy from habit or impulse, to secure status or prestige, to follow culture trends or symbolism, and so forth. This makes their sales highly influenced by advertising and other marketing strategies. Since some services are necessities (at least according to our culture), there is a tendency for services to be regulated.

Services is the fastest growing of the three classes of products, with between 40 and 50% of the consumption expenditures being for this class. As a result, many companies have now entered the services field. However, there has been relatively little market or other research done on services, so that few generalizations or factual statements can be made.

Examples of new services are closed-circuit and cable TV, the servicing and maintenance of "orphan" computer installations, rental housing for the elderly and low-income families, the provision of legal services for the disadvantaged, campgrounds, and urban transportation systems. Older, more established types of services include public utilities, banks, automobile repairs, recreation, medical services, insurance, and consultants.

Here are five of the more important concepts that must be considered in forecasting the demand for services.

1. The more man-centered the service, the more it departs from conventional treatment of the product element in marketing. Also, the more regulated or more professional the service, the greater the difficulty in relating the service product to the typical marketing view.

2. The success or failure in service-product performance may be dependent in part on the buyer. Thus the way he or she receives or uses the service will influence quality and subsequent sales.

3. Professional, technical, or entrepreneurial skills are the major inputs to convert the service (idea) into a marketable product. Except for the giants in communication and utilities, most services require only modest amounts of capital other than that necessary to acquire the appropriate skills.

4. Services have life cycles. For example, motion pictures, vaudeville, rail passenger service, watch repairing, and domestic services appear to have passed their peak growth.

5. There are consumer and industrial services, and the durable-nondurable dichotomy applies. Health care and insurance are durable services, while haircuts and entertainment are nondurables. This dichotomy can be of help in choosing the best forecasting technique.

New service products "happen"; they are not developed. The limited financial and manpower resources of most services prevents large expenditures for organized development. Thus, unless a large expenditure is necessary to provide the small level of services for introduction and testing, relatively little can be spent on forecasting in the product development stage.

TYPICAL PRODUCT DEVELOPMENT CONSIDERATIONS

At this point in the product life cycle, the major questions that must be answered are: Should we enter this business? If so, in what sectors of the total market? Forecasts of potential sales, R&D expenditures, manufacturing costs, distribution costs, and capital expenditures must be made to estimate in a macro way the potential profitability and return-on-investment for the product. Marketing strategies may be vague at this time, and they could change significantly later. But some assumptions must be made, so that evaluations can be performed and the required action taken.

For example, it may be necessary (a) to start building a distribution system during the product development stage, (b) to design the initial plant with the size and location based on some estimates of the total sales at steady state and how long it will take to reach steady state, and/or (c) to estimate how much the company can afford to spend on R&D and what the major types or areas of development should be. As a minimum, these decisions require "ball-park" estimates of sales and profitability.

The degree of accuracy and type of forecast will depend on whether the product under development will be a proprietary or nonproprietary one. For a proprietary product, timing is less critical and most analytical effort is directed toward the ultimate sales, whereas timing is a critical component for nonproprietary items.

The main difference between this development stage and the pre-product stage is that the product has been defined and the major technical breakthroughs have occurred. Because the product characteristics and the total market in which the product will compete are generally known, it is possible to use techniques that involve product comparisons, market testing, and analysis of market potential by market segment. The ability to do each of these well depends on good market research.

Market research is an important part of forecasting for all stages of the product life cycle. It generates valuable information about the significant factors, other interrelationships, market characteristics, and how the consumer makes his or her buying decision. And all of these serve as inputs for deriving the forecasts and measures of accuracy.

For example, changes in consumer attitudes and preferences will change the factors the consumer considers when buying, as well as their relative importance, so that product choices will shift and new products will be in demand. Entirely new market segments may also emerge, such as the increasing emphasis on age differentiation for products within a given market. Market research is an extremely broad area in which there have been considerable advances in recent years, and we shall give an overview only of those aspects relating to forecasting.

Market Research

One of the major problems in marketing is that the social sciences, as contrasted to the physical sciences, have yet to develop invariant laws. In the physical sciences, where there are well-developed and invariant laws based on deductive reasoning, models can be built and the laws tested by feedback systems—often by utilizing electronic computers because of the sophistication of the models and the statistical techniques employed.

One well-known application of this has been the successful exploration of outer space, where physical laws and theories were used to construct models that were in turn tested by space vehicles with elaborate equipment and feedback mechanisms. However, because we still understand so little about consumer behavior and other marketing factors, much of the market research must be empirical and exploratory.

In exploratory market research, there are two important aspects to be considered: (1) the *design and collection* of marketing information; and (2) the *analysis and interpretation* of the information. These are equally critical, and failure to do either one completely and correctly will usually lead to inconclusive or erroneous results. Much of the effort in the past has been focused on the design and collection of marketing information, with the attitude being that if this were done correctly, analysis could be accomplished by relatively simple tabulation and statistical methods.

However, it is now becoming apparent that because of the complex marketing structures, more powerful methods must be used to properly interpret the information collected. The improvements in electronic computing capabilities and the associated reduction in cost have made it possible to use many of the sophisticated statistical techniques that have been available for years, along with recently developed ones.

According to J. N. Sheth, two facilitating conditions have emerged that ensure large-scale diffusion of sophisticated statistical analyses in marketing in the future.[17] The *first* condition is that, after three decades of systematic data gathering, marketing research has learned the art of data collection. Procedures now exist for drawing accurate samples from populations, training interviewers and respondents, receiving cooperation from respondents, designing structured questionnaires, and coding and tabulating collected data.

Evidence of the acceptance of current data-collection methods is the credibility given to public surveys conducted by Nielsen, National Family Opinion (NFO), Roper, and others, which are generally considered to reflect unbiased consumer and public opinion. Such surveys incorporate sound statistical sampling with well-constructed and tested questioning methods. An extension of these public surveys has been the statistically designed monitoring of television watching, which provides the basis for television networks to evaluate program effectiveness, to add or drop programs, and to direct the type of advertising according to the type of television watcher.

[17] See "The Multivariate Revolution in Marketing Research," *Journal of Marketing* January 1971, p. 13–19.

The *second* condition that has enhanced the application of sophisticated statistical analyses is the recognition that the marketplace is a complex phenomenon, and that many factors intervene between the marketing activities of companies and market responses. Attempts are constantly made to examine these factors and how they mediate between marketing activities and market responses. This has resulted in the collection of information that corresponds to the complexity of the phenomenon.

Data Design and Collection.   The way in which data are collected and analyzed will depend on what previous work has been done and on the level of understanding of the market. Even in an existing market, knowledge about the relevant factors may be limited, and years of market research are required before there is a good understanding of the relevant factors and their interrelationships.

Edward Vogel, former vice-president of Anheuser-Busch, states that it took six years of extensive market research to understand sufficiently the effects on sales of different advertising media and the intensity of advertising and promotion before his company could more intelligently allocate advertising expenditures and thus significantly reduce the marketing cost per unit sold.

The best approach to market research is an evolutionary one, where each step is intended to add some new knowledge about the market. If little or no market research has been previously done, the first step is to identify factors that might be relevant (i.e., that can have a significant effect on sales).

Because there are generally many factors that could potentially be significant, collection of data for varying levels or changes in all of these factors through experimentation is costly and time-consuming. Instead, conversations should first be held with "experts," who at least have some intuitive feeling for identifying the relevant factors. This should narrow down the list of potential factors and may even make experimentation feasible.

An alternative or supplementary approach is to conduct a "pretest," where a small number of consumers are questioned at length to get some idea about the ways in which they react to various products and conditions, and about what factors might be important.

Experimentation implies the systematic variation of the levels (possible values) of each of the factors. However, it is frequently not feasible to vary systematically and intentionally the factor levels, because of reluctance to make any substantial changes that could negatively affect sales. As contrasted to manufacturing processes, where there is some willingness to make changes in the process parameters, marketing managers are seldom prone to make changes in market parameters.

Therefore, the information collected may be either what is called designed or undesigned data; designed data are obtained from experimentation, while the undesigned are measurements of the "natural" market (i.e., where no deliberate changes are made). The amount of data to be collected, the types of statistical analyses, and the ability to establish precise relationships are frequently quite different for the two situations.

When *undesigned data* are collected, the objective is to determine which system factors are most likely to cause a change in the factors under consideration (e.g., sales and quality). Thus, if there is an increase in one factor, will it cause a positive or negative change in another factor? Undesigned experiments usually require more information. They do not usually provide any sound basis for drawing definite conclusions but do give direction for further experimentation. However, there is little interference or disruption of the system being studied.

The main drawback or disadvantage in collecting undesigned data is that there may be little or no change during the data-collection period in significant factors. Therefore, the statistical analysis will show that these factors have no significant effect on the system being studied.

In the *designed data* experiment, where the levels of each factor are systematically varied, it is important to estimate first how large a change in a factor is required to influence any decision. That is, how sensitive to a decision is the sales estimate and, therefore, how much of a change in each factor will probably have to occur to affect sales that much? In a sense, this is a "bootstrap" operation because the impact of each factor on sales is what we are trying to estimate. Nevertheless, it is still advantageous to make "best" estitmates of the relationships so that an economic sample size can be determined and the possibility of having to extrapolate rather than interpolate is reduced.

In many instances, market research is required to determine what factors most significantly affect sales so that new product characteristics or specifications can be determined and incorporated into the new-product design.

For example, Kodak learned that the biggest headache for homemovie makers was all those blinding artificial lights with which they had to contend. This led Kodak's researchers to work on methods to avoid the use of artificial lights, which had to be accomplished by modifying both the camera and the film. The willingness of the consumer to pay the higher camera price that would have to be charged and his or her acceptance of the reduced picture quality (researchers thought the quality was "awful," but the consumer did not) were two new factors that had to be evaluated through market research.

Consumers frequently have to make trade-off decisions, such as convenience versus price or quality, and the types of trade-offs that will be made after the product is introduced can be determined through market research.

Thus Kodak found consumer dislike for artificial lighting so strong that it became apparent the total homemovie market would increase substantially with the introduction of a new product. It would generate new sales in two ways: (1) from consumers who already had moviemaking equipment but were willing to "obsolete" it for an improved product, and (2) from those who had not previously bought a movie camera because of the shortcomings of the existing ones. However, while Kodak sales forecasts gave estimates that the introduction of its new homemovie camera would be quite profitable, the success of it surprised virtually everyone.

In many instances, market research can at best provide indications of directions or preferences and establish bounds for them, with the exact magnitude being uncertain.

Market research is an effective way of identifying changes in consumer preferences—prior to those changes being observable through time-series analysis of sales—and thus avoiding the introduction of a new product in a declining market situation. This is especially true in the garment industry, where style changes occur quickly. A new product, while gaining the anticipated market share, can have significantly less sales than forecasted if the market for that style has dropped off. Changes in consumer preferences will not be immediately reflected in manufacturer's sales to retailers and distributors. This is because the first reaction at the retail-and-distribution level usually is to ignore changes in sales and to keep purchases constant, thus increasing inventories.

The problem of the interaction of many market factors must be considered in analyzing the results of market research. In the liquor industry, American distillers became concerned because their products were losing market share to imported Scotch and Canadian whiskies, as well as vodka. Market research pointed out that the consumer preferred a lighter taste, a characteristic not then present in domestic whiskies. The findings further showed that women, who shop for half the liquor sold and are more inclined than men to try new products, like the idea of "light whiskey." This led to the development of a new light whisky, which is distilled at a higher-than-normal proof of 160 to 190 and is aged four years or more in used barrels that impart less wood flavor than do new barrels. Large volumes of the light whiskey were distilled in 1968 and are now being introduced into the market.

However, there seem to be some problems on the horizon for the light whiskey. The 1968 total liquor industry growth of 6% was reduced to 3% in 1970 and 1971, and views of the distilleries have changed considerably. Reasons for the overall reduction in liquor sales must be investigated, along with the fact that light taste is only one of several factors that the customer takes into account. Early sales indicate that market penetration of light whiskey into the import business may be less than anticipated, and further market research of these factors will precede the introduction of light whiskey products of some of the distillers.

Data Analysis and Interpretation.   There are many things to consider in selecting the right statistical technique for the analysis of marketing data. Perhaps the most important consideration is the number of "dependent" variables or predicted factors, such as sales, market share, and product preference, to be explained by the independent variables. The latter are the factors that are measured and provide the equation basis for estimating the value of the dependent variables. Independent variables, also called explanatory or predictor variables, usually are "independent" only in a mathematical—not statistical—sense, since variations in one independent variable may cause or be related to changes in another independent variable.

Market research may involve *no* dependent variables; instead of a factor to be predicted, the objective is, say, to identify what elements are important in sorting consumers into homogeneous groups (how to distinguish between the buyer and nonbuyer, who is a repeat buyer, and the like). An example of *one* dependent variable is the prediction of sales (the dependent variable) by the use of independent variables (factors), such as number of consumers in each socioeconomic group, the growth of the economy, and the difference in product quality between the new and competitive product. There can be *two or more* dependent variables when the objective is to forecast several factors simultaneously taking into account their interdependence, such as new sales and repeat sales, or sales of black-and-white television sets and color sets for primary and secondary sets.

The techniques used in examining market data for exploratory analysis will also depend on the way in which the data are collected (designed versus undesigned), whether they are qualitative or quantitative data, and whether the interrelationships of factors are critical. The more sophisticated statistical methods are primarily of value when relationships of predictor factors are not independent (i.e., a change in one independent variable can lead to changes in several other independent variables, or the significance of a relationship is not usually obvious after tabulation).

In some cases, simple tabulations will show the relevance of a factor and sophisticated statistical techniques are not necessary. However, as we indicated earlier, since marketing structures are often complex, relationships that appear to exist from simple tabulations may disappear when interrelationships are considered.

The use of statistical techniques in exploratory analyses and the sequence in which the analyses are performed are illustrated in Figure 6.1. Only the major statistical techniques are shown, with brief descriptions of those in Figure 6.1 and other techniques given in Appendix B. These techniques are all included in multivariate statistical analysis, where the complex interactions of many variables can be simultaneously considered. Univariate (one dependent variable) and bivariate (two independent variables and one dependent variable) analyses are omitted from Figure 6.1, since exploratory market research normally involves many variables that are interdependent, because of the assumed complexity of the market being studied. Also, these are no more than special cases of the multivariate analysis.

Simple tabulations are included in Figure 6.1 as a part of the statistical analysis of marketing data, since some analysts feel that they can—through inspection of tabulations—eliminate certain factors, and direct subsequent analyses so that their costs are reduced. The ability to do such preliminary screening depends on the individual analyst's skill and intuition, the amount of previous market research, and the accuracy required.

Qualitative data, referred to by statisticians as nonmetric data, are descriptive in the sense that they tell whether a certain characteristic is contained (yes or no), give some verbal measure of a factor (such as color, male or female), or are a grouping of quantitative data (such as age group and economic class). In contrast, quantitative data (called metric data) have numerical values assigned to each variable. It may be necessary to use a rating scale to convert a qualitative factor to a quantitative scale. When marketing data in their collected form are both qualitative and quantitative, the usual procedure is to convert the qualitative data to quantitative data, so that quantitative techniques can be used. In most exploratory market research, qualitative data are analyzed; the following descriptions and examples of the most commonly used techniques are for quantitative data.

As we indicated earlier, the objective of the market research may not be to obtain a predictive equation but to sort a population into homo-

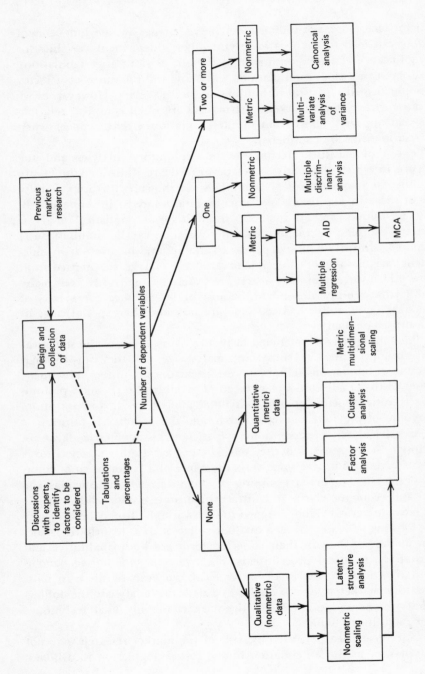

Figure 6.1. Statistical analysis of exploratory marketing data

116

geneous groups, as is done when there are no dependent variables. This grouping can then be the basis for subsequent market surveys or for directing marketing effort. (From a forecasting viewpoint, the grouping can lay the foundation for a disaggregated marketing model and for estimating how specific groups and, hence, overall sales will be affected by a particular marketing strategy.)

Univariate and bivariate analyses (special cases of multivariate analysis are appropriate when there are only two or three variables) are not commonly used in marketing research because of the complex market structures. If it is assumed that there are no interactions of the independent variables, then the simpler techniques that incorporate primarily regression analysis and tabulations for example, should be used.

Other Techniques

As we have just seen, market research is valuable in establishing relationships between factors and in generating inputs for the various techniques used in forecasting for the product development stage of the life cycle. However, it is sometimes not possible, because of timing or the need to maintain secrecy, to conduct market research in some areas. In such cases, other techniques must be employed to attempt to quantify expert opinion about qualitative factors. One of the better techniques for doing this is rating-ranking, which has a variety of applications in forecasting and decision-making situations.

Rating-Ranking Method. When introducing a new product into an existing market, it is extremely important to know how superior the new product is to those which are already being marketed or which the competition can potentially introduce, since market share is directly proportional to the product differences. These differences are usually expressed only in qualitative terms, such as "significantly better" and "substantial improvement." On the basis of such statements, estimates are then made that show a large market share for the new product, the charging of premium prices, or very rapid market penetration. When the product differences are expressed on a quantitative scale, there is a sounder basis for estimating market share and subsequent sales.

Product-difference measurement is accomplished in three ways: (1) by identifying the factors that influence the consumer's buying decision, and the relative importance of these factors; (2) by rating each existing, new, and potential product for each of these factors on a scale of, say, one to

10, where 10 connotes that the product meets the consumer expectations completely; and (3) by multiplying the factor weights by the ratings and summing these quantities for each product so that overall scores are obtained. The absolute scores for each product cannot be used to compare products, in the sense that an overall score of 100 for a product does not indicate that a product is twice as good as one with a score of 50. However, the differences do provide a basis for determining whether one product is definitely better when compared to other products. When qualitative comparisons are made, the evaluator is prone to give too much weight to the product characteristics for which the new product is better than existing ones and to give too little or no consideration to other factors that might be equally or more important to the consumer.

There might be just a few or many factors that are important in the buying decision. For an automobile windshield, there are at least 10 important factors in evaluating products, among which are impact resistance, ability to keep a person in the car upon collision, concussion likelihood, and visibility. For a medical instrument, the factors might be the likelihood of detecting a disease, the variability in the measurements, the time required for analysis, the cost of the test, and the skill required to use the instrument.

Table 6.1 illustrates how one can rate various products. Five products are being considered, with A, B, and C being existing products, D the new product to be introduced, and E the product the competition is most likely to market within two years after the new product has been introduced. The factors used to compare the products have been identified through market research, along with their relative importance to the

Table 6.1 Use of Rating-Ranking Method for Estimating Product Differences

	Factors and Relative Weights					
Product	Quality (6)	Ease of Maintenance (5)	Cost (8)	Performance (10)	Product or Corporate Image (4)	Overall Score
A	7	6	8	6	7	224
B	8	7	7	5	6	213
C	6	5	10	6	4	217
D	9	9	6	10	9	283
E	9	9	7	9	7	273

consumer (given below each of the factors). Several experts have been asked to rate each of the factors for each product, with the ratings given in the appropriate cells. The ratings have been multiplied by the weights, and overall scores are given at the end of each product row.

It can be seen that the new product, D, is definitely superior to A, B, and C, since there is little difference among these three (comparisons of the ratings with sales data can be a way of validating the rating method). However, product E is estimated to be only slightly inferior to D, which means that the competition will have an almost comparable product within two years.

Sales forecasts should consider not only the product differences, but the effects of product or corporate image and relative selling prices in estimating the rate of market penetration and eventual market share.

A side benefit of this approach is that the results of a rating-ranking exercise may give direction to further R&D and to improved product concepts, since the ratings will show where a product needs improvement and which factors are most important. Ideally, a rating-ranking of existing products before the product development stage would aid in directing the R&D effort prior to product introduction, pointing out the factors most important to the consumer and the way each existing product satisfies the desired product characteristics.

Further market research or analysis to determine how readily the consumer will accept the superiority of one product over another one will also enhance the forecasting accuracy. If the product has a short life and if improved quality, or longer life, or both are the distinguishing characteristics of the new product, the penetration rate will be much more rapid than if the product has a long life, because then it will take the consumer several years to detect the difference. Judgments must still be made in determining the significance of product differences, but these type of measurements force consistency into the evaluations and subsequent forecasts.

Although the rating-ranking method is not a precise technique, it is very useful for establishing bounds and checking assumptions. If there are considerable differences among the experts concerning the factor weights or ratings, these differences should be resolved through discussions (the Delphi method is applicable here) or further market research.

Disaggregate Marketing Model. There is often a tendency to look at a market only in its entirety, rather than to break it down into its components and to forecast what type of penetration can be expected in each component.

For example, while the total market for a product may be $1 billion, it is possible that as much as 75 to 90% of the market may be captive. There are two reasons for this: (a) for a product that is a component, the OEM's (Original Equipment Manufacturers) might make a very high percentage of the product themselves, or (b) for an end product, a large portion of the distribution outlets (e.g., wholesalers) might be controlled by the competitors. In this case, it is meaningful only to consider that portion of the market that is open or available.

Another similar situation is where the original equipment market is inaccessible, and the replacement market is all that is available, with a large portion of that also controlled by the OEM. This is particularly true for many automotive parts, as illustrated in the situation of small tire manufacturers, who are not able to supply the automobile manufacturers; they can only compete in the replacement tire market. The availability of data will determine the extent to which disaggregation is possible.

The disaggregation of a total market may also reveal trends that can have positive or adverse effects on a new market. In the illustration of the tobacco industry given in Chapter 2, the shifts in consumer preference to menthol and filter cigarettes (shown in Table 2.4) considerably reduced the potential for a new nonfilter, nonmenthol cigarette. Even if market research and a product-differences analysis had shown that a new nonmenthol, nonfilter cigarette was definitely superior to the cigarettes being marketed, it would still have difficulty in gaining sales in a declining market (depending on the marketing strategies employed by the competition).

Similarly, the introduction of light whiskey has been at a disadvantage because of both the trend of the market toward Scotch and gin, and a slowdown in the overall growth of the liquor industry. Not only is the available market smaller than anticipated, but there will undoubtedly be stronger competition within that market, since the only way for sales of existing products in that segment to grow is by increasing the market share.

Disaggregation by type of consumer is important for two reasons: (1) in understanding and accurately forecasting the penetration rate, and (2) in being able to track the forecast against what ultimately happens. Market researchers have found that consumers vary according to whether they will buy a product, and when they will buy it. These decisions depend on how long a product has been on the market and on how well consumers accept it. (The types of consumers are discussed in greater detail in Chapter 8.)

One such group is called innovators. These people have a high probability of buying any new product if it has sufficient appeal; that is, if it appears to have better product characteristics than competitive products. Innovators may give an initial surge to sales. And if—on the basis of a market test in which innovators made the most purchases—a smooth statistical projection is made, this forecast could lead to an excess or a shortage of capacity in the early stages of the product life cycle and also to revisions in strategy because of sales exceeding or not meeting expectations.

In the case of forecasts for color television, market disaggregation by different geographical areas and levels of income have provided a sound base for making accurate forecasts. Rather than assume one S-shaped curve for the total market, projections of S-shaped curves have been made for each segment and then aggregated to get the total forecast.

It often happens that certain geographical areas are more receptive (i.e., tend to buy) at an earlier stage than other areas. These are lead-indicators of national acceptance of a product: hence, penetration by area should be considered.

This is particularly true for products that are related to the weather, such as lawn supplies, air conditioning, outside building supplies (e.g., roofing and exterior siding), and swimming pools. Sales of new and established lawn products in the south in the late winter and early spring months are highly indicative of sales to the northern states a few months later.

Disaggregation for new-product purchases versus replacement sales can be of value when considering what market is available. The new product may be able to rapidly penetrate the new sales market (i.e., where the consumer is buying the product for the first time), whereas it may take much longer to penetrate the replacement market (i.e., where the consumer has some brand loyalty). In the appliance market, many of the segments are largely replacement sales. One manufacturer, GE, said that 75% of its washers and 60% of its refrigerator sales in 1972 were replacements.

Trends toward modularization and the extent to which this concept is built into a new product may change the size of the market. For example, in many major appliances and automobiles, repair parts are often obtained from salvaged parts, such as television tubes, generators, and brakes. As modularization takes hold, the repair-parts market will grow considerably, which is particularly relevant to the component-parts supplier.

Finally, disaggregation is essential when considering the introduction of a new product in a market that is not fixed (i.e., the market size can be changed if the new product is sufficiently different). Whereas market penetration may be particularly high for a given time, the new product may be sufficiently attractive so that the consumer is willing to acquire a second or third of the same item.

Moreover, the new product may have features that will not only extend its overall market penetration, but that will also capture all or most of the new consumers in addition to replacement and repeat sales. This was true of the entry of Corning Ware into the housewares market, where housewives were willing to have several vessels that served the same function but were different aesthetically. Likewise, color television increased the total percentage of disposable income spent on such a major appliance, because of households adding a second or third set. And similarly, the introduction of the Xerox copier radically changed the copying or duplication industry.

When a disaggregated market model is constructed, it is possible to look at each market segment separately and to make realistic projections for the total market. For example, while the number of households owning an item may not change, the percentage of multiple owners may increase dramatically. Also the new product may temporarily change the "life" of a product, where the consumer will scrap an item that still functions adequately to obtain one with improved features.

Similar-Product Analysis.   Since little data may be available and, say, for secrecy purposes market testing is inadvisable, it may be necessary to rely primarily on the technique of similar-product comparison. Here, one can compare a projected product with an "ancestor" that has similar characteristics.

In 1965, for example, we disaggregated the market for color television by income levels and geographical regions, and compared these submarkets with the historical patterns of black-and-white television market growth. This approach was based on the assumption that color television represented an advance over black-and-white TV analogous to (although less intense than) the advance that black-and-white television represented over radio. The analyses of black-and-white TV market growth also permitted us to estimate the variability to be expected—that is, the degree to which our projections differ from actual figures as the result of economic and other factors.

In developing our long-range forecast for color television penetration on a national basis, we considered the prices of black-and-white TV and other major household appliances in 1949, consumer disposable income in 1949, the prices of color television and other appliances in 1965, and consumer disposable income in 1965. The success patterns of black-and-white TV then provided insight into the likelihood of success and sales potential of color television.

In the case of the gas turbine, the sales experience of the diesel engine when it was first introduced gives some basis for projecting gas turbine sales, although there are now two basic types of engines instead of only one as when the diesel was introduced. Today, the likelihood of the Wankel engine being extensively marketed also changes such a comparison. The product differences (e.g., diesel versus gas, gas turbine versus diesel) as well as other factors, such as potential improvements and cost-reduction programs, must be taken into account. However, since it rarely happens that an exact comparison can be made, the "ancestor" product history serves as a starting point from which adjustments can be made.

For example, when Corning introduced its new flat surface cooktop (The Counter-That-Cooks®), the only product comparison that could be made was the self-cleaning oven. The significantly higher price of the flat surface cooktop and the fulfillment of a different customer want had to be considered in extrapolating from the earlier experience of the self-cleaning oven.

Input-Output Analysis.   Although this theory was first conceived in the seventeenth and eighteenth centuries, the first working input-output (I-O) model of the United States economy was produced by Professor Wassily Leontief of Harvard University just before World War II. It was not until electronic computers were generally available, however, that I-O became a real working tool of the economist. There have been very few applications of Leontief's work to business forecasting until recently. Now many companies are exploring how they might apply his I-O model to business planning.

This technique is primarily appropriate when the new product is to compete in a large market segment that can be related to the broad industry categories of the United State government input-output tables, or when the market for the new product has been in existence for several years and sufficient data are available to develop an I-O model for segments of the total industry. However, detailed data for much finer breakouts than those given by the United States Government tables are now available for many industry segments, from sources such as Arthur D. Little and MAPTEK. This has led to extended applications of I-O.

As early as 1970, a survey indicated that 50 major United States corporations had taken up work on I-O models, and projections showed that this number would increase to 500 in three or four years.[18] However, difficulties in being able to apply the I-O figures to specific products has slowed down this anticipated increase in applications. They have been found to be more appropriate to forecasting total company sales or sales of major segments of a company, where meaningful relationships can be established.

An example of the application of I-O that has appeared in published form described the experiences of a refractories division of a large United States corporation, Combustion Engineering, Inc.[19] I-O analysis was used to estimate the effect of different economic forecasts on industry growth rates by providing quantitative consistency both between the GNP forecast and the growth rates of 90 different industries and between different industry growth rates and those of refractory markets.

In that study, the primary input to a long-range plan was a single forecast of industry growth, such as steel production, based on I-O analysis, interviews with industry personnel, and company estimates. Input to the model was final demand—total government purchases of goods and services, personal consumption expenditures, capital spending, and net exports. The output was industry growth in 1958 dollars for each of the 90 industries and their market growth rates. The model included changes in technology, such as the quantity of steel used in automobiles, as obtained from external sources.

In the case of new products in an existing market, it may be possible to estitmate by I-O analysis the total market in which a product will compete, although it is unlikely that there can be any degree of disaggregation by I-O itself. Input-output analysis is most effectively used in determining long-term trends in the components of an industry (the inputs into that industry from other industries, and vice versa) through analyses of the trends of the coefficients in the I-O table. It is possible to readily spot how one material is being substituted for another, or how the consumption of a particular material by an industry is increasing or decreasing.

The application of I-O to sales forecasting for specific businesses is still in the development stage, and many companies have found that considerable effort and money are required to obtain their own I-O models. Furthermore, the resulting forecasts have limited use in the decision-making process.

[18] *Wall Street Journal,* February, 17, 1970, p. 1.
[19] E. D. Ranard, "Use of Input/Output Analysis in Long Range Planning"; and S. W. Yost and C. E. Stowell, "Using Input/Output for Evaluating Profit Center Performance," Windsor, Conn.: Combustion Engineering, Inc.

Production Costs

Although most research breakthroughs will have occurred before product development, there are usually several engineering, marketing, and other developments that still must take place. All critical events in the development, manufacturing, and sales areas should be identified. Also, estimates should be made of the effort and time required and the likelihood of success. These critical events should be linked together through a flow chart to ascertain dependency and consistency.

While the computer techniques of PERT and CPM are applicable, we have found that TGRIP (Tasks, Goals, and Resources Integration Program, which is a modification of the IBM Project Control System to permit the inclusion of goals) is more effective in checking feasibility and consistency. It essentially involves the identification of the goals that must be met at specific points in time to achieve a forecast and its related plan, the determination of the tasks that must be performed to achieve the goals, their interrelationships and required timing, and the resources needed to accomplish the tasks.

If the resources are not available as required, or the timing is impossible because of interdependency of the tasks, the goals and the related forecasts will have to be revised. The TGRIP technique, along with some examples, is presented in more detail in Chapter 7.

It is often difficult to estimate manufacturing costs during the product development stage, especially for the first few units that are made. Given that there is some estimate of unit price, one approach is to use similar-product analysis to determine what the profit-margin percentage has been at a "mature" point of the product life and what type of production-cost learning curve has been experienced for similar products.

This information can be used to estimate the production costs for an identical point in the life cycle of the new product and to project backwards, via the learning-curve methodology, to get the costs for units produced earlier in the life cycle. The critical events for manufacturing processes can then be considered to find out if the projected learning curve is feasible or if delays are likely to cause less learning (i.e., a higher percent learning curve, where the percent learning is subtracted from 100% to get the learning-curve percentage).

In applying both the TGRIP and learning-curve techniques, the variability of the estimates of timing, resources, and cost should be computed so that the overall variability can be included in the sensitivity or risk analyses for the new product. The variability in the likelihood of success for accomplishing the goals should be directly tied in with the sales and other estimates in computing their variability.

IN SUMMARY

If the new product is to be sold in an existing market, there is considerable information available (or that can be generated) to provide a basis for forecasting. Qualitative techniques, such as product-differences measurement, are used to make subjective estimates more objective. Market research can add considerably to what is already known to establish relationships and market understanding, and to reduce the number of assumptions that must be made.

Chapter VII

The Product Development Stage:
A New Market

When integrated circuit (IC) technology was first developed, it was apparent that products would emerge from it that would yield an overall high sales volume for the technology. While it was not clear just what the applications would be, it seemed almost certain that many new products, not previously feasible with the semiconductor technology then available, would become technically and economically practical.

As correctly anticipated, many new and quite revolutionary products were subsequently introduced. These included high-speed electronic computers, desk computers and calculators, and other electronic devices. And new developments, leading to new products, continue to arise to make use of that technology. For example, small pocket computers that utilize large-scale integrated circuits experienced such high demand in 1972 that the IC industry could not keep pace with it.

While the IC situation illustrates how it is economically desirable to proceed with development of a technology even when the specific products that will utilize the technology are not known, the pocket computer also demonstrates how new products can run ahead of technology. Although the integrated circuits for this minicomputer were commercially available, the semiconductor manufacturers could not build enough of the large-scale ICs, which are the heart of the pocket computer, to keep up with the demand.

The ultimate shortage of these components virtually stopped some of the end-product manufacturers, while slowing down others. The blame for the trouble was placed on the advanced design of the large-scale integrated (LSI) circuits for the pocket computer; the product developers had tried to leapfrog the industry by designing a product that required advanced ICs, and that led to the need for six redesigns.

Proper analyses of what had to be accomplished, and the time and effort associated with these critical events, could have signaled the ultimate shortage situation.

When Corning Glass Works first developed Pyroceram® a high strength, high-temperature resistant material, it was predicted that this technology would provide substantial profits to the company, even though the specific products that could utilize the new material were then not known. The characteristics of the material were believed to be of sufficient value to the eventual consumer to justify further process development. The successful introduction of Corning Ware confirmed this evaluation. Subsequently, Corning Glass introduced Counterange™ and building products applications, which are other examples of how the Pyroceram technology made new products possible (the Corning ·Glass products cited above and elsewhere in this book are registered trade names.)

From the time the first breakthrough in laser technology occurred, it has been predicted that there would be many significant new products utilizing the ability to narrow precisely the laser's beam of coherent light. The initial laser products provided substantial benefits to the users for the various applications, but produced relatively small profits for the manufacturers.

However, researchers now see potential use of laser technology in disease diagnosis and prevention. Arthur Vassiliades, senior research engineer at Stanford Research Institute, says "The laser is becoming extremely useful and valuable in medical research. Its future importance is hard to overestimate."[20] Already it has been demonstrated that the laser can explore the makeup of a cell and manipulate genes and chromosomes, diagnose certain diseases such as cancer, and identify disease-causing bacteria in a fraction of the time taken by conventional methods.

In the foregoing examples, the key to determining whether development funds should be expended—and, if so, how much—was not in the prediction of specifically which new products or markets would emerge from the technology. Rather, it was whether the technology would inevitably lead to acceptable profit returns within a reasonable time frame.

In new-product or new-technology situations, where the market does not exist or is not reasonably well-defined, forecasting for the product development stage is often quite difficult. Nevertheless, there are tech-

[20] "The Laser's Bright Future in Medicine," *Business Week*, July 15, 1972, p. 50.

niques and approaches that make it possible to obtain forecasts of sufficient accuracy for decision-making purposes. Among these are identification, timing, and tracking of critical events; market research; bounding techniques; and the rating-ranking method.

Two major types of forecasting situations arise during this stage:

1. The technology has been developed and the problem is to identify and *choose among product alternatives.*

2. The product concept has been developed and forecasts of sales and profitability are needed so that the decision of whether to introduce the product can be made; thus it is usually possible to *establish bounds* for some broad total market, thereby reducing the problem to the determination of what portion of that total market will buy the new product.

We shall consider both of these forecasting situations in the balance of this chapter.

CHOOSING AMONG PRODUCT ALTERNATIVES

In many cases, a material or technology has been developed for which there are potential applications that might have significant payoffs. The problem is first to identify the specific product opportunities, and then to determine which, if any, should be exploited and whether those products selected should be developed simultaneously or in sequence.

Because forecasting is sometimes an integral part of the selection method, as is the case here, we shall describe the overall approach to selecting among new product opportunities, rather than attempt to separate the forecasting technique from the total methodology. Two approaches are presented here: the choice of either depends on the time and personnel available for analysis and the number of potential products identified.

Combined Delphi/Rating-Ranking Approach

When either (a) the technology is not proprietary and must be exploited rapidly, the manpower is not available, and there are a large number of products from which to choose, or (b) the overall payoff does not appear sufficient to justify an intensive selection effort, then the approach that can be taken is a combination of the Delphi method and the rating-ranking technique.

With this approach, it is possible that the best opportunity might be overlooked or given a low ranking because of limited available information, since the objective is to make the best use of both (a) the information that is either available or that can be readily obtained, and (b) the experience of the personnel participating in the selection process. No technique has yet been developed that circumvents the need for good information.

As the first step, several separate groups of experts are asked to list all possible product applications that could utilize the new technology. The experts are encouraged to stretch their imaginations as best they can and to ignore potential development, marketing, and manufacturing problems. This probe of applications should include specifications (product requirements) for each market, and ratings (on a scale of 1 to 10) of how well the new product, the existing product, and other potential products meet the specifications.

The factors to be used for evaluating the opportunities are also rated or weighted according to their relative importance. A list might include these factors.

- Size of the market.
- Gross new additions to the operating margin.
- Relative advantage of the new product over existing or potential ones (based on the specifications and relative importance of each specification).
- Effort required to develop a marketing system.
- Degree of commitment by potential customers (if the product is to be sold to an OEM).
- R&D effort necessary to develop the process and product required for competitive pricing.
- Capital intensity of the business.
- Time span for the product to become profitable.
- Price sensitivity of the market.
- Degree of completeness of the marketing and development information.
- Amount of control over the events necessary for success.
- Expected ROI (based on a 10-year planning horizon).

The potential products are rated by each of the experts, along with their individual reasons for such ratings and how well-qualified they feel they are for each rating (e.g., well-qualified, some basis, or no basis). Where there are significant differences in the ratings, the experts will be provided additional information from other experts and given an opportunity to change their ratings. An average rating for each product for each factor is thus obtained, and overall scores for each product are computed by multiplying ratings by the factor weights and adding them. (This is very similar to the illustration in Table 6.1.)

This procedure will produce a ranking of the new-product opportunities. The list of products that should be simultaneously developed is compiled by determining how much resources are available, and by selecting the top-ranked products in order until the resources are exhausted.

Flow-Charting Approach

Another and more comprehensive methodology can be used when either (a) only a few products have been identified, or (b) the list has been reduced (as outlined in the foregoing discussion), and there are sufficient resources and time available to do a more exhaustive evaluation. This approach basically involves flow-charting of the critical events, timing, resources, and goals for each product. The objective is to establish a sound basis for ranking the products and also for determining how the available resources can be most effectively used, taking into account scheduling or sequencing problems.

This approach requires a precise definition of project goals, the assumptions made, the events that must happen for the assumptions to come true or the goals to be met, the sequence in which the events must occur, and the resources required to accomplish these events. The flow-chart information can thus serve as input for a variety of computer-oriented techniques designed to analyze such information.

As we discussed in Chapter 6, we have utilized a computer program called TGRIP that shows, in a way similar to PERT, the schematic relationships of goals and tasks and determines the resource requirements over time.

The optimum allocation of resources is then made by considering factors such as the short- and long-term economic implications of each new product, risks involved, resources required and available, and capital investment. Next, a rating-ranking technique similar to that given for the previous approach can be utilized to obtain the ranking of projects. Finally, the detailed resource requirements for each project are considered to see if the scheduling of the projects is still feasible over time, considering short-term fluctuations.

The initial step of establishing goals, and putting into a flow chart the critical events for accomplishing these goals, the timing, and the event dependency will prove valuable in three ways. *First,* it will show whether the timing implied in the forecasts is feasible. Often, the flow chart makes it apparent that the assumptions or timing are unrealistic. *Second,* the flow chart will provide a good basis for estimating risks for marketing, and manufacturing, for example. *Third,* it will also show how many of the critical events are subject to control—as contrasted to being dependent on other forces, such as legislation, sociological actions, changes in consumer preferences, and technical breakthroughs that must occur.

The addition of resources to the flow chart may reveal that short-term savings in resource requirements make the overall timing infeasible. Although the use of a computer will enhance the analysis and give a basis for tracking developments versus the plan, the major benefits are derived from the discipline of preparing the flow chart and the various estimates.

An example of how even very simple flow charting can provide valuable insight into forecasting and estimation of related risks is shown in Figure 7.1. This reveals some of the critical events that were necessary in 1968 to achieve widespread acceptance of an artificial kidney machine.

Under the conditions prevailing at that time, home dialysis cost $12,000 to $15,000 for the first year, which included training and machine cost, plus $5000 per year for maintenance and supplies. Dialysis at a hospital cost $20,000 to $25,000 per year; and the cost of a transplant operation was about $10,000, with availability of good kidneys being an additional problem. Statistics further indicated that over 50,000 persons were added each year to those needing dialysis, while only about 5000 were able or willing to avail themselves of the treatment.

In order for the market to increase significantly, and to penetrate this potential demand, it became apparent that certain critical events had to occur. Consider: government funds were necessary to set up and conduct training courses; insurance policies had to be changed (which required the efforts and influence of labor unions); people had to be willing to locate themselves geographically so that it would be possible to give them prompt service when their home unit failed; and there had to be improvements in the kidney-machine design to make it more economically attractive.

Interviews with doctors, insurance executives, congressmen and senators, labor union officials, and other persons indicated that each of these events was unlikely to take place for several years. This led to a substantial downward revision of previous sales estitmates.

Consideration of the large overall expenditures required, and of the

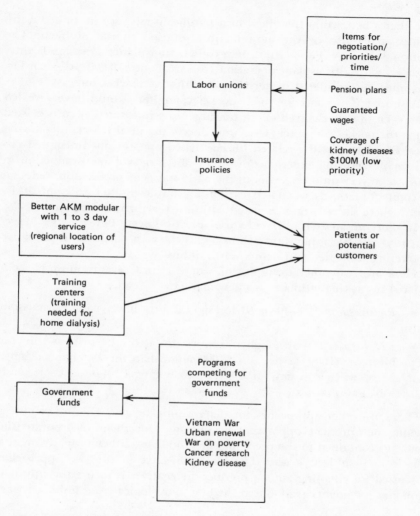

Figure 7.1. Flow chart of critical events for expansion of artificial kidney machine (AKM) market.

inconvenience and the psychologically unattractive nature of home dialysis, also suggested high risks because of the basic consumer reaction that a kidney machine was unacceptable. (Even the introduction in 1972 of a portable kidney machine, which provides more mobility, appears unlikely to have a large market, because it costs $5000 per year to operate, in addition to the $4500 purchase price.)

Either a better oral treatment or a significant advance in kidney transplants appears to be the most feasible solution to the problem. The National Kidney Foundation states that transplants are significantly cheaper, with a transplant operation costing about $10,000. All such factors must be considered in deriving an objective market forecast.

A similar flow chart for small pocket computers would have revealed that, even though the technology for large-scale integrated circuits existed when the pocket computers were introduced, the need for manufacturing breakthroughs and the related timing (based on previous integrated circuit manufacturing experience) would cause large-volume production in 1972 to be very unlikely. Also, in the early stages of production, redesign is commonplace, as we noted earlier for minicomputer integrated circuits, where six redesigns occurred within a year of introduction.

In short, an analysis of risks by use of critical event flow charts will frequently suggest a high probability of delays in facilities expansions, marketing strategies, and manpower buildups.

Here are two other examples of where critical events must be considered in making estimates for new markets.

- *Picturephones*®—the need for significantly lower cost transmission lines.
- *Video cassettes*—although introduced in 1972, the price is thus far prohibitive ($1600, or perhaps $1000 more than the average consumer might be willing to pay for a leisure-time gadget). The lack of standization is also critical.

There are other approaches for determining how to allocate resources among new-product opportunities, but most of them incorporate the concepts contained in the preceding methodology, either formally or in a less formal, subjective way. The main objective of the two approaches discussed for choosing among product alternatives is to use the information and judgments available in the best, most logical, and unbiased way.

ESTABLISHING MARKET BOUNDS

As we noted earlier, it is usually possible to establish a bound or an upper limit, and then to estimate by various methods what portion of that upper bound can be realized. In the case of therapeutic devices, the upper limit will be the number of persons afflicted with the disease to which the device applies. For industrial products, this limit might be the number of factories, or the amount of product produced divided by equipment capacity. For programmed learning methods or teaching machines, the bound is the number of schools (or some multiple, depending on the potential number per school).

In other instances, the new product may be one that can potentially be bought by each household, each child, each woman, and so on, so that only a very large upper limit can be set. The ability to determine the minimum upper bound is critical, and thorough analysis can substantially reduce the forecasting error.

For example, the potential market, or upper bound for electric ranges and electric dryers in the New York City area is not the number of residences that have electric wiring. Rather, it is the number of residences that have 220-volt outlets or in which the installation of 220-volt outlets is permissible.

When the market segment in which the new product will compete is a very large one and cuts across many industrial sectors, the input-output technique might help establish the upper bound for sales. Again, the government I-O tables are much too macro to do any reasonable bounding, and more definitive industrial sections are vital to establishing any reasonable bounds.

Input-output is primarily of value for long-range projections, but even there accuracy is questionable. This is because I-O methodology relies heavily on assumptions of future technological changes, which are usually kept secret until they are near introduction. The impact of inventions such as the Xerox copier, Poloroid camera, and the electronic computer have had very important effects on markets relating to them.

Comprehensive Market Research

The next step after bounding is to determine the conditions under which someone will buy the new product, and to estimate—by some form of rating method—how well these conditions will be met. This provides the basis for estimating the penetration level. Unless a careful and thorough analysis is performed, it is possible to grossly overestimate the level of penetration.

Virtually all objective methods incorporate some form of market research, whether it is consumer-oriented, or accomplished by questioning "experts." However, it is important to be aware that the type of market research for new markets is quite different from that of existing markets. Customer wants are more clearly defined, and product comparisons can be made for existing markets, whereas consumer needs, preferences, and trade-offs for new markets must be established through market research.

Exploratory research is often necessary for new markets before more definitive investigations can be made. It is also essential to determine not only how a consumer will react to a product and whether it will meet his or her needs, but also to determine whether the customer will be able to purchase it.

Identifying Market Needs.   Theodore Levitt has described several situations in which markets that had very high upper limits were not successfully exploited, because of lack of sound market research, even though the new product was intuitively a solution to the market need.[21] He cites examples where there can be a need but no market, or a market but no customer.

In automated education, for example, a field predicted by many to yield substantial profits by the early 1970s, General Electric and Time organized the General Learning Corporation in 1965 with elaborate fanfare, expecting to capitalize on the electronic equipment capability of GE and the educational materials from Time.

The reason for the massive failure of this and other similarly optimistic competitors was not that the forecasters were wrong, since there is potentially a huge education market, but that the existence of a market does not assure the automatic existence of a customer. It was found that there are no customers large enough to buy very much of the elaborate new educational technology visualized by scientists and educators.

General Learning did not distinguish between the existence of a vast number of eager prospects and the nonexistence within those ranks of any solvent customers. The product it tried to introduce, a one-year basic high school physics course employing sophisticated equipment and feedback mechanisms, cost over $12 million to develop. This product was much too costly to produce and hence to buy, compared with the $30,000 or so it costs a publisher to produce a conventional physics book.

Levitt also referred to predictions that may be grounded in some imminent truths about science and life, and yet not apply to new products because of customer wants. The sea may harbor a huge food supply but the consuming public is not likely to exhibit any great fondness for strange new foods. Food habits are among the most difficult of all habits to change, even in the case of extraordinary privation.

Consider the disappointments suffered in recent years by companies that created new, low-priced, high-protein foods for consumption by

[21] See "The New Markets—Think Before You Leap," *Harvard Business Review*, May-June 1969, p. 53.

Table 7.1 How Housewives Spend Their Time on Housework and Their Attitude Toward It

Women's Housework	Percent of Housework Time	Rank of Dislike (1 = Most)
Wash Articles	3.2	1
Miscellaneous housework	7.1	2
Garbage	0.6	5
Vacuum	6.4	5
Dry laundry	3.8	5
Clean house	16.0	8
Trash disposal	1.3	11
Iron laundry	11.5	3
Miscellaneous laundry	1.9	4
Wash laundry	6.4	8
Wash, dry dishes	24.4	12
Cleanup	2.6	8
Dust	6.4	12
Sweep	2.6	14
Fold and sort laundry	5.8	15

undernourished masses in South America and India. The companies found that they did not understand how such people live, what they value, and what must be done to change their accustomed habits.

Market research that identifies market needs and the degree to which a new product satisfies them can circumvent such product failures as those just described and their associated bad forecasts. In the case of household appliances and labor-savings devices, one method is to consider how a housewife spends her time doing housework, what tasks she dislikes most, and therefore what types of trade-offs and choices she is likely to make. (As we indicated earlier, the overall amount spent on household appliances is relatively stable, although the allocation among products may vary significantly.)

The results of research performed by Nelson Foote in the mid-1960s (see Table 7.1) show the percent of housework time spent on each task and how the tasks rank according to dislike.[22] Foote's research revealed a complex pattern of time used in performing specific household activities, with these findings giving suggestive data for understanding the need for appliances.

[22] "The Time Dimension and Consumer Behavior," in Joseph W. Newman, editor, *On Knowing the Consumer* (New York: John Wiley and Sons, Inc. 1966), pp. 38–46.

The extent to which a new household appliance eliminates the housewife's dislike for performing a task, and the degree of innovation—compared with existing products—can be measured by the rating-ranking technique. This measurement, along with the historical sales data for that type of appliance, gives the forecaster the foundation for estimating market penetration.

The service that the new product performs must be compared with the cost of that service and the willingness of the consumer to pay the price for an acceptable profit. As we saw earlier, the artificial kidney machine performs a valuable service to the person who has malfunctioning kidneys, but most "customers" are not willing or able to pay the costs of that service. Either the cost of the machine and maintenance (operation) must be substantially lowered, or the costs must be covered by insurance in order for the market to expand significantly. Although vital to life itself, the product must be considered a luxury that only the wealthy can afford.

However, as our standard of living and life-style change, what is a luxury at one point in time often becomes commonplace or a necessity at some later time. We see such an evolution for products, such as garbage compacters, pocket calculators, photographic equipment, and color television. Drug-detection devices will become a necessity as new drug laws are passed.

Detecting Market Patterns. Valerie Free and Dr. Thomas Neman have described how electronic computers greatly extended the power of marketing research, so that it is now possible to store and manipulate large amounts of data more economically, and to perform complex calculations for sophisticated statistical analyses.[23] The primary targets thus far have been mass-market items, where larger samples are possible so that the sampling error is reduced, thus increasing the researcher's confidence in the results.

Attitudinal and life-style profiles can help identify characteristics of potential customers, suggesting ways to shape a product or promotional theme. For example, the major purchasers of a certain type of product may prove to be young mothers in the 20 to 35 age range. Psychographic studies may help to separate this group into distinctively different segments, each with individual product perceptions and buying habits. This will enable the forecaster to identify the potential buyer, thus establishing a good estimate of what portion of the upper sales bound will be realized.

[23] "Market Research Matches Products to Consumers," *Computer Decisions*, May 1972.

Comprehensive market research analyses will help determine what types of products the consumer perceives a new product to be similar to, so far as consumer preference is concerned. This establishes a basis for historical-analogy analysis, where the sales and profit patterns for the analogous products can be studied and forecasts for the new product made, taking into account dissimilarities as well as similarities.

Other Market Tests

If consumer preferences, trade-offs, and major product characteristics cannot be determined or evaluated, some other form of market test is necessary. Here, the best basis for forecasting the penetration level is expert opinion, either from a group of marketing experts, or from one expert who has demonstrated considerable market insight.

Products for which only gross upper bounds can be established, and for which there has been little sound basis for forecasting prior to early introduction, include cable television, minibikes, xerography, leased cars (a new concept although not a new product), and video cassettes. The decisions to introduce these products were primarily made from analyses that showed that even the most conservative estimates would yield handsome profits.

IN SUMMARY

Forecasting for products to penetrate new markets will generally have to rely on bounding techniques or an analysis of critical events to establish the soundness of assumptions and related estimates. Whenever possible, qualitative statements and intuition should be converted to a quantitative form by rating-ranking methods or other approximate measure-of-value techniques. Market research is also critical to reduce macro bounds and to check assumption validity so that reasonable profitability analyses can be performed.

Chapter VIII

The Testing and Introduction Stage

When the Olivetti Company introduced a new portable typewriter in 1950, it was faced with the question of whether its existing sales policy was adequate or whether some new sales policy would have to be adopted. The company believed that it would be possible to create a large market for portable typewriters in private households. (Hopefully, this would be good advertisement for Olivetti's bigger machines, which would in turn help its sales for office use.)

To achieve this result, certain conditions had to be fulfilled: the sales price had to be rigidly controlled and kept below the monthly salary of a clerk; advertising was needed to stress the usefulness of typewriters; a wide knowledge of typewriters should be fostered; and lastly, distribution arrangements should be tightened to bring the machine to the notice and within the reach of passersby.

Olivetti conducted a market research experiment in both Trieste and Milan of sales through retailers of household electrical goods. The results were encouraging: portable typewriter sales were mainly to clerks, artisans, students, and women; and sales of the company's own branches were not affected. The company chose electrical goods' shops for its test because, even in small towns, they are numerous, they have good display windows, they have regular customers with high purchasing power, and they are organized for lease-purchase sales.

In view of the successful outcome of the experiment, Olivetti adopted a policy of sales through these retail outlets, bolstered by promotional measures such as advertising and the formation of typing schools. In five

140

years, the volume of sales of this portable typewriter model was increased to a figure four times higher than that of its predecessor. The market research, as is true in many new-product introductions, had provided a sound basis for forecasting future sales and consumer reactions.

TYPICAL DECISIONS

Among the important questions that need to be answered at the testing and introduction stage are: What should the marketing plan be? How much manufacturing capacity is needed? How should capacity be added? How should R&D be allocated over time?

The answers require forecasts of when the sales rate will move upward into the rapid-growth stage, what the rate of market penetration will be, and what the ultimate penetration or steady-state sales rate will be. Significant profits are dependent on good forecasts and the right answers.

In the testing and introduction stage, sales and other marketing information are available for the first time in the product life cycle. Thus a major expenditure can be justified to validate the various assumptions and the occurrence and timing of critical events.

Whereas the bounds (upper and lower limits) for the forecasts prepared earlier may have been quite broad (but acceptable for the decisions being made then), the analyses at this stage can substantially reduce those bounds. In fact, they must reduce the forecasting error, since the decisions to be made will require greater accuracy. It may be possible for the first time in the new-product analyses (a) to substitute knowledge gained from market experience in place of expert opinion, and (b) to disaggregate the market and prepare forecasts for each segment.

Statistical techniques are of limited value for analyzing trends and making projections. This is because the decisions to significantly expand capacity must be made well in advance of the point in time at which the sales rate begins its rapid move upward. However, the use of statistical techniques at least gives a belated signal and, while such an approach might be considered as too late, it is still better than doing nothing, as we shall discuss later in this chapter.

Pilot production facilities, rather than new plants, usually provide the manufacturing resources for producing the volume needed for the testing and introduction stage, since this stage may extend for several years or more.

(There are, of course, exceptions to products having a long introduction period, such as cereals, apparel, toys, and "fad" items, where the total life cycle may only last a few months to a few years. Here, it is important to recognize that the fad product will have a very short introduction period. Thus the primary problem is to estimate the length of the life cycle and the penetration rate.)

Furthermore, there may still be considerable uncertainty, so that large facilities expenditures cannot yet be justified. For example, the uncertainty about when the rapid growth would begin and what the peak sales rate would be led to the decision to produce Corelle® Livingware in a pilot facility, even though there would have been significant economic advantages if every critical event occurred in the shortest possible time. A comprehensive analysis revealed that a large-scale expansion was not feasible until after several critical events had taken place.

Therefore, the major emphasis during the introduction stage will often be on forecasting the length of the introduction stage (or the time to rapid growth) and the growth rate during the rapid-growth stage. The two main approaches involve (1) market research to learn who the consumer will be and the quantities he or she will purchase, and (2) the tracking of critical events to determine when they will most likely occur (if at all).

MARKET RESEARCH

This approach encompasses all investigations and analyses that are made to learn more about the marketplace and how the new product will perform in that environment. Most of the market knowledge gained during this part of the product life cycle will be derived from surveys, experiments, and other forms of market testing.

Because of the costs associated with market testing, this kind of research will usually be done in only one or a few geographical areas, depending on how much variability there is in consumer preferences throughout the potential market segments and how many assumptions or hypotheses must be tested. The primary objective of market testing at this stage is to determine (a) if the new-product characteristics will be as well received by the consumer as the assumptions indicate, and (b) if not, what must be done to make the product successful (e.g., what will make the consumer "switch" from his or her present product choice).

For example, forecasts prepared in the late 1960s projected that sales of Picturephone would be in the rapid-growth stage by 1973. It was assumed that the product features and price would be sufficiently appealing to the customer, and that the method of transmission would be both feasible and economical.

The Picturephone was subsequently introduced for market testing in Pittsburgh and New York City. The market test showed both that the demand was extremely low because of the high cost and other related problems, and that significant improvements in transmission methods were needed to achieve lower costs and to make large volumes feasible.

While a large market for picturephones is still likely, it will probably not emerge until at least the late 1970s, and then—as the test indicated—the initial market will be for communications within and between corporations.

With the high number and percentage of new-product failures, it is dangerous and frequently inadvisable to proceed with a strategy that strongly depends on the accuracy of all assumptions and related projections. There should be contingency plans that can be quickly implemented if any of the critical assumptions prove to be incorrect.

Blunders can be reduced or eliminated through extensive market research. Such was the case for a new concept in roofing, where market tests indicated that the product, while aesthetically appealing to the customer, did not have sufficient advantages to warrant the price that would yield an acceptable profit.

Market research should show not only why the consumer is or is not buying, but who the consumer is, and how he or she is using the product. In many instances, the consumer does not use a product primarily for its intended purpose. This happens frequently with housewares products, where the housewife finds an end use that had not even been considered when the product was introduced, such as a storage vessel or an ornament instead of a cooking vessel.

Once the different uses have been identified, forecasts must be revised to take into account the potential and market share for the new applications. (Segmentation may be quite different than originally conceived, since the types of buyer may change when the end use changes.)

A similar situation arises when the profile (sociological factors) of the consumer is established through market research. The forecasts may have assumed that the main consumer would be a white, middle-class person, whereas in reality the product is primarily purchased by lower-income persons with no race differentiation. Consider the Cadillac and the Volkswagen, which are often bought by persons with quite different sociological characteristics from those for whom the vehicles were originally designed.

Likewise, many new apparel goods, toys, and other consumer and industrial goods are bought by people of different age and income groups, residential and geographical areas, and race and sex from those initially assumed in sales forecasts. Unless the sociological profile of the consumer is obtained from market research, it is possible to base new forecasts on old or erroneous assumptions.

Factors Affecting Sales

Since World War II, several developments have led to the decline of traditional socioeconomic variables (e.g., education, occupation, sex, marital status) as good predictors of consumer brand and product choice. Among these are the dramatic increase in consumer discretionary power (causing a widened attitude of consumer choice) and the situation where product innovation has become a dominant marketing strategy.

As a consequence, consumer behavior is approached as a decision process, rather than as the result of a decision process, which has led to added emphasis being placed on such factors as motivation, perception, cognition, learning, and influences. In turn, these factors are measured by factors such as attitudes, mobility, life-style, social class, and other personal characteristics.

Market researchers are now working with behavioral scientists, who supply hypotheses that are testable in consumer behavior contexts. This approach identifies factors that are more nearly related to the choice the consumer ultimately makes, thus providing the factors that can be incorporated into a forecast to make it more accurate.

However, there is generally little if any information for such consumer behavior factors for the total population or for particular geographical areas. Thus it is often necessary to either obtain estimates of the behavior-factor mix for each area through sample surveys, or to correlate the behavioral factors with sociological and demographic factors, for which information is readily available.

Consumption Patterns. Ronald E. Frank, William F. Massy, and Harper W. Boyd conducted a study in mid-1960 to determine the validity of the assumption that socioeconomic and demographic variables are correlated with product consumption.[24] Their primary objective was to pro-

[24] See "Correlates of Grocery Product Consumption Rates," *Journal of Market Research*, May 1967.

vide a better basis for determining marketing strategy, where the major marketing effort would be directed toward that portion of the population which would be most likely to buy a particular product.

Market research has shown that a relatively small proportion of households determine a large proportion of total sales in many food and cosmetic product categories. In fact, the 50% of the households above the median of household usage of a product may account for as much as 80 to 90% of its total dollar volume.

In their investigations, Frank, Massy, and Boyd analyzed the relationship between socioeconomic-demographic variables and consumption for each of 57 grocery products. They also collected information to clarify other questions about the characteristics of the buyers of these products. Here are the results of their study.

1. There is little relation (degree of correlation) between the standard socioeconomic and demographic variables and total household consumption in each of a variety of product categories.

2. Families who are heavy users of a product in one time period remain heavy users in subsequent periods.

3. A household's consumption of one kind of product can be predicted to some extent by its consumption of other products.

Thus the consumption of a new product (primarily nondurable goods) can be forecast (a) by identifying the consumption patterns of various products by different types of consumers or households, and (b) by determining which other products have similar market characteristics so that the purchases of the new product can be related to the historical patterns of the established ones.

Income Levels. The conclusions reached by Marcus Alexis, Leonard S. Simon, and Kenneth M. Smith on the significance of socioeconomic factors in sales of specific products are quite similar.[25] Their findings are related to the importance of income for predicting food expenditures. High-income families not only buy more goods that have positive income elasticities, but in many cases they also buy better quality in those products.

The sensitivity of various commodities to family income is shown in the accompanying table. Each column heading denotes how the amount

[25] See "Some Determinants of Food Buying Behavior," *Empirical Foundations of Marketing* (Chicago: Markham Publishing Company, 1969).

of product purchased by a family changes with an increase in family income.

Increases	Remains the Same	Decreases
Frozen orange juice	Onions	Bread
Frozen vegetables	Fresh milk	Pork chops
Fresh tomatoes	Margarine	Pork and beans
Fresh fruit	Catsup	Canned soup
Cartoned orange juice	Peanut butter	Canned orange juice
Regular coffee	Laundry soap	Canned milk
Butter		Spam
		Chicken
		Canned vegetables
		Potatoes
		Instant coffee
		Tea
		Powdered milk
		Jelly
		Rice
		Sugar

However, only 32% of the variation in total food expenditures could be explained by socioeconomic and demographic factors. This percentage included car ownership, equivalent number of adults (i.e., children were also counted, being weighted by age, according to percent of food eaten, compared with adults), family income, and race. Thus the remaining 68% of the variation must be explained by other factors. Although Alexis, Simon, and Smith did not, in their investigation, determine what these additional factors are, it is highly likely that they are life-styles, psychographics, family life cycle, and so on.

Common Needs and Wants. William D. Wells took a somewhat different approach when he studied who buys various products and which consumer groups they belong to.[26] His objective was to identify products whose usage is correlated and which are purchased because of common sets of needs and wants.

His research methodology was a questionnaire survey of 12,500 housewives concerning their purchases of 104 products for *family* use and also

[26] See "Backward Segmentation," Chapter 6, in Johan Arndt, editor, *Insights into Consumer Behavior* (Boston: Allyn and Bacon, Inc., 1968).

of 40 products for their *personal* use. In addition, the study contained questions about buying plans for 21 durable items, reading of 54 magazines, viewing of 48 daytime television programs, and viewing of 118 nighttime and weekend television programs.

Wells analyzed the questionnaire responses by using a multivariate statistical technique called factor analysis (see Appendix B for details of this technique) to determine what the independent variables had in common with one another.

Table 8.1 shows the five most significant groupings for products purchased for family use. (Wells included 16 groupings in his published

Table 8.1 Groupings of Products Purchased for Family Use

Group Factor	Product Families	Loading[a]
Large family	Laundry soap, detergent	78
	Toothpaste	70
	Toilet tissue	69
	Amount spent weekly at supermarket	68
	Shampoo	65
	Cold cereal	61
	Toilet soap	60
	Peanut butter	58
	Frankfurters	56
Wrappers and savers	Plastic bags	69
	Plastic wrap	68
	Aluminum foil	55
	(Wax paper bags)[a]	(43)
Babies	Diapers purchased	84
	Strained baby food	82
	Soap for baby clothes	79
	(Cotton swabs)	(47)
Dieters	Artificial sweeteners	70
	Diet soft drinks	69
	(Liquid dietary—Metrecal, Sego, etc.)	(43)
Canned menu	Canned luncheon meat	66
	Canned spaghetti	65
	Canned beef stew	61
	Canned pork and beans	51
	(Casserole mixes)	(44)

[a] The arbitrary cutoff point is 50; loadings less than 50 are in parentheses.

paper.) The numbers given with each product are their "loadings," which represent the degree to which that product "participates in" or "is typical of" the dimension measured by the factor. Similar groupings (seven in all) were obtained for products purchased by the respondents for their personal use.

Let us look briefly at the five basic conclusions drawn from the group factors shown in Table 8.1. The results of this analysis were cross-tabulated by the demographic characteristics to determine which of them help to single out the heavy users of the various groups of products. Consider these factors.

FACTOR 1.   LARGE FAMILY.   Common sense suggests that these products go together because all are used heavily by families with a higher-than-average number of children. This diagnosis is confirmed by the fact that a respondent's position on this factor correlates higher with total family size than with any other demographic variable. The demographics also reveal that income is highly important. Heavy purchasers of these products are not just large families; they are large families with a greater-than-average amount of money to spend. To the maker of packaged goods, the mother of a comparatively well-off large family is worth much attention.

FACTOR 2.   WRAPPERS AND SAVERS.   This grouping, sufficiently independent of the first grouping to form a separate factor, consists of products used to wrap and save food. (In the exhibit, one product that did not quite make the arbitrary cutoff point of 50 is included because it helps clarify the meaning of the factor.)

This factor is interesting for two reasons. First, it shows commonly used household items that do not correlate to total family size—at least not as consistently as do the items that load heavily on Factor 1. A possible explanation is that large families with many appetites have few leftovers to wrap, and that such leftovers are not saved long enough to require plastic or aluminum coating. Second, the products that load highest on this dimension—plastic bags and plastic wrap—might a priori be considered substitutes for each other. Thus it might be expected that high use of the one product would go with low use of the other. But this is not so; usage of these two products is positively correlated.

FACTOR 3.   BABIES.   Combinations like this increase our faith in the meaningfulness of less obvious combinations. Note the sharply lower loading of cotton swabs, suggesting either that this product does not get heavy use in all families with babies, or that families blessed with babies are not the heavy users.

FACTOR 4. DIETERS. The variable behind this group of products is also clear. Here again one of the loadings is sharply lower, suggesting either that there are other uses of liquid dietary, or that many calorie-conscious consumers who are willing to cut down on sugar are unwilling to make the greater sacrifice required by a liquid diet. The philosophy seems to be that half measures are better than no measures at all.

FACTOR 5. CANNED MENU. The surprising thing about this grouping is that the products did not load heavily on the "large-family" factor. All are foods eaten by children, and all are relatively inexpensive. The demographic relationships make the reason clear. These products tend to be most heavily used by families further down on the economic scale than the families that are the heaviest users of the products on *Factor 1*. In addition, blacks tend to be heavier users than whites of the products on *Factor 5*, while a race difference did not appear to be significant for *Factor 1*. These two differences identified this group of products as a separate set.

In short, the analysis shows that consumer products fall into meaningful groups that help to illuminate the roles, customs, attitudes, and sometimes the personality characteristics of distinct groups of consumers. This information is extremely helpful in redesigning a product and in advertising and promotion.

Repeat Purchase Rates. As we suggested earlier, sales of nondurable goods come primarily from "heavy buyers," who may account for a greater percent of the product class *volume* than of the product class *buyers* they represent.

David H. Ahl describes research of this type, where a consumer mail diary panel was used within a test area.[27] Through cumulative trials (sequential responses), he obtained measures of the cumulative percent of the population trying a brand or product after various points in time.

His analysis of the repeat purchase rate for various buyers indicated that, in general, the ultimate repeat level can be accurately estimated after one-half of the projected ultimate triers have been active in five subsequent periods. This will occur either during the introduction or rapid-growth stages, permitting a sound basis for forecasting later sales. Ahl also found that seasonality is important, a consideration often overlooked in market testing and analysis.

[27] See "New Product Forecasting Using Consumer Panels," *Journal of Marketing Research*, May 1970, pp. 159–167.

From the foregoing examples, it can be seen that it is difficult to extrapolate from previous market research (although it gives at least a good basis for experimentation). Thus market testing is generally desirable to identify the factors that affect sales rates and can be used for market disaggregation. However, in some instances, it is possible to avoid such market testing, and primarily to track sales for specific market segments.

Lead Sectors or Indicators

Sometimes it is possible to identify lead areas (geographical) or economic groups that are good indicators of penetration or sales rates for the total product sales. This can be done in situations where (a) seasonality causes one geographical area to lead others in product sales, (b) one area is more fashion-prone or likely to accept a product before others, or (c) price will result in the product first being bought by high-income groups (i.e., the product is not a necessity and its sales will depend initially on the buyers having disposable income).

The lawn-products market provides an example of why seasonality is the reason for one geographical area being a lead indicator. For several years, Scott Seed has utilized a representative stratified sample for estimating field sales within one week after they occur. (A stratified sample is one where a population to be sampled is divided into meaningful homogeneous subpopulations before sampling.) In its sampling system, the Scott dealers are grouped by size, type, and area of the country.

For most Scott products, and particularly for those with a short seasonal life (e.g., Halts for crabgrass control, which has most of its sales in an eight-week period), it is critical to estimate within the first two weeks of each product's seasonal life span what its total sales will be. The southern region provides the basis for such an estimate.

For fashion apparel and similar-type goods, one or two geographical areas, such as New York City and Los Angeles, will often buy a new product at a rapid rate before it is accepted in other areas. (However, this may be a result of the innovator-imitator mix, which we shall discuss further in the next section.) Close tracking of sales in such areas will produce a good indication of what sales will be in all other areas.

Many higher priced, durable goods are first bought by the high-income groups. For these products, both the length of the introduction stage and the penetration rate may differ for various economic groups. Age might also be a basis for lead-lag disaggregation, but this is often because of the mix of income levels within an age group.

This is shown in Table 8.2, which tabulates the 1971 color-TV penetration levels by age and economic group.[28] While it appears that there are distinct differences by age groups, the actual difference is due to income level, where the differences for the same income levels in the various age groups are not very large.

The overall penetration rate and by income level over time is given in Figure 8.1. The shapes of the curves, which indicate the penetration rates, are different for the lower three income levels as contrasted to the upper three levels.

Innovator-Imitator Sales

Earlier in this book, we described the buyer as either an innovator or imitator. As we saw, the innovator is the type of buyer who is willing to try most new products, while the imitator is representative of the large majority of consumers who wait until the product is tested and proven by the innovator before they will buy it.

This classification is actually an oversimplification, and a better dichotomy is presented by Everett M. Rogers in his discussion of the theory of adoption and diffusion of new ideas or new products by a social system.[29] He describes the major classes of adopters, based on the timing of adoption by the various groups, as innovators, early adopters, early majority, late majority, and laggards.

Rogers defines innovators rather arbitrarily as the first $2\frac{1}{2}$ percent of the adopters, with the innovators characterized as venturesome and daring. Innovators also interact with other consumers, but they are not influenced in the timing of purchase by other members of the social system.

Our intent here is not to describe the various adoption groups in detail (the reader can learn more about them from Rogers' book), but to show that it is dangerous only to track early sales, and not to look at the types of buyers. Innovators may quickly buy a new product, giving it a significant sales pattern, only later to become disenchanted with the product and discourage the imitators from buying.

The length of time required for the innovator to test the product, prove its worth to his satisfaction, and communicate this to the rest of

[28] The statistics for this exhibit, along with other data relating to TV sales, are contained in a NICB August 1972 publication dealing with "The TV Household: A Profile" by Fabian Linden. This type of situation illustrates where the AID technique, shown earlier, might be applied to identify which factors are most significant in penetration rates.

[29] See *Diffusion of Innovations* (New York, Free Press Glencoe, 1962).

Table 8.2 Television Ownership by Age of Household Head and Income, 1971

	Owning Color Television
All Households	43.3%
Under 25 years	25.5
Under $5,000	13.7
$5,000–$10,000	30.2
10,000–15,000	42.9
15,000 and over	42.9
25 to 34 years	47.3
Under $5,000	26.6
$5,000–10,000	44.6
10,000–15,000	58.0
15,000 and over	64.4
35 to 44 years	52.4
Under $5,000	24.8
$5,000–10,000	48.8
10,000–15,000	57.2
15,000 and over	72.7
45 to 54 years	50.6
Under $5,000	16.9
$5,000–10,000	47.5
10,000–15,000	60.1
15,000 and over	72.9
55 to 64 years	44.1
Under $5,000	20.9
$5,000–10,000	46.2
10,000–15,000	60.6
15,000 and over	72.4
65 years and over	29.1
Under $5,000	21.2
$5,000–10,000	42.2
10,000–15,000	64.4
15,000 and over	69.3

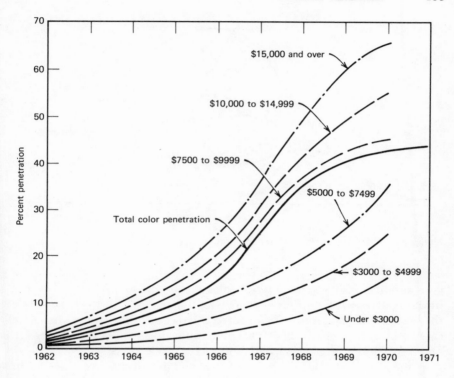

Figure 8.1. Yearly color penetration versus income.

the consumers will be a controlling factor in determining when the product will pass into the rapid-growth stage. This time interval can be estimated from (a) early questioning of the buyer or an analysis of characteristics and life of the new product and (b) comparisons with similar but older products. When the consumer testing period nears the end, market surveys are needed both to ascertain what the innovator thinks of the product and to start monitoring closely subsequent sales to non-innovators.

The error that can be made by not differentiating consumers in this way can be seen by considering Figure 8.2, which illustrates the sales to each type of consumer and their effect on total sales. (This figure is only an example; it does not give a true relationship between the different types of buyers.)

If the overall S-shaped curve, referred to as the Gompertz curve and discussed further in Chapter 9, is first established on the basis of analo-

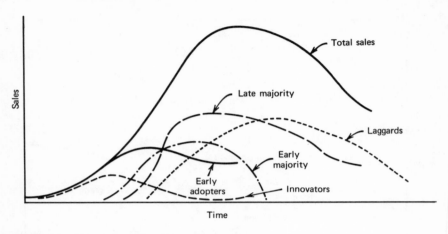

Figure 8.2. Sales curves for different adoption types.

gous product analyses, and initial sales are found to follow closely the initial relatively flat portion of the curve, the analyst will likely conclude that the earlier assumptions were correct. However, the form of the curve cannot be firmly established until non-innovator purchase patterns are observed and extrapolated from consumer-attitude polls.

While the total sales curve is smooth and nondecreasing (except for the phasing-out stage or fluctuations due to economic conditions or competitive actions), this exhibit shows that the sales patterns for the different types of consumers vary considerably.

Other Types of Disaggregation. In addition to the previously mentioned ways of sorting out and separately handling forecasts for the different types of consumers, or of relating sales of one product to sales of another product, the forecast must take into account the sales of units to "new" owners (those who buy for the first time) and replacement sales (Figure 8.2).

Figure 8.3 illustrates the need for considering new versus replacement sales for ·TV sets. Here, the annual new-sales curve peaked in 1973 and, to maintain a constant or increasing sales rate, the future decreases will have to be offset by increases in replacement sales. Note that the S-shaped curve is not the unit sales per year, but the total (cumulative) sales over time, since the annual sales curve turns down in the phasing-out stage. Occasionally the annual sales curve appears to be S-shaped, but this occurs when the steady-state phase extends over a long period of time be-

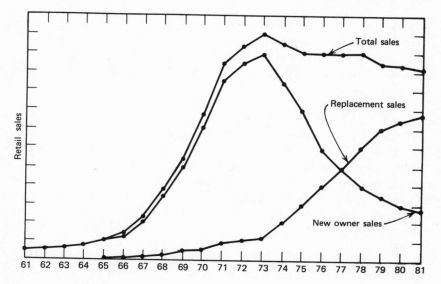

Figure 8.3. TV-set sales by year.

cause of replacement sales. However, the penetration curve does follow an S-shape, with penetration plateauing at an upper limit determined by economics, utility, and so forth.

The demand by new owners or the penetration rate is a function of technical development, market price, economic conditions, and consumer priority. These factors should be incorporated into a forecasting equation to get the new-owner sales.

The replacement sales are a function of the life or mortality of the product. Early failure and replacement data can be analyzed to estimate mortality, with distribution curves (such as the Weibull or truncated normal curve, which we shall describe later) providing the basis for life extrapolations.

In the absence of good mortality data, the percent of total sales represented by replacement sales can be estimated by examining the percentages for similar-type products. For established appliances, the replacement percentages for older products is high—for example, refrigerators (84% replacement sales in 1967, 69% in 1968) and clothes washers (72% in 1967, 68% in 1968). This contrasts with the low replacement percentages for new appliances, such as room air conditioners (15% in 1967, 18% in 1968) and dishwashers (13% in 1967, 17% in 1968).

In estimating the percent of total sales represented by replacement sales, the forecaster should be mindful that these percentages will also be affected by the introduction of models with new features and economic conditions (consumers will delay purchases when economic conditions are bad).

Similar-Product Analysis.   Another form of disaggregation is to break the total market into smaller segments for bounding purposes, and to establish trends for each of these segments, as well as for the total market. Table 8.3 contains the total expenditures on appliances in relation to expenditures on all consumer goods from 1947 to 1968. Column 4 shows that total expenditures for appliances were relatively stable over periods of several years; hence, new appliances had to compete with existing ones, especially during the business recessions of 1948-1949, 1953-1954, 1957-58, and 1960-61.

Certain specific fluctuations in the figures of Table 8.3 are of special significance. When black-and-white TV was introduced as a new product in circa 1950, the ratio of expenditures on radio and TV sets to total expenditures for consumer goods (column 7) increased about 33% (from 1.23 to 1.63%) as against a modest increase of only 13% (from 1.63 to 1.88%) in the ratio for the next decade. (A similar increase of 33% occurred in the 1962-1966 period as color TV made its major penetration.)

In all probability, the acceptance of black-and-white TV as a major appliance in the 1948-1951 period caused the ratio of all major household appliances to total consumer goods (see column 6) to rise to 4.98%; in other words, the innovation of TV caused the consumer to start spending more money on major appliances about that time.

Our expectation in mid-1965 was that the introduction of color TV would induce a similar increase. Although this product comparison did not provide us with an accurate or detailed forecast, it did place an upper bound on the future total sales we could expect.

The next step was to look at the cumulative penetration curve for black-and-white TVs in United States households (Figure 8.4). We assumed color-TV penetration would have a similar S-curve, but that it would take longer for color sets to penetrate the whole market (i.e., to reach steady-state sales). Whereas it took black-and-white TV 10 years to reach steady state, qualitative expert-opinion studies indicated that it would take color twice that long; this accounts for the more gradual slope of the color-TV curve.

At the same time, studies conducted in 1964 and 1965 showed significantly different penetration sales for color TV in various income groups,

Table 8.3   Expenditures on Appliances Versus All Consumer Goods

Year (1)	All Consumer Goods[a] (2)	Household Appliances[b] (3)	Radio, TV, and other[b] (4)	Totals of columns 3 and 4 (5)	Column 5 Divided by Column 2 (6)	Column 4 Divided by Column 2 (7)
1947	110.9	3.18	1.43	4.61	4.16%	1.29%
1948	118.9	3.47	1.48	4.95	4.16	1.23
1949	119.1	3.13	1.70	4.83	4.06	1.43
1950	128.6	3.94	2.46	6.40	4.98	1.91
1951	138.4	3.87	2.26	6.13	4.43	1.63
1952	143.3	3.82	2.37	6.19	4.32	1.65
1953	150.0	3.99	2.61	6.60	4.40	1.74
1954	151.1	4.02	2.74	6.77	4.48	1.81
1955	162.9	4.69	2.79	7.48	4.59	1.71
1956	168.2	4.89	2.87	7.76	4.61	1.71
1957	176.4	4.63	3.00	7.63	4.33	1.70
1958	178.1	4.44	3.07	7.51	4.22	1.72
1959	190.9	4.86	3.42	8.28	4.34	1.79
1960	196.6	4.74	3.62	8.36	4.25	1.84
1961	200.1	4.77	2.76	8.53	4.26	1.88
1962	212.1	5.01	3.94	8.95	4.22	1.86
1963	222.5	5.24	4.54	9.78	4.40	2.04
1964	237.9	5.74	5.41	11.15	4.69	2.27
1965	257.4	6.03	6.01	12.04	4.68	2.33
1966	277.7	6.77	6.91	13.68	4.93	2.49
1967	288.1	7.09	7.41	14.50	5.03	2.57
1968	313.9	7.80	7.85	15.65	4.99	2.50

[a] Data obtained from *Survey of Current Business*, Personal Consumption Expenditure Tables (U.S. Department of Commerce, July issues).

[b] Data obtained from the *Survey of Current Business Statistics* (U.S. Department of Commerce, 1969 Biennial Edition).

rates that were helpful to us in projecting the color-TV curve and in tracking the accuracy of our projection.

With these data and assumptions, we forecast retail sales for the remainder of 1965 to mid-1970 (see the dotted section of the lower curve in Figure 8.4. The forecasts were accurate through 1966 but too high in the following three years, primarily because of declining general economic conditions and changing pricing policies.

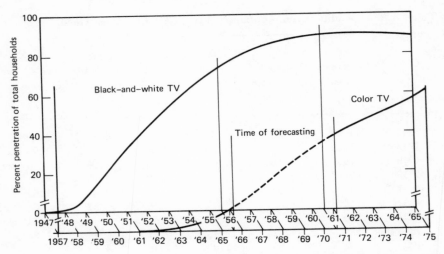

Figure 8.4.   Long-term household penetration curves for color and black-and-white TV.

We should note that when we developed these forecasts and techniques, we recognized that additional techniques would be necessary at later times to maintain the accuracy that would be needed in subsequent periods. These forecasts provided acceptable accuracy for the time they were made, however, since the major goal then was only to estimate the penetration rate and the ultimate steady-state level of sales. Making refined estimates of how the manufacturing-distribution pipelines will behave is an activity that properly belongs to the next life-cycle stage.

CRITICAL EVENTS

In the testing and introduction stage, the tracking of signals that indicate whether critical events will occur or to what extent they will be achieved can be significant in estimating when the rapid-growth stage will begin and how rapidly sales will grow thereafter. The color-television set, for example, was introduced in 1954, but did not gain acceptance from most consumers until late 1964. This was because the color-television set could not leave the introduction stage and enter the rapid-growth stage until the major networks had substantially increased their color programming.

Tracking the signals of network behavior and stated intentions provided an early warning of when sales would start growing rapidly. On the other hand, several critical events still have to occur before Picturephones will achieve significant sales levels. Following the progress of these events will give ample lead time for those companies that will participate in the manufacture of the various picturephone-system components.

Statistical Techniques

While of little value for predicting when a radical change will occur, statistical techniques can be of value in tracking what is happening to ensure that turning points have not been overlooked through poor market research or failure to detect signals. Failure to analyze the historical information (however limited it might be) of a new product can result in very late detection of turning points and the inability to react in time to changes in market conditions.

Time-series analysis techniques, and especially the Census Bureau X-11 method, will provide a good method for identifying when the rapid-growth stage begins. Several years of data (at least three) after rapid growth begins are needed to establish statistically how rapidly sales are growing. A detailed discussion of the use of time-series analysis is given in Chapter 10.

Essentially, time-series analysis will measure what the current sales rate is and how rapidly it changes. These two factors are of interest at this stage, and they should be forecast. However, detection and measurement at the time turning points take place is essential when other techniques have not been effective in forecasting these changes.

One other statistical technique is worth mentioning here. Failure rates of components or the life of the product itself are critical to the sales volume of the product. The validation of failure rates will require considerable data when complete life histories are utilized to establish the mortality curves.

Experience shows that most failure rates follow the Weibull, truncated-normal or log-normal probability distributions, for which special graph paper has been constructed so that the rates yield straight lines. Relatively little failure data are required to establish the failure curve—and even this amount of data is reduced if assumptions are made on the basis of similar products and the objective is to test the hypothesis that the failure rate follows a specific probability curve.

This approach is applied not only in the testing and introduction stage, but also during product testing in the lab. Automobile companies, manufacturers of engines, aircraft companies, and many other industries have been using these curves for years to predict failure rates.

IN SUMMARY

The testing and introduction stage provides the opportunity to validate assumptions and to expand on earlier forecasting models. Good market research is the main vehicle for doing this, and a variety of market tests can be performed to get the desired information. From this stage on, a variety of tracking methods are used to validate trends and assumptions, and to detect changes. Such data will permit the application of comprehensive statistical models.

Chapter **IX**

The Rapid-Growth Stage

An analysis of the history of nylon shows that its booming sales life was repeatedly stretched out through the introduction of new products that utilized its distinct material characteristics. The first nylon end uses were primarily military—parachutes, thread, and rope. It then entered the circular-knit market via the hosiery business, where it experienced steadily increasing sales and profits.

Much of nylon's sales growth was the result of imaginative and well-timed marketing strategies that several times revived a sales pattern that appeared to be flattening out. New uses such as warp knits in 1945, tire cord in 1948, textured yarns in 1955, and carpet yarns in 1959, further extended the nylon sales curve. Whereas the initial uses of nylon might have caused it to reach a saturation level in 1962 of 50 million pounds annually, the consumption of nylon in 1962 actually reached 500 million pounds.

This type of situation illustrates one of the several kinds of problems that arise during the rapid-growth stage of the product life cycle. Here are some of the questions that must be answered by the forecaster.

- Is the growth rate approximately what was forecasted during the introduction stage or is it significantly different?

- At what saturation level and point in time will the sales rate level off?

- Will the sales pattern follow some statistical pattern or will marketing and other strategies extend the product life cycle?

- Are the aberrations in the growth rate of a temporary nature due to conditions such as changes in the economy and short-term changes in consumer preferences, or are they signals of a slowdown or buildup in the sales rate?

• How will pipeline filling and subsequent fluctuations affect the sales rate?

The largest expenditures made during the product life cycle will generally occur at this stage (except for drugs and other products that have low manufacturing costs and require relatively small facilities' investment). Thus commensurate forecasting and tracking efforts are justified. Whereas the signaling of the rapid upturn in the growth rate is done in the introduction stage, and often leads to major investment in original plant and equipment, the prudent timing of the majority of capital expenditures for further facilities' expansion depends on accurate forecasts or analyses that answer the above questions.

Cost analyses show that production facilities must have 80% or more utilization to provide adequate returns on investment when there is strong competition. Conversely, it is still possible to achieve acceptable profits at lower levels of utilization when there is relatively little competition because of patent protection. Similarly, forecasts on the low side can lead to loss of market share when there is competition, while underestimation has much less severe implications when the new product has patent protection. The ability to achieve and maintain economical inventory levels depends on accurate forecasts from this point in time in the life cycle.

Furthermore, profitable incremental increases in sales as a result of special marketing tactics are dependent on correctly forecasting what the sales level and its rate of change will be without the use of such tactics. For example, if a marketing tactic in the form of a price decrease is implemented while the sales rate is growing, it is possible to conclude falsely that sales have increased significantly because of the price decrease, even though a large portion of the growth would have resulted anyway from the sales trend.

In one such situation, a price decrease for a laboratory glassware product was followed by a 200% increase in sales, which made the tactic appear to be very profitable. However, a later analysis indicated that over two-thirds of the sales increase would have occurred without the drop in price, which made the tactic unprofitable.

Since the decisions made during the rapid-growth stage can have a substantial impact on profits, large amounts of money can be spent on the forecasting techniques that are justified for this stage, either for generating primary forecasts or for verifying estimates derived by other methods.

FORECASTING THE GROWTH RATE

As color TV entered the rapid-growth stage, it was very clear that sales would grow rapidly thereafter for several years. However, the change in the sales rate at that point in time (1964) could not be measured statistically until some time after it occurred. A plot of the data up to 1964 showed that the sales-rate trend could have had a slope within a large range, so that the growth rate could not be accurately evaluated.

The methods most appropriate for measuring the growth rate are basically the same as those described in Chapter 8—market research and market disaggregation. But here, at the beginning of the rapid-growth stage, there is a sounder basis for determining the validity of the assumptions and projections through the tracking of critical events.

The turning point for color TV was signaled by both the increase in color programming hours and the turning point in the market penetration for the high-income group. As for most major appliances, the market penetration rate for a new product will be more rapid initially in the high-income group, leading the total market penetration by a period of three months to over a year.

Accordingly, the change in color-TV market penetration for the high-income group provided an early measure of the growth rate of the total market. A disaggregated market model, which had been developed for initial estimates, and market surveys of purchases and the ways the set was used by various income groups gave a basis for tracking the previous forecasts. Interestingly, there were no significant differences or consistency in either the overall market penetration patterns or the saturation levels for the different income groups above $5000 per family per year: the lead-lag relationships in the curves were the major difference (Table 9.1).

Continued tracking of the characteristics of the consumers of a new product is valuable for obtaining a better reading of the penetration in the early part of the rapid-growth stage. The proportion of buyers who are imitators and the percentage who are repeat buyers are important in estimating both the penetration rate and the steady-state sales rate.

The replacement purchases will indicate the life of the product (i.e., the mortality curve for nonconsumable goods), which affects most sales at the steady-state stage. (Other purchases during the steady state will result from consumers increasing the number of items of a product that they own at any one time, such as automobiles, shoes and other apparel, and appliances.)

Hence the way the product is used is also important. New uses may be only temporary since the product may be considered a substitute item for a product need that has not yet been met adequately.

Table 9.1   1970 Consumer Profile—Television Sets (in millions)

Household Income	Households	Households With Black-White TV	Households With Color TV
Under $3000	10.1	1.9	1.1
$3000–$4999	7.4	2.8	1.6
$5000–$6999	7.6	6.7	3.9
$7000–$9999	11.9	11.3	6.4
$10,000–$14,999	14.9	14.9	8.6
$15,000 and over	12.2	10.6	6.0
Total	64.1	48.2	27.6

	1964	1965	1966	1967	1968	1969	1970	1971
Households (million)	57.0	58.0	58.7	60.2	61.3	62.7	64.1	65.3
TV homes (million)	52.9	53.9	55.0	56.8	58.2	59.7	61.2	62.5
TV sets per TV home	1.21	1.25	1.29	1.33	1.37	1.4	1.44	1.48
TV sets in use—homes	64.3	67.3	71.0	75.5	79.6	83.9	88.1	92.3
Color sets in use —homes	2.8	5.2	9.1	14.0	19.3	24.5	29.1	34.6
Black-and-White sets in in use—homes	61.5	62.1	61.8	61.5	60.3	59.4	59.0	57.7
Black-and-white set sales to public	8.0	8.4	7.3	6.2	6.6	6.8	6.5	7.1
Color-set sales to public	1.3	2.6	4.2	5.4	6.0	5.9	5.6	6.9
Black-and-White Sets Imported	0.7	1.0	1.3	1.3	2.0	3.1	3.6	4.2
Color Sets Imported	0.02	0.05	0.2	0.3	0.7	0.9	0.9	1.3
Black-and-White sets sales to public—under 13″ sets	0.8	1.4	1.8	1.6	2.4	3.0	3.2	3.3

Statistical techniques are of limited value for estimating the growth rate in the first few months after the rapid-growth stage has begun. This is because of the lack of sufficient data to accurately estimate seasonals or to identify any other patterns. Also, aberrations such as changes in the economy, competitive actions, and pipeline filling are difficult to measure or to separate from long-term trends.

Usually, seasonal patterns cannot be firmly established until three or more years data have been collected. If less than 30 months data are available, it is unlikely that any statistical technique will estimate the seasonals with any degree of confidence.

However, because seasonals can be quite important for tracking the sales rate and estimating when the product will enter the steady-state stage, special efforts should be expended to measure them. One approach is to use a product-comparison, historical-analogy method, where seasonals for similar and older products are assumed to apply for the new product, and statistical tests are utilized to determine the validity of this assumption.

Table 9.2 illustrates this approach. It tabulates the percent of a year's demand by month for appliance retail sales. These percents are composed, of course, of both seasonals and trends. Product comparisons may indicate how much of the seasonals and trends implicit in these percentages are applicable for a new product. These estimated seasonals can then be applied to the raw sales of the new product to estimate trend direction and changes.

FORECASTING WHEN LEVELING OFF WILL OCCUR

Failure to determine when the growth rate will decline and sales level off is one of the major causes of overcapacity. Also, forecasts of early leveling off that prove to be incorrect can lead to loss of market share.

Although good statistical methods are valuable at this stage in helping to detect a turning point, they should be used primarily to signal changes that have not been correctly identified by other methods. If facilities and profits are to be maximized, forecasts of the time and level at which sales will enter the steady state must be made well in advance of the turning point.

Earlier forecasts may have included similar-product analysis, where the sales patterns for products with analogous characteristics (e.g. type of market, degree of innovation, distribution system) were used as a basis for estimating the parameters of the sales pattern for the new product. Most sales patterns follow what are called the Gompertz curve or S-shaped curve, similar to those shown in the previous chapter (Figures 8.3 and 8.4).

These curves are of a general exponential form with three constants or parameters, and are characterized by: (1) low sales with small growth in the early part of the product life, (2) rapid growth after a breakthrough occurs, and (3) then a plateau. Estimates of the three parameters, which are set by studying the curves and related parameters of similar products, fix the shape of the sales pattern curve, and provide estimates of when and at what penetration level the sales will level off.

Table 9.2 Seasonality Data for Major Appliances (Retail Sales Percent by Months)

Appliance	Year	January	February	March	April	May	June	July	August	September	October	November	December
Refrigerators	1968	7.1	7.5	6.9	7.2	8.2	9.1	10.3	10.8	8.8	8.2	7.7	8.2
	1967	7.2	7.2	6.9	7.5	8.2	9.2	10.1	10.1	9.3	8.7	7.4	8.2
Freezers	1968	6.8	6.4	6.7	6.6	8.2	9.0	11.8	11.7	9.5	8.3	8.1	6.9
	1967	6.6	6.4	6.4	7.1	8.3	8.8	11.3	11.8	9.5	8.7	7.1	8.0
Ranges	1968	7.4	7.6	8.1	7.7	8.6	8.7	8.2	8.6	8.2	8.6	8.9	9.4
	1967	7.6	7.5	7.8	8.0	8.5	8.5	8.2	8.1	8.6	8.7	9.3	9.2
Water heaters	1968	8.6	7.7	7.9	9.0	7.7	9.2	7.5	8.9	8.1	8.0	7.8	9.6
	1967	9.0	7.8	8.2	8.0	7.9	8.1	8.1	8.4	8.0	8.0	7.8	10.7
Washers	1968	8.3	8.1	8.1	7.5	7.8	7.4	8.2	9.6	9.0	9.2	8.8	8.0
	1967	8.1	7.9	7.9	8.0	7.8	7.9	8.0	9.6	9.2	8.9	8.5	8.2
Dryers	1968	9.3	7.9	7.1	6.1	6.1	6.4	7.3	7.5	9.5	10.6	11.5	10.7
	1967	9.0	7.5	6.6	6.6	6.3	5.9	7.1	7.3	9.7	11.4	1.13	11.3
Dishwashers	1968	8.1	7.0	6.8	6.7	8.4	8.0	7.7	7.9	7.7	8.0	10.2	13.5
	1967	7.0	6.6	6.7	7.2	8.2	7.6	7.3	7.6	8.8	8.5	10.3	14.2
Air conditioners	1968	3.8	5.1	4.7	6.5	9.1	12.5	23.1	14.0	4.8	2.6	2.5	2.3
	1967	3.7	4.1	5.2	7.5	12.8	24.8	18.6	10.6	4.6	3.2	2.7	2.2
Black-and-White television	1968	8.3	7.6	7.3	6.5	6.8	7.3	7.5	8.1	8.3	9.1	9.9	13.3
	1967	8.7	8.2	7.5	7.0	7.3	7.3	7.6	7.5	8.5	8.8	9.5	12.1
Color television	1968	8.7	8.0	6.6	6.2	5.5	5.8	6.2	7.4	9.5	9.9	11.3	14.9
	1967	7.9	6.7	6.4	6.5	5.7	5.3	5.6	7.6	10.3	11.1	11.5	15.4
Total TV	1968	8.8	8.1	7.5	5.6	6.2	6.4	6.9	7.6	9.1	9.2	10.6	14.0
	1967	8.9	7.6	7.3	6.2	6.4	6.2	6.7	7.2	9.1	9.9	10.2	15.0

By the middle of the rapid-growth stage, enough data are available to estimate mathematically the parameters of the curve and to compare them (preferably, to test them statistically) with the earlier estimates. However, the reader should note that the saturation or steady-state level will move up and down as the data are gathered and the parameters are estimated. This will be a result of the sensitivity of the curve to the values of the parameters, which themselves may be functions of economic or competitive variables. Therefore, other techniques should be used to validate the statistical estimates.

Graham F. Pyatt and other economists have tested and validated the theory that the rate at which you actually approach an expected or eventual penetration level is a function of technology, economic factors (price, general economy, and interest rates), and what is called a priority pattern, which is a function of perceived product utility to the consumers.[30] The measure of technology can be obtained from a Delphi exercise; the economic factors are available from government and marketing sources; and the priority pattern can be estimated by experts and a consumer panel.

The slope-characteristic method is a more complete and comprehensive technique that describes the sales pattern from the testing and introduction stage through the phasing-out stage. The Gompertz curve and many other life-cycle curves are special cases of the general curve fitted by the slope-characteristic technique. It is of particular value in forecasting when a product will pass from the steady-state stage to the phasing-out stage, as we shall discuss in more detail in Chapter 12. Considerable data are required for the slope-characteristic curve, and it is generally difficult to obtain accurate estimates until late in the rapid-growth stage.

During the rapid-growth stage, sufficient data will become available to accurately estimate the product life (or mortality curve should the need arise for the distribution of the times between sales and scrapping). However, it is important to determine whether the expected product life and its probability distribution curve will decrease or vary over time, since most products experience an increase in time to failure or replacement over the product life cycle. As the sales rate approaches the steady-state stage, it is important to forecast accurately the replacement rate, since a large portion of the subsequent sales will be derived from replacement sales.

Statistical techniques, and particularly time-series analysis (discussed in detail in Chapter 10), can be effective in identifying a slowdown in the

---

[30] See, for example, Graham F. Pyatt, *Priority Patterns and the Demand for Household Durable Goods* (London: Cambridge University Press, 1964).

sales rate and the ultimate leveling-off point within a few months after they occur (effective use of the Census Bureau X-11 technique can make it possible to spot turning points as they occur).

However, the concurrent identification of turning points will usually be too late to avoid significant losses of profit because of late or wrong decisions. Therefore, statistical techniques are primarily of value as checks in the event that other signals are not detected. Market research and the other techniques described in this chapter are more effective for timely forecasts.

EXTENDING THE RAPID-GROWTH STAGE

The S-shaped approach assumes that sales will follow some smooth, well-behaved curve. While this may be true for many new products, it is a dangerous assumption for many others. Consider the example in Figure 9.1, where the original uses of the product would have led to a leveling off of the growth curve at point A. However, new uses have caused the sales for the new product to follow curves 1, 2, and 3, instead of entering the steady-state stage at points B and C.

The example of nylon, given at the beginning of this chapter, illustrates such a situation for the history of a material in which there were new uses of the same product and new products made from the same material.

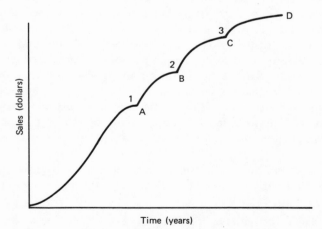

Figure 9.1. Hypothetical life cycle of a new product.

In forecasting the sales pattern, the analyst must endeavor to learn about the marketing strategy and potential product variations (new uses of the material or product), and not to assume a smooth sales pattern if such extensions should appear likely.

The maturity date (leveling-off time) can be postponed by various strategies. Theodore Levitt has described how the sales life of a new product can be extended in four ways.

1. Promoting more frequent usage of the product among current users.
2. Developing more varied usage of the product among current users.
3. Creating new users for the product by expanding the market.
4. Finding new uses for the basic material.[31]

The first major new nylon product, after its initial military applications, was women's hosiery. If no changes had been made to the initial marketing strategy for nylon, the sales curve would have leveled off at a time similar to point A in Figure 9.1. This is also the hypothetical point at which the first systematic effort was made to extend the product's life. (Earlier action might have produced less of the plateauing effect.)

DuPont studies had shown an increasing trend toward "bare-legged-ness" among women, which was coincident with the trend toward more casual living and a declining perception among teenagers of the "social necessity" of wearing stockings. Hence, one strategy could have been to reiterate the social necessity of wearing hose at all times, which would have been a costly strategy. Instead of encouraging more frequent use, DuPont promoted the "fashion smartness" of tinted hose and subsequently of patterned and highly textured hosiery.

There are other ways that the leveling-off point can be delayed, such as the customer becoming a multiple owner (i.e., owning both primary and secondary units). In the TV field, good marketing and improved consumer economics (more disposable income and lower prices) led to an increase in the average number of sets per family. Hence, although the household penetration rate approached the saturation level, the sets sold as multiples, and the increasing number of failures (because of more sets in the field and therefore more replacement units beings sold) extended the rapid-growth stage by several years. Automotive manufacturers attempt to do the same thing by strongly promoting second-and third-car ownership.

[31] Theodore Levitt. *The Marketing Mode* (New York: McGraw-Hill Book Company, 1969).

SIMULATING THE PIPELINE

We have thus far been considering the penetration rates and leveling-off points for consumer sales. The buildup and fluctuations of inventories in the pipeline (at the dealer and distributor levels) will significantly change the manufacturers' sales rates over time and, particularly, when the consumer sales enter the steady-state stage.

In addition to merely buffering information, in the case of a component product, the pipeline exerts certain distorting effects on the manufacturer's demand; these effects, although highly important, are often illogically neglected in production or capacity planning.

While the ware-in-process demand in the pipeline has an S-curve as in retail sales, it may lag or lead sales by several months and thus distort the shape of the demand on the component supplier.

Figure 9.2, which is based on color-TV sales and inventories, shows the long-term trend of demand on a component supplier as a function of distributor sales and distributor inventories. As one can see from this exhibit, supplier sales may grow relatively sharply for several months and peak before retail sales level off. The implications of these curves for facilities' planning and allocation are obvious.

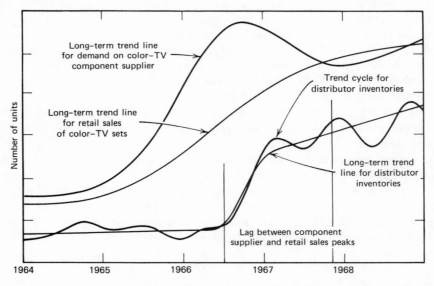

Figure 9.2. Patterns for color-TV distributor sales, distributor inventories, and component sales. Scales are different for component sales, distributor inventories, and distributor sales, with the patterns put on the same graph for illustrative purposes.

In this illustration, we are using components for color-TV sets because we know from our own experience the importance of the long flow time that results from the many sequential steps in manufacturing and distribution. There are more spectacular examples; for instance, in the case of truck engines, it is not uncommon for the flow time from component supplier to consumer to stretch to two years.

To estimate total demand on Corning Glass Works' production, we used a retail demand model and a pipeline simulation. The model incorporated penetration rates, mortality curves, and the like. We combined the data generated by the model with data on market share, glass losses, and other information to comprise the corpus of inputs for the pipeline simulation. The simulation output allowed us to apply projected curves like the ones shown in Figure 9.2 to our own component-manufacturing planning.

Simulation is an excellent tool for these circumstances because it is essentially simpler than the alternative—namely to build a more formal mathematical model. Simulation bypasses the need for analytical-solution techniques and for mathematical duplication of a complex environment and allows experimentation. Simulation also informs us how the pipeline elements will behave and interact over time. Such knowledge is very useful in forecasting, especially in constructing formal causal models at a later date.

Tracking and Warning

This knowledge is not absolutely "hard," of course, and pipeline dynamics must be carefully tracked to determine whether the various estimates and assumptions made were indeed correct. Statistical methods provide a good short-term basis for estimating and checking the growth rate and for signaling when the turning points will occur.

In late 1965, it appeared to us at Corning that the ware-in-process demand was increasing, since there was a consistent positive difference between actual TV-bulb sales and forecasted bulb sales. Conversations with product managers and other personnel indicated there might have been a significant change in pipeline activity; it appeared that rapid increases in retail demand were boosting glass requirements for ware-in-process, which could create a hump in the S-curve similar to one in Figure 9.2. This humping provided additional profit for Corning in 1966 but had an adverse effect in 1967. We were able to predict this hump, but unfortunately we were unable to reduce or avoid it because the pipeline was not sufficiently under our control.

The inventories all along the pipeline also follow an S-curve (Figure 9.2), a fact that creates and compounds two characteristic conditions in the pipeline as a whole: (1) initial overfilling, and (2) subsequent shifts between too much and too little inventory at various points—a sequence of feast-and-famine conditions.

For example, the simpler distribution system for Corning cookware had an S-curve similar to the ones we have examined. When the retail sales slowed from rapid to normal growth, however, there were no early indications from shipment data that this crucial turning point had been reached. Data on distributor inventories gave us some warning that the pipeline was overfilling, but the turning point at the retail level was still not identified quickly enough, as we have mentioned before, because of lack of good data at that level. Corning now monitors its field information regularly to identify significant changes, and to adjust its shipment forecasts accordingly.

Another example of severe overfilling of the pipeline occurred at the O. M. Scott Seed Company in the early 1960s. Rapid growth took place from the mid-1950s to 1960, when consumer sales entered the steady-state stage. However, Scott's salesmen were able to continue achieving the company's historical growth by building up inventories at the distributor level, so that the distributor inventories in 1961 were almost equal to annual sales. The next two years resulted in drastic decreases in Scott's dealer sales while the field inventories were reduced (The field sales continued to grow, however, but at a significantly lower rate than during the rapid-growth stage).

The need to consider properly the pipeline implications in forecasting cannot be stressed too strongly, since it has frequently been the cause for building excess capacity.

IN SUMMARY

The decisions made during the rapid-growth stage can have greater effects on profitability than those made during any other stage of the product life cycle. Thus, commensurate forecasting effort should be expended. Market research proves very valuable in verifying assumptions and in permitting further market disaggregation. Statistical methods can be used, but these will still have limited value. Caution must be given to false signals, since there are several ways that the rapid-growth stage may be extended after it appears to be leveling off. Pipeline considerations are crucial and must be given adequate attention.

Chapter X

The Steady-State Stage:
Time-Series Analysis
and Projection

Several years ago, personnel of a company participating in a rapidly growing industry were forecasting divisional sales for the new fiscal year to be approximately 70% greater than the year earlier. This forecast was based primarily on data that showed that during the last quarter of the then current year sales had almost doubled over sales of the preceding year. This same situation continued for the first quarter of the new fiscal year and, in fact, the rate of sales even increased slightly. Hence the forecasters were highly confident that their earlier estimate was not only correct but possibly conservative.

A detailed statistical analysis of the sales data revealed that most of the sales increase was due to a rapid-growth pattern that had taken place in the middle and latter part of the preceding year. The analysis indicated that the business had a low growth rate at that time (the end of the first quarter), and the trend was such that there would probably be little growth in the sales rate for the next four or five months.

On the assumption that existing patterns would continue into the near future, and with no special or additional information such as about orders or marketing strategies, the forecasters estimated that sales for the current year would be only about 10 to 15% higher than the preceding year. Extending this finding, and assuming an upturn after the middle of the year, we see that their revised projection for the entire year gave sales of approximately 30% more than the previous year, compared with the earlier divisional forecast of a 70% increase.

Subsequent sales proved the statistical approach to be very accurate, with ultimate sales within 5% of the estimated projections.

When a product enters the steady-state stage of the life cycle, there are usually sufficient data available to perform quantitative statistical analyses and enough knowledge about the nature of the market to establish causal relationships. Failure to make good use of these data may lead to inaccurate forecasts and wrong decisions. There are two ways in which the data can be analyzed to derive forecasts:

1. To make projections from time-series analyses, where the sales and growth rates are obtained statistically and forecasted from projections of these rates.

2. To establish causal relationships from which forecasts can be derived.

In this chapter, we shall describe time-series analysis and projections; causal techniques shall be presented in Chapter 11. However, let us first consider how both approaches are applied—individually and in combination—before directing the discussion to time-series analysis and projection.

TYPICAL DECISIONS

At this stage of the life cycle, the decisions the manager makes are quite different from those made earlier. Most of the facilities' planning has been done, and trends and growth rates have become reasonably stable. It is possible that swings in demand and profit will occur because of changing economic conditions, new and competitive products, pipeline dynamics, and so on. Thus the manager will have to maintain his tracking-and-warning activities and possibly even introduce new ones. However, he will generally concentrate his forecasting attention on these areas:

- Long- and short-term production planning.
- Setting standards to check the effectiveness of marketing strategies.
- Projections designed to aid profit planning.

In planning production and establishing marketing strategy for the short and medium term, the manager's primary focus is usually on having accurate estimates of both the present sales level and the rate at which this level is changing. The forecaster is thus called on for two related contributions at this stage.

1. To provide estimates of trends and seasonals, which obviously affect the sales level. Seasonals are particularly important for overall production planning and for inventory control. To do this, he needs to apply time-series analysis and projection techniques—that is, *statistical* techniques.

2. To relate the future sales level to factors that are more easily predictable, or that have a "lead" relationship with sales, or both. Therefore, he needs to build *causal models*.

The type of product under scrutiny is very important in selecting the techniques to be used.

In situations where the levels of the distribution system are organized in a relatively straightforward way, for example, statistical methods can be used to forecast shipments and field information to forecast changes in shipment rates. Further investigation can also include incorporating special information—for example, marketing strategies and economic forecasts—directly into the shipment forecasts, which may lead to a causal forecasting model.

On the other hand, a component supplier may be able to forecast total sales with sufficient accuracy for broad-load production planning, but the pipeline environment may be so complex that his best recourse for short-term projections is to rely primarily on salesmen's estimates. In such cases, the best role for statistical methods is to provide guides and checks for salesmen's forecasts.

TIME-SERIES ANALYSIS

At this steady-state point in the life cycle, sufficient time-series data are generally available and enough causal relationships are known from direct experience and market studies so that the forecaster can indeed apply these two powerful sets of tools. Historical data for at least the past several years should be available, and he will use all of it, in one way or another.

We should mention a common criticism at this point. People frequently object to using more than a few of the most recent data points (such as sales figures in the immediate past) for building projections. Since the current situation is always so dynamic and conditions are changing so radically and quickly, they argue that earlier historical data have little or no value.

Our experience indicates this point of view has little validity for medium- and high-volume items. (Low-volume items will often show a random pattern, in which case the demand from month to month will not be related.) A graph of several years' sales data, as shown in Figure 10.1a, gives an impression of a sales trend that could not be possibly obtained from looking only at two or three of the latest data points.

In practice, we find that overall patterns continue for a minimum of one or two quarters into the future, even when special conditions cause sales to fluctuate for one or two (monthly) periods in the immediate future.

For short-term forecasting of one-to-three months ahead, the effects of such factors as general economic conditions are minimal and cause no radical shifts in demand patterns. And because trends tend to change gradually rather than suddenly, statistical and other quantitative methods are very good for short-term forecasting. The use of one or only a few of the most recent data points will mean that the nature of trends, cycles, and seasonal fluctuations in sales will not be given sufficient consideration.

Granting the applicability of the techniques, let us now discuss the means by which the forecaster identifies precisely what is happening when sales fluctuate from one period to the next and how he forecasts such fluctuations.

Sorting Trends and Seasonals

Obviously, a trend and a seasonal are quite different and must be handled separately in forecasting.

Consider what would happen, for example, if a forecaster were merely to take an average of the most recent data points along a curve, combine this with similar average points stretching backward into the immediate past, and use these as the basis for a projection. For example he might easily overreact to random changes, erroneously taking them for evidence of a prevailing trend; or he might mistake a change in the growth rate for a seasonal.

Furthermore, the executive needs accurate estimates of both trends and seasonals to plan broad-load production, to determine marketing efforts and allocations, and to maintain proper inventories—that is, inventories that are adequate to meet customer demand but are not excessively costly.

Before proceeding, it might be well to illustrate what such sorting-out looks like. Figures 10.1 *a, b,* and *c* show the initial decomposition of raw data for factory sales of color-TV sets between 1965 and mid-1970. Figure 10.1a presents the raw-data curve. Figure 10.1b shows the seasonal factors that are implicit in the raw data; this is a fairly consistent pattern, although there is some variation from year to year. Figure 10.1c shows the result of discounting the raw-data curve by the seasonals of part b; this is the so-called "deseasonalized data curve." Next, in Figure 10.1d we have drawn the smoothest or "best" curve possible through the deseasonalized curve, thereby obtaining the trend-cycle. Furthermore, the differences between this trend-cycle line and the deseasonalized data curve represent the irregular or nonsystematic random component that the forecaster must always tolerate and attempt to explain if at all possible by other methods, such as those incorporating special knowledge.

In sum, then, the objective of the statistical technique used here is to do the best possible job of sorting out trends and seasonalities. Once this has been accomplished, the current sales rate and the way it is changing can provide the base for projecting into the future. The two most common methods of projection are (1) to extend visually, from the graph, the sales rate curves, or (2) to determine the mathematical equation of the sales-rate curve and compute the projections by the equation. However, these methods are not very sensitive to recent changes in the sales rate.

We have found a third approach that gives better results. To obtain as accurate a projection as possible, it is important to determine not only the trend, but also the way the trend is changing direction. This is shown in *Part e* of Figure 10.1 where the first differences, or month-to-month *changes* in the growth rate are plotted. The forecasting accuracy will increase when it is possible to identify the peaks and valleys, or what we call the turning points (i.e., the places on the sales curve where the growth rate reverses direction). When these turning points are correctly identified, the points in time at which there is no significant change in sales can be forecasted.

Estimating Seasonals.   There are three problems that arise in estimating the seasonal factors for a time series.

1. It is usually difficult to sort out a seasonal from a trend, since both influence any particular point in the time series. One of the more common (and inaccurate) ways of computing a seasonal is first to divide the monthly (or quarterly) sales by the total sales for the year, and multiply by 12 (or four). When the figure for a particular month is greater than 1, it means that the sales are seasonally high, and when the seasonal is less

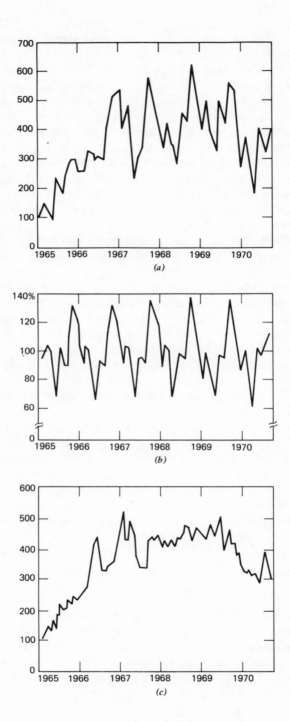

(a)

(b)

(c)

178

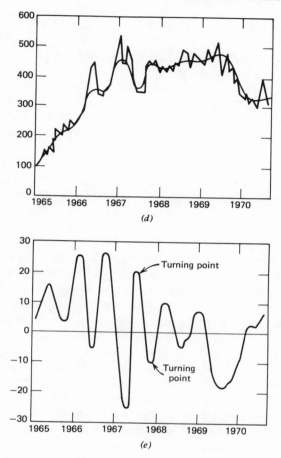

Figure 10.1 *(a)* Raw data for factory sales of color-TV sets (in thousands). *(b)* Seasonals for factory sales of color TV (percent of average monthly sales rate). *(c)* Factory sales of color-TV sets (deseasonalized) (in thousands). *(d)* Final trend-cycle of factory sales of color-TV sets (in thousands). *(e)* Changes in final trend-cycle (growth rate) of factory sales of color-TV sets (in thousands).

than 1, it means that sales are lower than the average rate. Repeating this procedure for several years and averaging the seasonals for the same month of each year will then give estimates of the seasonals.

A major source of error in this method is that the trends are also reflected in the seasonals. For example, when there is a sales trend that has been upward during the year spanned by the data, the seasonals for the early months of the year will be less than they should be and the seasonals for the last months of the year will be greater than they should be. An accurate splitting out of seasonals and trends requires a more sophisticated mathematical approach.

2. There can be a trend in the seasonals (i.e., they may be increasing or decreasing from one year to the next). While it is possible to get some estimate of seasonals with as little as two or three years of data, at least four or five years are needed to identify and estimate trends in seasonals with any accuracy.

As in the foregoing situation, when trends in the sales rate are not distinguished from the seasonals, there may appear to be a trend in the seasonals when in fact there is a gradual change in the trend of the sales rate. A similar problem arises when there are shifts in seasonals because of strategy changes.

For example, in the case of Corning Ware, special promotions had occurred for several consecutive years in March, with the computation of seasonals reflecting this. When the special promotions were shifted to February, the time-series analysis did not recognize the change in the seasonal factors, but indicated a significant upward change in the sales rate. It took several months before the sales rate adjusted to the new seasonals.

Ideally, estimates should be made of the impact of changes in strategy and adjustments made to the data. It is possible to estimate the effects of the change in strategy if a similar change has taken place previously, since the fluctuation would be reflected in the time-series analysis.

3. A difficulty arises from random fluctuations. This is where, for reasons that are not normally repetitive, the random "blip" in sales has occurred at the same time of the year for the past two or three years. The solution to this situation, and the others given earlier as well, is not to accept any seasonal estimates on the basis of statistical analysis alone, but to consider the seasonal factors as valid only when there is some rationale for their being above or below average and for changing in a particular way.

In the case of electric power consumption, the seasonals are now above average for the summer months, in contrast to a significantly below-average condition some years ago, because of increases in air conditioning and summer recreation activities, for example. Thus, if there have been no changes in marketing strategies, competitive actions, environmental conditions, and so on, then an apparent radical change in sales may be due to a random fluctuation rather than a causal event.

TIME-SERIES TECHNIQUES

We shall now consider some of the primary time-series analytical techniques that are extremely important in forecasting for the steady-state stage of the product life cycle. These techniques, which include moving average, exponential smoothing, adaptive forecasting, the Box-Jenkins method, and the X-11 routine, are particularly useful for estimating seasonals and trends for sales.

Moving Average

This technique is the arithmetic average of consecutive data points, with the length of the moving average defined as the number of points used in calculating the moving average. The purpose of the moving average is to either remove seasonals (or other cycling) from the data or to remove the randomness ("smoothing") from the data. In other words, the moving average is an estimate of what we have earlier described as the trend-cycle.

To remove the seasonals from the data most effectively, the length of the moving average should be equal to one-year's data, (e.g., 12 if the data are in months and four if in quarters). This will also provide a basis for estimating seasonals, since the ratios of raw data to smoothed data for each month can be averaged to obtain seasonals. However, this is only an approximation method, for the reasons stated in the preceding section.

When the moving average contains more or less data points than those for a year, the effect of seasonality is not completely removed. An approach frequently taken is to obtain estimates of seasonals by another, more comprehensive technique, and to remove the seasonal component before smoothing the data with the moving average. After the moving averages for a number of "sets" of points are computed, a curve is fitted to the points and estimates are obtained by projecting this trend line. The estimates from the trend line then are multiplied by the seasonals to obtain forecasts.

A more apparent error in this technique is that the moving average will "lag" the current sales rate for a time period of one-half the length of the moving average. To get a current reading, corrections should therefore be made by projecting the moving average this length of time.

Another weakness of the moving-average technique is that it is relatively insensitive to recent trend changes, since small or even large changes in the most recent data points will be dampened by the moving average. To overcome this problem, the tendency is to shorten the length of the moving average. This results not only in more sensitivity to recent changes, but also in more response to noise (random fluctuations rather than true changes in the sales rate).

The problem is therefore to choose the length of moving average that will most often identify changes in trend but that will not overact to random or unusual fluctuations. The "optimum" length of a moving average, which depends on the characteristics of the market and other factors influencing sales, must be determined from an analysis of the data.

An effective way to respond to changes in the trend line is to give more importance to the most recent data points. This is achieved by weighting the various points in the time series, with larger weights given to the most recent points. This is what exponential smoothing does, as we shall discuss shortly.

Still another problem arises with moving averages. It is possible that there are cycles in the data, because of fashion changes or consumer preferences occurring at regular intervals of time or because of other anomalies in the market. A moving average can remove such cycling, especially if the moving average is long when compared to the cycling. Conversely, there is the danger of artificially inducing cycles, and the analyst must be alert to avoid such a possibility. The approach to computing a moving average can best be described by the example included in the appendix at the end of this chapter.

Virtually all time-series techniques employ some form of a moving average. The distinguishing features are the ways in which the seasonals are treated, the length of the moving average, and the weights given to each data point. As indicated, the technique that produces the most accurate forecast for a particular series depends on the way in which the data vary.

We shall now turn our attention to one of the best-known weighting techniques.

Exponential Smoothing

This technique derives its name from the method of assigning weights to each point in the time series—namely, that the moving average includes all points in the time series, with the weights varying according to an "exponential-decaying" function. In other words, the older the data point the less weight it receives in the average.

Various forms of exponential smoothing have undoubtedly been in use for many years, since the concept or desirability of giving a decreasing weight to the older, less recent data points becomes apparent to any analyst who has spent much time in forecasting. However, the mathematical theory was formally developed, applied, and published in the 1950s by R. G. Brown, who was then employed by Arthur D. Little, Inc. It was especially needed at that time because of the emerging situation of rapidly expanding product lines and the need for good forecasts for inventory control purposes. A related problem was that electronic computers were a new product, had little storage capabilities, and were very slow compared with today's computers.

Thus there was a demand for a forecasting technique, especially when several hundreds of items are to be forecasted, that had these six characteristics.

1. It should not require the maintenance of huge data storage files. (That is, it would not be necessary to keep the entire sales history of the item in storage.)

2. The computations required when forecasting with the technique should take very little computer time.

3. It should have the ability to identify seasonal variations in the data and to take these properly into account when forecasting. (Also, it would be very advantageous if the technique could test the statistical significance of the seasonals.)

4. It should have the ability to fit adequately the most recent data.

5. It should give more recent data more weight in determining the forecast.

6. It should do a very respectable job in forecasting all of the items. (Given any time series, it is always possible to find *the* technique or forecasting model that is more optimal than any other. When considering several hundreds of items, however, they are usually so different in this characteristic that the same technique or model would not be optimal for all of them. What must be done, then, is to find that model that does an adequate job on all—or at least relatively large subsets—of them even though it might not be optimal on any of them.)

Many methods have been developed that have some or all of the foregoing characteristics, but most such techniques take the form of what we call exponential smoothing. While there are various kinds of exponential smoothing, all have one thing in common: the equation contains the feature (in one form or another) where the new forecast is equal to the old forecast plus some fraction (alpha) of the last forecast error.

The analyst's job is to determine two things: (1) the *weight* to be given to the most recent data point, and (2) the *type of smoothing*—that is, the way in which the current trend is to be projected. The length of the moving average is not specified, since all data points are given some consideration (weight), although for practical purposes the chronologically older points are ignored when the weight for the most recent point is very large. Since an exponentially-decaying weighting method is used, the specification of the weight for the most recent data point (alpha, which is the same as the weight given to the last forecasting error) determines the weights to be given to all of the other points.

Determining the Weight. Most exponential-smoothing computer programs (the calculations can be done by hand but they are time-consuming) have a feature for determining an approximately optimum weight that will maximize the forecasting accuracy, assuming that future data points will vary in the same way as in the past. A weight that is large (varying between 0 and 1, with a typical weight being about 0.05 to 0.20) will tend to track noise, while a smaller weight will not respond to changes in the sales rate rapidly enough. The optimal value of the weight will increase as the trend changes direction more frequently.

From a mathematical viewpoint, exponential smoothing has the convenient feature of permitting a new forecast to be based on the last forecast and the error in that last forecast. This means that once the weight is established, the only information that must be retained is the last forecast and weight, thereby eliminating the storage of all previous data points.

The disadvantage of doing this, however, is that the nature of the environment may change, which will necessitate that the value of the weight should be updated. This is an important consideration in determining what should be included in the data base, since every forecasting technique—no matter how accurate when implemented—should be continuously tracked to see if the technique or the parameters (e.g., the weight and the type of smoothing) should be changed because of the changing character of the time series. D. W. Trigg and A. G. Leach have developed a method whereby the weight adaptively changes as the forecasting error increases.[32]

Because of randomness and the cost of computing the best weight for each time series, the approach most commonly taken is to determine the optimum weight for a group or class of products, and to use that value

---

[32] "Exponential Smoothing With An Adaptive Response Rate," *Operational Research Quarterly*, Vol. 13, No. 1, pp. 53–59.

for all of the products in that group. The total for the group is then the basis for tracking and updating the weight. Also, the total for the group may be analyzed by other time-series techniques (e.g., the X-11 routine), and when turning points are identified, either a new weight is computed or an adjustment factor is applied to the new forecast.

We have found that in designing an automated forecasting system it is important to include manual override features (on an exception report basis) in the computer program. This will permit adjustments for turning points and revisions to the forecasting parameters to account for special events, such as new marketing strategies and strikes, which are not included in the forecasting model. Because of the likelihood of changes in the factors affecting sales, maintenance of the forecasting system is also very critical.

Determining the Type of Smoothing. The other important aspect of exponential smoothing, the degree or type of smoothing, is dependent on the stability of the environment and the sales-rate trend. *Single* smoothing assumes that there is virtually no change in the sales rate, with the forecast equal to the current rate (adjusted for seasonals). *Double* smoothing is essentially a linear projection of the sales rate, with the recent changes in the rate being the basis for projection. *Triple* smoothing incorporates a curved trend, and basically is a quadratic fit and projection-type of smoothing. Triple smoothing should be used only for short-range forecasts, since quadratic projections result in rapidly increasing or decreasing sales estimates that are usually quite inaccurate.

Because of the way in which each type of smoothing makes projections, exponential smoothing should not be used for deriving forecasts for more than three to six months into the future. To obtain acceptable accuracy beyond this period of time, it is usually necessary to build long-term stability into the forecasts. This long-term stability is usually done via a secondary exponential smoothing of 12-month totals. The one-month ahead forecast is strictly short term, the 12-month forecast is long term, and all months in between are a mathematical combination of the two methods, as illustrated in Figure 10.2.

The short-term trend line in Figure 10.2 has more weight assigned to the latest data points, thereby being more responsive to short-term swings. Whereas there is definitely an upturn at the present time, the long-term trend indicates decreasing sales. We combine these two trend lines to obtain a "best" forecast.

Single smoothing is most applicable to mature products that are experiencing small, if any, changes in long-term sales rates, while triple

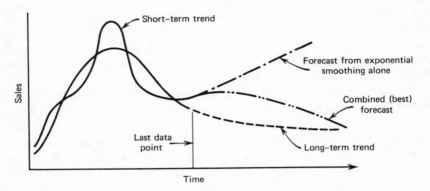

Figure 10.2. Exponential smoothing where short- and long-term trends are combined.

smoothing is applicable to products that have dynamic growth patterns. When the growth pattern is in a constantly increasing or decreasing state, double smoothing is most appropriate.

For most exponential smoothing applications, the technique is slow to recognize turning points, and will take three to six time periods to adjust completely to a change, although the errors will not be too large unless a very significant change has occurred. It does react quicker to changes, however, than a moving average.

The most extensive application of exponential smoothing has been in the area of production and inventory control, where the technique is used for obtaining forecasts for large numbers of items. When incorporated into a production-planning system, including a model for computing safety stocks and reorder quantities, the forecasts and reorder points and quantities can be calculated for a maximum of a few cents each and often for less than one cent each.

The simplicity and low cost of deriving forecasts has led to an increasing use in other areas, especially in the financial functions. The major weakness of exponential smoothing is its lack of direct calculation of seasonals, which expedited the development of the next technique.

Adaptive Forecasting

This technique is an extension of exponential smoothing, with some form of a mathematical feature for computing seasonals. (Although exponential smoothing and moving average are in a sense adaptive, we prefer to define adaptive smoothing in this way.) Several different seasonal computational routines have been developed; the major ones are *harmonic regression, Fourier analysis,* and *simple ratios.* The first two routines are relatively sophisticated mathematical techniques. The problem of getting the best combination of parameters is increased significantly (versus exponential smoothing), and it is usually necessary to establish the parameters for large groups of time series, as well as to obtain seasonals for low-volume groups.

In our discussion of exponential smoothing, only one smoothing parameter (weight) was used. When there is a trend in the data, a suitable replacement for double exponential smoothing is called either a three-factor adaptive or Holt's method.[33] The three factors are called the rate, trend, and seasonals, each of which is separately predicted by single exponential smoothing, using its own smoothing parameter. It so happens that the rate plus the trend are the same as the trend-cycle, which is multiplied by the seasonals to obtain forecasts.

We have used a three-factor adaptive method, with the factors being the trend cycle and seasonals. The trend-cycle is forecasted using Holt's method and the seasonals are predicted using single exponential smoothing based on Fourier estimates of the seasonals, and then being exponentially updated. This approach requires three smoothing parameters; however, through simulations of artificial time series, we have found that the forecasts are not very sensitive to the value of the seasonal's smoothing parameter over relatively large ranges.

R. G. Brown has developed a method called "general adaptive forecasting," based on *harmonic regression.* This method takes into account both trend and seasonals and requires only one smoothing parameter.[34] The main difficulty with this technique is that—in order to describe the seasonals adequately—a relatively large model is needed, which can possibly cause a sluggish response to changes in the sales pattern.

The *Fourier analysis* approach was developed by P. J. Harrison.[35] This is the approach we prefer (with modifications) because the seasonals (a) can be statistically tested for significance, and (b) are unbiased estimates that have good "response to change" characteristics. The ratio approach used in Holt's method mentioned earlier is basically what the name im-

---

[33] This method is discussed in several of the books and articles listed in Appendix A. For example, see P. J. Harrison, "Short-Term Sales Forecasting," *Applied Statistics,* Vol. 14, Nos. 2 and 3, 1965.

[34] *Smoothing, Forecasting and Prediction* (Englewood Cliffs, N.J.: Prentice-Hall, Inc., 1962), p. 158.

[35] "Short-Term Sales Forecasting," pp. 102–139.

plies, a technique whereby the *simple ratios* of actual data to trend data are computed to obtain seasonals.

In many companies, historical data for time series do not exist for more than two to three years, making the potential variability in the estimates of the seasonals high. In this case, it is important to include a capability for testing the significance of seasonals and for overriding individual seasonals with group seasonals. (Unless the time series contains relatively large and stable numbers, it is advisable to use group seasonals rather than individual seasonals.)

Furthermore, seasonal computations in many techniques include division by the seasonals, which may lead to large errors (or system "blow-up") when they are abnormally low because of poor estimates. This happens when sales data are either highly volatile or influenced by wide inventory swings.

In several situations, we observed that more than 20% of the time series had no consistent variation and could be considered random data. For these situations, we had to provide tests for randomness, and the capability to use straight arithmetic averages or order statistics to estimate the probabilities of attaining given levels of sales when randomness was identified.

As indicated earlier, we have developed an adaptive forecasting routine that incorporates such features along with double smoothing. We have also produced significantly better forecasts than with other techniques and previous methods.

Since several variations of adaptive forecasting have been developed in recent years, we shall therefore consider next the one technique that generalizes most of the time-series forecasting methods.

Box-Jenkins Method

At the present time, this is the most powerful and comprehensive technique available for prediction and control. It includes all of the features described earlier, as well as several others. Because it was designed to do a thorough job of time-series analysis, it is still too difficult—given the current state of the art—to be applied on a large-scale production basis.

Basically, it optimally designs the moving-average features (length of moving average and weights) for a particular time series. This is in contrast to most other techniques, where the length of the moving average is either fixed, limited to a few choices, or must be specified. The Box-Jenkins method has sophisticated modelling features, such as auto-regression and difference filters. It also allows for the incorporation of extraneous information (e.g., number of trading dates, price changes, leading indicators, and other special events) with adjustments being made based on such information.

These features permit some very interesting applications of the Box-Jenkins technique. For a company in which most of its products are several steps back in the pipeline from the consumer, economic factors will explain only about 20 to 30% of the variation in shipments; the remaining, unexplained portion of variability is composed of many other factors. A convenient way of handling this problem is to forecast the unexplained portion statistically, and then to add an adjustment (perturbation) due to the relevant economic factors. Both of these can potentially be accomplished simultaneously by the Box-Jenkins technique. Because of these comprehensive characteristics, virtually all moving-average techniques are special cases of the Box-Jenkins method. However, for a particular technique, such as exponential smoothing, the various parameters in the Box-Jenkins model take on specific values.

The Box-Jenkins method, compared with other time-series techniques, is more costly to use. Several commercial firms sell computer programs for performing the computations, which cannot be performed manually, and other institutions—such as the University of Wisconsin—are now making similar computer programs available to business and industry. As computer technology progresses and becomes less expensive, the Box-Jenkins technique will become more acceptable for making large-scale time-series projections. Until that happens, one of the best techniques available today in the trade-off of forecast cost versus accuracy is the Shiskin routine or Census Bureau X-11 technique.

The X-11 Routine

We have found that this technique, which was developed by Julius Shiskin of the U. S. Census Bureau, is an extremely effective tool for analyzing historical data in depth to determine seasonals, sales rates, and growth.[36] It simultaneously removes seasonals from raw information and fits a trend-cycle line to the data. Shiskin developed it primarily as a method for deseasonalizing government data, and it has been used for many years for this purpose.

[36] R. L. McLaughlin, "Time Series Forecasting," Marketing Research Technique, Series No. 6, American Marketing Association, 1962.

The X-11 routine is very comprehensive: at a cost of less than $10 per time series, it provides detailed information on seasonals, the trend-cycles, and several other measures. It is the most accurate method known for estimating seasonals.

The Shiskin routine is basically an iterative procedure, where computations are alternately performed on the seasonals and trend-cycle until a best overall fit of seasonals and trend-cycle is obtained. It recognizes and fits trends to the seasonals as well as to the sales rate. Unweighted moving averages are used to remove seasonals, and weighted moving averages are used to smooth the randomness out of both the seasonals and trend-cycle. The moving averages that generate the trend-cycle are designed so that each weighted moving average fits (via least squares) a cubic polynomial to the points in the averages. Also, because of the particular weights that are chosen, the moving averages do not lag; they give current least-square estimates of the trend-cycle of the latest data points.

Extraneous information, such as number of trading dates in a month and strikes, can be incorporated into the analysis and adjustments can be made for them. Sales that are significantly different from the overall pattern, because of randomness or some special event not included as input, are statistically adjusted by upper limits. The graphs in Figure 10.1 were obtained from the X-11 routine.

Although the X-11 was not originally developed as a forecasting method, it does establish a base from which good forecasts can be made. However, there is some instability in the trend line for the most recent data points, since the X-11, as we mentioned, utilizes some form of moving average. We have therefore found it valuable to study the changes in growth as well.

In particular, when recent data seem to reflect sharp growth or decline in sales because of some market anomaly, the forecaster should determine whether any special events occurred during the period under consideration—for example, promotions, strikes, and abrupt changes in the economy. The X-11 provides the basic instrumentation needed to evaluate the effects of such events.

Generally, even when growth patterns can be associated with specific events, the X-11 technique and other statistical methods do not give good results when forecasting beyond six months, because of the uncertainty or unpredictable nature of future events. However, for short-term forecasts of one to three months, the X-11 technique has proved reasonably accurate, and has given good results up to one year or more into the future, depending on the stability of the sales pattern.

The method by which a sales forecast is derived from the trends, seasonals, and other data obtained from the X-11 is basically as follows.

• Graph the rate at which the trend is changing. See the graph in Figure 10.1e. It describes the successive ups and downs of the trend-cycle shown in part d.

• Project this growth rate forward over the interval to be forecasted. Assuming we were forecasting back in mid-1970, we should be projecting into the summer months and possibly into the early fall.

• Add this growth rate (whether positive or negative) to the present sales rate. This might be called the unseasonalized sales rate.

• Project the seasonals of Figure 10.1b for the period in question, and multiply the unseasonalized forecasted rate by these seasonals. The product will be the forecasted sales rate, which is what we desired.

In special cases where there are no seasonals to be considered, this process is of course much simplified, and fewer data and simpler techniques may be adequate.

We have found that an analysis of the patterns of change in the growth rate gives us more accuracy in predicting turning points (and therefore changes from positive to negative growth, and vice versa) than when we use only the trend-cycle.

The main advantage of considering growth change, in fact, is that it is frequently possible to predict earlier when a no-growth situation will occur. The graph of change in growth thus provides an excellent visual base for forecasting and also for identifying the turning point.

Rather than dwell on the methodology, we can best understand the value of the technique by considering the following applications, some of which directly involve forecasts, while others affect the forecasting accuracy.

In our most extensive application, we have used it to provide sales estimates for each company division for three periods into the future, as well as to determine changes in sales rates. We have compared our X-11 forecasts developed by each of several divisions, where the divisions have used a variety of methods, some of which take into account salesmen's estimates and other special knowledge. The forecasts using the X-11 technique were based on statistical methods alone and did not consider any special information.

The division forecasts had slightly *less* error than those provided by the X-11 method; howover, the division forecasts were slightly biased on the optimistic side, whereas those provided by the X-11 method were unbiased. This suggested to us that a better job of forecasting could be done by combining special knowledge, the techniques of the divisions, and the X-11 method. This is actually being done now by some of the divisions, and their forecasting accuracy has subsequently improved.

Here are three reasons for the satisfactory forecasting performance of the X-11 technique.

1. When forecasting only one to three periods into the future there is a good chance that patterns presently observed in the change in trend-cycle will continue into the immediate future. However, one to three periods are usually too short a time for anything of major importance to occur that would reverse the present direction of the trend line. Of course, the further into the future one projects, the less this holds true.

2. This technique allows the forecaster to make quasi-statistical projections and still use any special knowledge he might have about the sales.

3. When forecasting total company or division sales, which are themselves the sum of the sales of many products, the law of large numbers usually means less randomness in the data and therefore better forecasting accuracy. There is one qualification, however. If the components of the total tend to be heterogenous because they are in different markets, less accuracy may be obtained by aggregating. An example is Corning's subsidiary, Corhart Refractories, which sells refractory brick to both steel and glass manufacturers. Unless Corhart sales are forecasted by separating these two products, forecasting accuracy suffers.

In Figure 10.3, the raw data, trend-cycle, and change in trend-cycle are shown in part *a* for the situation where the sales rate has doubled over the past year. As this illustration shows, the current sales rate (period 3, 1968) is not due to good performance at that time (i.e., the last data point) but to growth in the preceding year. The rate of growth is declining (this would be difficult to see from the raw data alone), and it appears that there will be little growth in the immediate future.

This means that the ratio of sales for 1968 versus 1967 would be declining, since there was significant growth at the same time in 1967 (part *b*). Based on previous patterns, the forecast was for growth later in 1968. However, the forecast for the overall year of 1968 was for only a 30% increase versus 1967.

Another example involves an analysis of inventory turns for color-TV sets at the factory level, where the use of ratios based on raw data indicated that the inventory level was acceptable and would continue to be so in the near future. A subsequent statistical analysis with the X-11 tech-

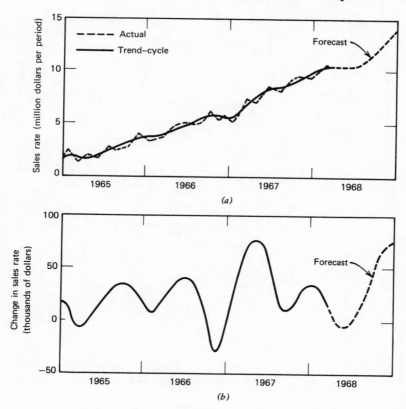

Figure 10.3. Raw data and trend-cycle for situation where sales rate doubled in previous year.

nique revealed that since the inventory-to-turn ratio had peaked, it would be declining in the immediate future, and—unless corrective action were taken—it would reach an unacceptable level. This analysis provided valuable information for forecasting future sales and for scheduling production of color bulbs.

In Figure 10.4, a graph of current and past inventory turns for factory inventories of color-TV sets, the trend-cycle and rate of change (part *a*) show that in early 1969 the inventory turns started to flatten. A projection of the change in turns (part *b*) indicates that they will experience a downward trend in the immediate future, they will continue to decrease, and they could reach a level comparable to that in 1967 of 10 or less turns, which was considered by the industry as unacceptable.

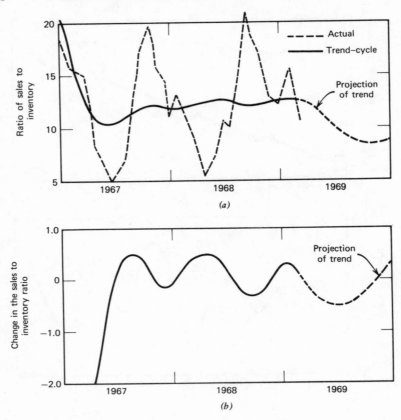

Figure 10.4.   Factory inventories of color-TV sets, 1967 to period 3 in 1969.

From an examination of the raw data it is not at all obvious that there is any particular cause for concern that inventory turns could be heading toward an unacceptable level. Furthermore, it can be seen that the use of the ratios in raw data form occasionally suggests a false trend (not shown by the time-series analysis).

In still another example, an analysis of the annual sales data (to establish a trend) and special information from salesmen were used to set the budget for the next year. Raw data for the past few years were then used to obtain seasonals and cycle the budget (i.e., break down the annual sales into period sales).

Through the use of the X-11 technique, an analysis was made of the sales data for previous years and the new budget. An examination of the

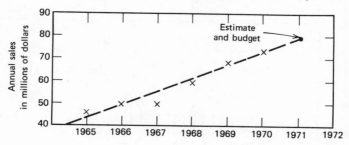

Figure 10.5. Establishment of budget based on projection of annual sales trend.

imputed growth pattern for the coming year indicated that both the total sales and the cycling pattern were unreasonable, taking into account the current sales rate and expected trends.

This is shown in Figure 10.5, where the annual sales data for the past six years (including an estimate made in period 11 for the 1970 sales) and a trend projection of the annual sales (on which the budget of $82.5 million was based) are given. Salesmen had indicated business was strong, based on the good increase in sales in 1970, and they felt that the current trend would continue.

However, the time-series analysis of period data given in Figure 10.6a shows that there was actually negative growth at the time the budget was set and that the sales rate going into 1971 would be $5.7 to $5.9 million per period. Stated in annual sales, the rate of $75 million was significantly lower than the budget, which meant that there would have to be considerable growth during 1971 for the budgeted sales to be achieved.

Inserting the budget data and cycling for the next year gave a pattern represented by Figure 10.6b. One can see that the budget required a growth rate significantly different from the current trend and from any growth pattern of the past three years (actually, data for earlier years, omitted here, were also included in the analysis). Furthermore, the high forecast (and budget) for 1971 actually caused an upward revision in the sales rate and growth pattern.

When these plots were shown to management, it was agreed that the budget objective was optimistic and that there was no strong reason (such as increased orders) to indicate a sudden upturn. In addition, there was not only a high probability of an industry strike in the fall (the budget did not reflect this possibility), but also economic forecasts were for the trend in the industrial markets involved to be flat or even negative in 1971. All of these factors suggested sales of 5 to 10% lower than budget, which proved true.

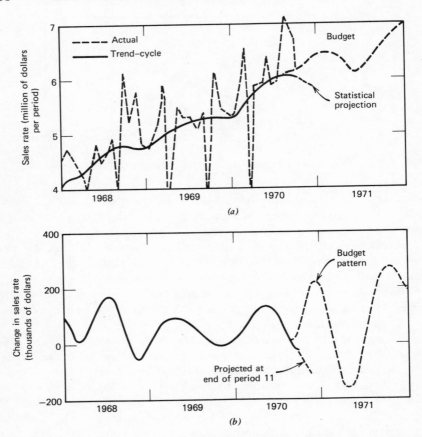

Figure 10.6. Time-series analysis of sales for period data and implications of the budget.

Other applications of the X-11 technique include the tracking of the growth pattern for actual sales versus the imputed pattern for budgeted sales, and estimating the effects of special events, such as pricing changes and promotions. David Goodman and Kavin Moody have described how the effects of promotions were measured with the X-11 technique and how the results of the time-series analysis were incorporated into a decision-making model.[37]

In our descriptions of exponential smoothing and adaptive forecasting, we suggested that a more sophisticated technique should be used for

[37] See "Determining Optimum Price Promotion Quantities," *Journal of Marketing,* Vol. 34, October 1970, pp. 31–39.

establishing group seasonals and identifying turning points (changes in trend). The X-11 Routine is an excellent technique to use in combination with less detailed time-series analysis techniques for analyzing and forecasting large groups of time series.

Other Analysis Techniques

In one sense, *regression analysis,* which is a form of trend projection, can be considered a time-series analysis technique when sales are regressed or correlated to time. This is, however, only one application of regression analysis, the discussion of which we have included in the next chapter on causal models. As a rule, regression analysis neither sorts out seasonals from other time-series components, nor does it directly consider cycles. When used primarily to consider time as the independent variable, it does a reasonably good job of determining how sales change over time, with the main time base being annual data rather than monthly or quarterly data.

Spectral density analysis is also a time-series analysis technique, although it is basically a statistical method for identifying the significance and length of cycles in the data. Cross-spectral density analysis has great value in establishing lead-lag relationships and in determining if there are cycles of similar length in different time series that might be correlated. A discussion of this technique has also been included in Chapter 11.)

Finally, *learning curves* might be considered a form of time-series analysis for production costs, where the learning rate and the unit costs at various points in time are established by curve fitting. Since numerous articles[38] have been published on the application of the learning curve to various industries, we shall omit any further discussion of this well-known technique.

IN SUMMARY

Time-series analysis techniques are extremely important in forecasting for the steady-state stage of the product life cycle and can be applied to earlier stages when sufficient data are available. These forecasting techniques determine the sales rate and the way in which it changes, thus

[38] For example, "Perspectives on Experience" (Boston: The Boston Consulting Group, Inc., 1968).

laying the foundation for the projection itself. There are various methods for projecting the current sales rate, and the techniques for time-series analysis and projection will depend on the nature (e.g., variability and consistency) of the data and the amount of money that can be spent for the forecast.

APPENDIX: EXAMPLES OF MOVING AVERAGE

The way a moving average is calculated and the inherent weaknesses of this method are illustrated in the following example. In Table 10.1, the actual sales have been divided by seasonal estimates to get deseasonalized sales. The estimates of seasonals were obtained from seasonal analyses for similar-type products. Seasonals can be derived from moving averages by computing the ratio of actual sales to the moving average for each month (of length 12 or 4, depending on whether monthly or quarterly data are used). However, this is at best only an approximation method for dealing with seasonality; it will not give best estimates of seasonals for reasons given earlier in this chapter.

The deseasonalized sales have been plotted in Figure 10.7; these are represented by the solid line. A moving average of length 7 has been used to remove the randomness from the data and to get an estimate trend-cycle. The data for the moving average are shown in part d of Table 10.1, and these are plotted in Figure 10.7, as shown by the dashed line.

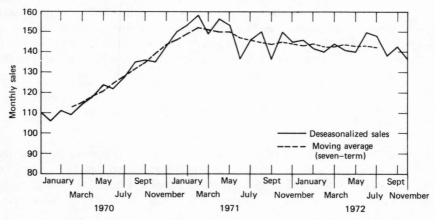

Figure 10.7. Graphs of deseasonalized sales and moving averages for illustrative time series.

Table 10.1 Data for an Example of the Calculation of the Moving Average

a. Actual Sales

Year	January	February	March	April	May	June	July	August	September	October	November	December
1970	107	104	118	109	115	127	117	118	123	134	135	138
1971	139	148	165	159	151	169	144	131	143	150	133	151
1972	141	146	155	141	146	155	132	141	146	138	136	137

b. Seasonals

Year	January	February	March	April	May	June	July	August	September	October	November	December
1970	0.97	0.98	1.06	1.00	1.01	1.08	0.94	0.97	0.97	0.99	0.99	1.02
1971	0.97	0.99	1.08	1.00	1.01	1.08	0.94	0.96	0.98	1.00	0.97	1.01
1972	0.97	1.00	1.09	1.01	1.01	1.10	0.94	0.94	0.97	1.00	0.95	1.01

c. Deseasonalized Sales

Year	January	February	March	April	May	June	July	August	September	October	November	December
1970	110	106	111	109	114	118	124	122	127	135	136	135
1971	143	150	153	158	149	156	153	137	147	150	137	149
1972	145	146	142	140	144	141	140	150	148	138	143	136

d. Seven-Term Moving Average

Year	January	February	March	April	May	June	July	August	September	October	November	December
1970	—	—	—	113	115	118	121	125	128	132	135	140
1971	144	146	149	152	151	150	150	147	147	145	144	145
1972	144	143	144	143	143	144	143	143	142	—	—	—

In part c, for example, the July 1971 value is calculated from the April to October values from part b for that year as follows:

$$\frac{158 + 149 + 156 + 153 + 137 + 146 + 150}{7} = 150$$

199

Note these four important points.

1. When a moving average of length 7 is used, three data points at the beginning and three data points at the end of the time series are lost; that is, there are no moving average values for the six points. Also, when a moving average of length 13 is used, six values are lost at each end of the time series. (When the length of a moving average is even, the resultant moving average must be centered by taking a two-term moving average of the even-term averages.)

2. Consider, for example, the moving average value for June 1970, which is the arithmetic average of March to September, inclusive. This moving average value for June is the least-squares estimate of the trend-cycle for June, the midpoint of the moving average, assuming a linear trend between March and September. In other words, the moving average is equivalent to a moving least-squares fit of the data.

3. The missing values at each end of the data, especially at the most recent end, lead most people to think that the moving average lags the current trend value—for example, we don't really have a good estimate of the trend-cycle for December 1972, the latest estimate we have is for September 1972. While this is true, it is not an insurmountable problem. Since each moving average is a least-squares fit, weights can be developed to obtain weighted moving averages,[39] which are least-squares fits for October, November, and December 1971, and even beyond for forecasts of the trend-cycle. This is how forecasts can be developed from moving averages. How these weights are developed is beyond the scope of the book; refer to books listed under moving averages in Appendix A.

4. We mentioned in (2) above that a linear trend is fit to the data included in the moving average. We are certainly not constrained to linearity, because weights can be again developed such that a weighted moving average of the data gives a least-squares estimate of the data, using nonlinear trends such as quadratic or cubic polynominals. This is exactly how the X-11 routine discussed earlier smooths the randomness from the deseasonalized data to estimate the trend-cycle.

---

[39] This is to be contrasted with the unweighted moving average in Figure 10.1, where each month receives equal weight in the moving average.

Chapter XI

The Steady-State Stage:
Causal Models

In late 1960, one of the major beer companies had a study conducted to forecast beer consumption for the next decade. There had been virtually no growth in total beer sales in the United States during the 1950s, but the general consensus was that, while the population had grown during that time, there was little change in the total beer-drinking population. The company executives felt that the 1960s would be "boom years" for the beer industry, since the war babies would come of age and be consumers of their product.

An analysis of the growth of population age groups and the beer consumption for each age group revealed that the beer-drinking population had in fact grown during the 1950s, although not as rapidly as the total population. An examination of liquor and wine sales indicated that their markets had grown substantially during the 1950s. When sales of all alcoholic beverages were converted to total equivalent alcohol sales, and the age groups were weighted according to market research findings about drinking habits, the results showed that the alcohol consumption had remained very stable over the past 10 years, although there was a small upward trend. Wine and liquor had been increasing their share of the total alcohol market over this period of time.

By using these results, government forecasts of population growth, and statistical proportions of market share and alcohol consumption trends, the analysts came up with a forecast of beer consumption for the 1960s. They then estimated the sales for the beer company conducting the study from an analysis of its market share of total industry sales. (The market share of the 10 largest beer companies had grown substantially over the previous 20 years.) The statistical projection of market share employed a weighting method for the points in the time series, with the most recent points receiving greater weight.

As time passed, the various factors included in the study were tracked, and the equivalent alcohol consumption per capita experienced a significant upward trend in the mid-1960s. Some of the other trends also changed direction during that period.

This knowledge of the dynamics of the market helped the beer company's executives to realize that future sales would not grow rapidly as a result of market momentum alone, and it also had an impact on their later strategy formulation.

Stafford Beer, who is well known for his research into the nature of viable systems and how they function, has ascribed three attributes to these systems: their innate complexity, the complexity of their interaction with the environment, and the complexity of their internal connectivity.[40] Although causal models may include factors from any of these attributes, in forecasting the greatest emphasis is placed on the second attribute. In causal models, we attempt to explain how various factors in the environment and other aspects of the system will affect sales or whatever it is we are forecasting.

In Chapter 10, we examined the historical data to identify the systematic or explainable variation in the data. We made no effort to determine why the data behave in a particular manner, but only to show that there is some consistency in the data (time series) that can provide a base for statistically forecasting the future. We did however indicate that the time-series analysis can provide help in establishing causal relationships, by identifying cyclical behavior that should be explained by related factors and by providing a base for measuring the effects of special events.

Furthermore, when attempting to determine whether there are any significant relationships between two or more factors, it is of value first to remove seasonality from the data (for all factors) since it is both difficult and not particularly meaningful to attempt to explain seasonality with predicting or causal equations. In addition, a nonseasonal movement in a causal variable may wrongly correlate with a seasonal movement in the dependent variable.

Quite frequently, it is necessary also to remove trends from the data. This is the case when the forecaster knows beforehand that the trends in both the dependent and independent variables are not causally re-

[40] *Decision and Control* (London: John Wiley and Sons, Inc., 1966), p. 257.

lated, but only coincidentally (e.g., as later shown in Figure 11.2, where plots of sales and the Federal Reserve Board (FRB) Index have similar trends).

While the decisions made in the steady-state stage may not be as economically important as those made in the earlier stages of the life cycle, which would suggest that extensive effort should not be expended in preparing forecasts for the steady-state decisions, there is another reason for the justification of large resources for establishing causal relationships. The marketing strategies, and those pertaining to other functional areas too, are dependent on how well the analyst understands the environmental factors. This means that knowledge of causal relationships is critical for most aspects of decision making in the steady-state stage; thus the expenditures are justified.

Market research, which we discussed at some length in Chapters 6 and 7, is often an essential step in obtaining data for identifying causal relationships. However, we shall not repeat the techniques and nuances of market research here, but shall center our attention on the techniques for determining whether a causal relationship is statistically significant in the data, whether the data confirm a logically deduced supposition about relationships, and how the relationships can be used for forecasting.

CAUSAL-MODELING TECHNIQUES

Probably the most commonly used technique for estimating the relationships between two or more factors is regression analysis. In the following discussion, we shall give a brief overview of regression analysis and other statistical techniques, with their strengths, weaknesses, special considerations, and applications. Because one aspect of regression analysis involves economic factors, we shall describe the incorporation of anticipatory and leading indicators in a forecast.

We shall then look at how econometric models are developed (industry and government), how input-output models can be applied to steady-state forecasting and, finally, how simulation models can be used in forecasting.

Regression Analysis

Although one of the most extensively applied forecasting techniques, regression analysis is also one of the most incorrectly used and abused techniques. The objective of regression analysis is to establish the best statistical relationships between two or more variables. These relationships are based on historical data and indicate the extent to which one or more "dependent" variables (factors to be forecast) have experienced a change as there have been changes in the "independent" variables (basis of forecast).

These related changes could have been the result of chance or because the variables being examined have been mutually affected by another variable, so that, in fact, there is no cause-and-effect relationship. Because of this, serious errors can arise when extrapolations are made (i.e., when the values of the independent variables are outside the range of the values used in establishing the regression equation).

Cause-and-effect relationships can never be positively established, apart from statistically designed experiments; they can only be hypothesized, and the probabilities of the hypotheses not being "accidentally" true can then be estimated by means of regression analysis. The data used in regression analysis are almost always undesigned (i.e., not derived from well-designed experiments) and the forecaster must accept the data available to him.

Since the estimated regression coefficient can be quite erroneous because of certain circumstances, this problem can be entirely eliminated only by using designed data obtained from a controlled environment. (This is usually not possible to obtain because of the unwillingness of marketing people to intentionally make changes that may not be optimal).

The methodology of regression analysis can best be described by the example in Figure 11.1, where we have plotted sales over time. The objective in fitting a line to the data is to minimize the sum of the squares of the vertical differences between the actual (plotted) data and the line. The line is called the regression equation, with sales being the dependent variable and the time, in this case, the independent variable.

(In one sense, when time is the independent variable, the regression analysis can be called time-series analysis, but since we are not breaking down the data into its components—seasonals, trend-cycle, and random— the term time series, as we have defined it, does not apply.)

In this exhibit, the line fitted to the data is nonlinear or curved. If there is a constant growth rate, even though the plot of sales over time may be curved, the regression line becomes linear when the logarithm of sales is the dependent variable in the equation.

When there are two or more independent variables, the approach is the same, but from a visual point of view we would be dealing with three or more dimensions, which is difficult to visualize. However, there are

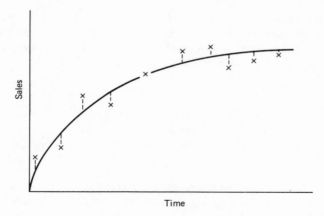

Figure 11.1.   Example of regression line.

mathematical techniques (and related computer programs) for obtaining regression equations or best fits to the data for any number of variables, and the increase in the prediction accuracy of the equation can be evaluated when new variables are introduced into the equation.

Potential Problems.   There should be some rationale for trying to get a regression equation or relationships between two or more variables—that is, the relationship should be hypothesized before the calculations are performed. Not only might there be no causal relationship between the factors in a regression equation, but there are four other potential problems of regression analysis.

1. The independent variables may not be statistically independent (they may be interrelated). This is called the multicollinearity problem and it causes biases in the coefficients of the regression equation.

2. The relationships may change. (The sizes of the coefficients and overall model characteristics are dynamic.)

3. There may be a limitation on the number of variables that can be included in an equation, based upon the amount of data available. (There must be fewer independent variables than data points or observations.)

4. The signs of the coefficients of the independent variables in the equation may be counter-intuitive and opposite to the true relationship, since the best fit to the data is obtained mathematically, regardless of the way the variables are most likely related. (However, there are meth-

ods for controlling or forcing the sign of a coefficient to be as desired.) The analyst must also consider that intercorrelations between the variables can cause the sign of the coefficient of a particular variable to be different from that expected. This again, is caused by the collinearity problem.

Recommended Steps.   Because of these potential problems, here are eight recommended steps for performing a regression analysis. (The manager should be aware of these steps so that he can evaluate the procedures by which a forecast has been obtained.)

1.   Remove seasonals and oftentimes the trends, by time-series analysis, from the data before attempting to perform a regression analysis.

2.   Identify the "logical" variables by expert opinion, as well as the most likely functional form (i.e., relationship to the dependent variable) and attempt to determine whether the independent variables are truly statistically independent.

3.   Graph each independent variable versus the dependent variable to determine the type of relationship (linear or curved) and type of curve. The independent variables should also be graphed against each other to see if there are any relationships.

4.   Convert variables to their necessary form. It may prove to be of value to combine several variables into one new variable, as we shall discuss later.

5.   Split the data into two groups, with one group being used to obtain the equation and the other group to test the validity of the equation.

6.   Perform regression and correlation computations.

7.   Check signs of the coefficients for reasonableness. If a step-wise regression is performed (i.e., new variables are added to determine their significance), see if the signs change from one iteration to the next.

8.   Test for predictability. See how well the regression equation predicts the future.

Illustrative Applications.   We shall now consider several applications of regression analysis to illustrate some of the foregoing points.

In establishing economic manufacturing quantities for new products and other products that will most likely have a significant number of design changes, it is necessary to predict the frequency and cost of such changes. In the aircraft industry, where there are many design changes, experience shows that the number of design changes for a contract can be forecast with sufficient accuracy by considering a few factors such as maximum speed of the aircraft, length of the contract, and extent to which the aircraft is "new."

In that same project, the frequency with which lots are split on the production line (i.e., a larger lot is subdivided into smaller lots) was determined to follow the functional form of the aircraft learning curve. It was critical in the lot-splitting project to hypothesize the relationship of splitting to the learning curve, because there were relatively few data points for establishing statistically the functional form of the relationship.

In many instances, a rather elaborate method is developed for measuring the state of a social system, and the changes in the measure over time or against other variables are then used in regression analysis for predictive purposes. Rensis Likert, director emeritus of the University of Michigan's Institute for Social Research, has long championed the concept that in measuring the value of its assets, a corporation should place a monetary value on its personnel.[41]

One aspect relating to this concept has been to show that future profits are a function of the overall personnel situation of a company. In measuring the "state" of a company's personnel, Likert incorporates into composite factors the answers to such questions as: Has a company's decision-making process improved or gotten worse? Are its performance goals higher? To what extent do its employees think that they have a say in how they do their job? Do its employees feel they have the support of management?

These factors have been incorporated into a regression equation for predicting a company's productivity and financial performance. According to Likert, on the basis of data from more than 75 companies, the factors will account for as much as two-thirds of the fluctuations in financial results and productivity gains from year to year.

In a similar way, the experience of several companies shows that composite indices for leading indicators and anticipatory data correlate very highly with sales, being lead-indicators for three months to two years into the future. Further discussion of these relationships is given in Chapter 13, since the primary application of the sales versus leading indicators or anticipatory data has been for the tracking and warning of sales rather than the forecasting of them.

An example of wrong inferences drawn from regression analysis is when sales are found to be highly correlated with R&D expenditures or marketing factors such as sales expense, advertising, sales manpower, and so forth. The coefficients of the factors such as R&D and advertising are

[41] "A New Twist to People Accounting," *Business Week*, October 21, 1972, p. 67.

then said to be an indication of how much R&D or advertising resources are needed to generate one dollar of sales. In many cases, this is the reverse of what actually happens, since the R&D budget and the marketing budgets are established as a fixed percentage (or within a narrow range) of sales, rather than the sales resulting directly from the expenditures.

Regression analysis has been applied in a variety of ways for estimating future profitability on the basis of marketing and other factors. It is possible to get accurate estimates of gross margins (profits) for manufacturing plants with several major factors incorporated into a linear regression equation.

The much-publicized General Electric SBU (Strategic Business Units) approach to allocation among business opportunities utilizes regression equations for estimating future profitability for each business. This approach takes into account such factors as market share, annual growth of the business, and return on sales for the total industry. This work has been extended by the Marketing Science Institute in a project called PIMS (Profit Impact of Market Share), where several industrial corporations are underwriting the project and supplying data for relevant businesses so that the coefficients of the regression equations can be estimated.

As suggested in the steps for performing regression analysis, the data should first be deseasonalized and often have the trends removed before establishing regression equations and estimating the accuracy of the relationships.

This is true for the sales of most companies when related to the GNP or FRB indices. In Figure 11.2 the left-hand graph is for the sales of a

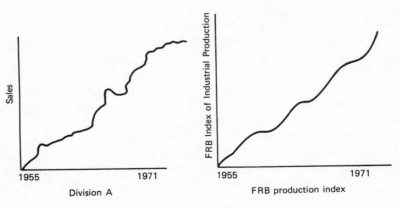

Figure 11.2. Graphs of sales and the FRB index.

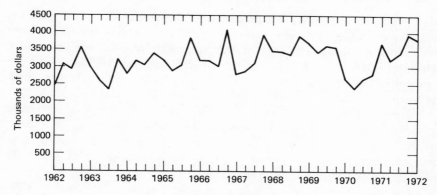

Figure 11.3.   Quarterly sales of the Widget Company.

business division within a company and the right-hand graph is for the Federal Reserve Board Index of Industrial Production.

If the forecaster were to perform a regression analysis relating the sales of Division A to the FRB production index, he would no doubt get a very good regression relationship. He would find that about 95% of the variation in the sales of Division A would be explained by the FRB index. However, when short-term sales forecasts are obtained from this relationship, the forecaster would be very disappointed in its performance.

Closer observation of these plots would show that the good relationship resulted because both time series happen to have the same trend (upward) over the long term, but that there is very little relationship over the short term. Those trends may not be causally related and, if the trends were removed from the time series before the regressions were performed, the 95% explained variation might drop to about 25%.

A very interesting and instructive example of the actual procedure in building a forecasting model via regression analysis is illustrated by Stephen J. Browne and Dennis O'Brien of Data Resources, Inc.[42] Figure 11.3 shows the quarterly sales (in units) by the Widget Company (actual name withheld for proprietary reasons) which is to be forecasted. Widgets are sold chiefly to the transportation and construction industries, and also are an important item in inventories.

The first step was to deseasonalize the sales in order to avoid spurious relationships that might arise from seasonal movements in sales with the

[42] Data Resources, Inc., Lexington, Massachusetts, presented this example at The Institute of Management Sciences Conference in November 1972 in a paper titled "Product Line Forecasting and Planning."

trend-cycle movement of the independent variables. When Widget's de-seasonalized unit sales were related to the FRB production index for the transportation industry, 54% of the variation in sales was explained. Housing starts were then added to the equation, further increasing the percent of variation in sales explained to 72%. When the change in inventories was also added, 77% of the variation was explained.

Figure 11.4 shows how well the sales predicted from the regression equation compared with the deseasonalized widget unit sales. In looking at this exhibit, we see that before the predicting equation could be considered adequate for short-term planning purposes, some additional missing variables would have to be found.

Note that the three variables in the equation up to this point—FRB transportation index, housing starts, and change in inventories—are general economic variables; none reflects factors such as pricing or advertising and promotion, over which management has control.

When relative prices, defined as $100 \times$ (company price of widgets/industry price), were lagged one quarter (i.e., sales at time t were related to relative prices at time t-1) they explained 17% of the *unexplained* variation. Likewise, when promotional activity was regressed against the predicting error of the original regression equation, it explained 65% of this so-called unexplained variation.

Lastly, since there was a strike in the automotive industry, to which widgets are sold, a dummy variable was created to estimate the effect of the strike on widget sales. For the four quarters of 1964 and 1970, the dummy was assigned negative values, -0.6 in 1964 and -1.0 in 1970, with their sizes indicative of the relative strength of the two strikes.

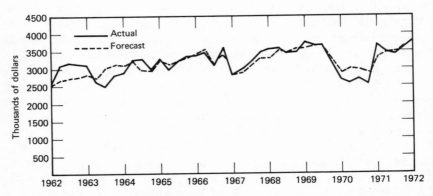

Figure 11.4. Actual deseasonalized sales for Widget Company versus predicted sales (derived from equation with three economic variables).

Also, positive values were assigned to the dummy in the two quarters following a strike, because of increased sales caused by postponed auto production (+0.3 in 1965, +0.5 in 1971, first and second quarters).

Figures 11.5 and 11.6 show how well the regression equation predicted deseasonalized sales of widgets without and with the strike dummy variables in the equation, respectively. The final equation was:

Deseasonalized Sales
of widgets (in units) =   3568.07 + 1555.25 (FRB Transportation Production Index) + 1041.40 (previous quarter's housing starts) + 45.80 (change in inventories) − 45.57 (relative price) + 2975.12 (advertising) + 410.23 (strike dummy)

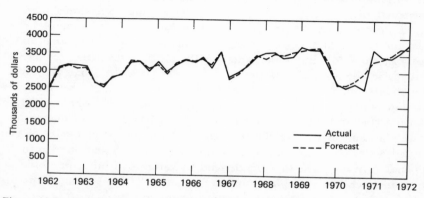

Figure 11.5.   Widget sales when relative price and advertising are included.

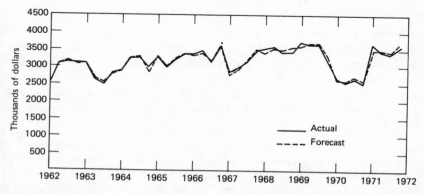

Figure 11.6.   Widget sales when economic factors, marketing factors, and strikes are included.

This equation explains 98% of the variation in deseasonalized widget sales. All of the variables are significant statistically. The coefficients are a measure of how a change in each variable will affect sales. For example, if the FRB transportation index increased by 0.1, widget sales would increase by 156 units. If the relative price increased from 80 to 81%, the company would lose 45.6 units of sale (note the negative sign).

The point of this example is that much forethought is put into a regression. The computer does not select the variables to be entered in a regression equation, the analyst does. The variables selected must be rational and causal in explaining the mechanics of the system to be forecasted.

Although it was possible in the preceding example to include all of the variables in one equation, it often happens that the system to be forecasted is too complex to be represented by one regression equation, and a more comprehensive approach must be taken. For example, consider the United States economy, with its many sectors, the United States steel or automobile industries, and the TV pipeline described earlier.

In these situations, the systems can be described by what are called econometric models.[43] These models consist of many interdependent regression equations. For example, in the flow chart of the TV pipeline shown earlier in Figure 2.2, each arrow is described by one or more equations; the same is true in the flow chart of the Wharton model of the United States economy shown in Figure 11.7. These equations are interdependent in the sense that the dependent variable of one equation may be an independent variable in another equation of the system. (This situation causes many statistical equation-estimation problems.)

Econometric Models

These models are now gaining increasing acceptance, both in specialized forecasting within a company and in large-scale national economic forecasting for projecting a large number of economic factors, which can then be used as inputs to the regression equation described in the preceding section. This trend has only taken place in recent years; as early as 1961, econometric models were viewed with apprehension and scepticism.[44]

[43] A much more extensive description of how economic data bases and the methodology for developing economic models can be applied is given by Otto Eckstein and Donald L. McLagan in "National Economic Models Help Business to Focus on the Future," *Computer Decisions*, October 1971.

[44] Edward G. Bennion, "Econometrics for Management," *Harvard Business Review*, March-April 1961, for a discussion of why econometrics were not experiencing widespread use at that time.

Final demand – Sector output – Employment – Unemployment

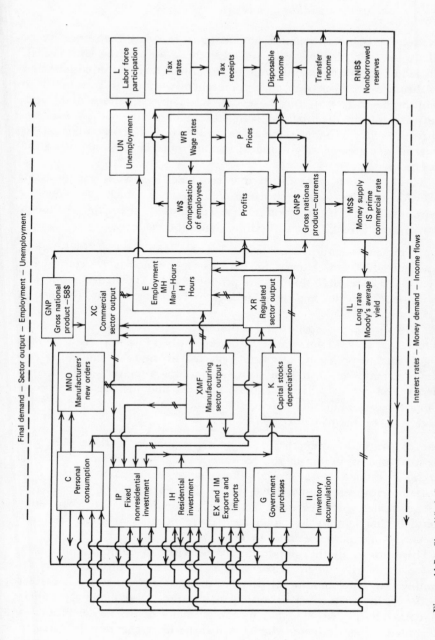

Interest rates – Money demand – Income flows

Figure 11.7. Simplified flow chart of the Wharton Mark III quarterly econometric model.

213

National econometric models have been in existence for several years. Perhaps the best known is Wharton's Economic Forecasting Unit (EFU). This model incorporates economic theory into a series of equations and uses historical information and comprehensive statistical routines to establish the coefficients for the equations. Their equations and coefficients are continually updated with current data and with new or recently expanded economic theory (e.g., Wharton recently updated its model to give greater weight and to include more factors relating to the monetary sector).

However, some people feel that econometric models cannot accurately forecast the economy because of the way in which the economic environment and its functioning are continually changing. Although their concern is real, these two points should be made.

1. Tracking techniques are employed to identify trends in relationships and significant changes; for this reason the models are continually updated. Also, research findings are producing new knowledge about how the economy operates, and these findings are incorporated into the models as they occur.

2. Because most social and economic systems have considerable momentum, they do not change instantaneously. (The impact of changes in government policy are often not reflected in the GNP and other economic measures until at least six to 12 months after they are put into effect.) The gradual changes can be detected and included in the economic forecasts. For this reason, the models can be quite accurate for projections of one to two years.

One of the main strengths of econometric models is their ability to identify turning points in the economy. They have varying degrees of success in estimating the overall effects, once turning points have been signaled. However, studies have shown that, for the long term, econometric models produce more accurate economic forecasts than other methods that employ less sophisticated quantitative methods and rely primarily on experience and judgment.

This leads to another important characteristic of economic forecasting and econometric models in particular. The accuracy ultimately lies (assuming the understanding of the way the economy functions is correct) in the ability to forecast or anticipate the fiscal and monetary policies that provide the basis for making the estimates of the model inputs (or judgmental-quantitative methods), which therefore generate the forecasts.

Most economic forecasters rely heavily on contacts with governmental officials and other knowledgeable people throughout the world to supply the necessary information for generating accurate economic forecasts. Because of the dependence of fiscal and monetary policy on these assumptions, the econometric model provides a vehicle for rapidly assessing the effects on the economy of errors or incorrect assumptions about these exogenous variables (i.e., factors, such as fiscal and monetary policy, that are extraneous to the accurate workings of the economic system but have a significant effect on it).

Through time-sharing computers, or by having economic forecasts for several sets of assumptions, the industrial economist can perform these evaluations himself. And, if he has established relationships between his company's sales and the economy, he will be able to estimate the effects or sensitivity of corporate performance to different sets of assumptions about government policy.

Wharton's Mark III Version. The overall detail of an econometric model can be seen in Figure 11.7, which is a flow chart of the Mark III version of the Wharton econometric model. This simplified flow chart depicts the main interactions in the Mark III model. Most of the lines connecting boxes on the flow chart represent current period (simultaneous) flows. When one sector affects another with a significant lag, the connecting line is broken with two slashes.

The boxes in the first column of the flow chart are the final demand values that help to determine manufacturer's new orders, capital stocks, and sector outputs. New orders also enter directly into the determination of sector outputs and indirectly affect the values for the nonmanufacturing outputs and capital stocks.

Given capital stocks and sector outputs, labor requirements can be obtained. From the labor requirements and (exogenous) labor force, we can obtain unemployment. Next, taking unemployment as a measure of conditions in labor markets, we can obtain wage rates and the wage bill. With these, we can determine the prices of goods, which in turn enables us to solve the identity for gross national product in current prices. This together with employee compensation determines profit-type income (PROF). Once we know the income items, we can solve for government tax receipts and personal disposable income.

As in most macro models, money supply and short-term interest rates are determined by supply and demand, with GNP in current prices being the most important factor affecting demand. Short-term interest rates determine the long-term rates with a lag, and these rates together with prices feed back into the demand equations for personal consumption, fixed nonresidential investment, and residential investment. Note the arrows feeding into the inventory accumulation box. In the Mark III model, inventory change is determined as the difference between inflow (represented by manufacturing production) and outflow (represented by the demand items).

There is actually a considerable amount of detail in the current model, with more than 100 economic factors being forecast two years into the future through the simultaneous solution of 250 regression equations. An even more extensive model has been developed by Data Resources, whose econometric model has 600 complicated, interdependent equations. Both the Data Resources and Wharton models are commercially available, as are several others, on time-sharing computers, along with data banks that include several thousand economic time series.

Models for Specific Businesses.   The 1969-1970 economic situation made many companies aware of the need to do (or have available) economic forecasting and to establish relationships between their sales and the economy. As in the earlier example, it is sometimes possible to get relatively good regression equations for company sales as a function of economic factors. However, this has not normally been our experience; we have found it necessary to develop econometric models for specific businesses, incorporating the approach described earlier for doing this.

As indicated, the first step should be to identify the factors that are most likely to affect the dependent variable (sales). Michael Evans, who directs the Chase Econometrics activity, states that some of the relationships between businesses and specific economic factors are:

Automobiles:	Disposable income, relative price, unemployment, stock of autos, and credit.
Other Durables:	Disposable income, stock of durables, and consumer attitude.
Nondurables and Services:	Disposable income, consumption of nondurables and services (this reflects attitude) in previous time periods.

One of the major problems in developing an econometric model for forecasting sales for a business within a corporation is the difficulty in obtaining the required data. Although time series for many economic factors can be obtained through the government or any of several economic consulting groups that offer such services on time-sharing facilities, there are other types of needed data, such as household penetration for the product line, total product-class sales over time (e.g., housewares), and new versus replacement sales.

Unless there are industry data services, these types of information must be obtained through market research. (It is possible to omit such factors from the econometric model, but to do so will reduce the accuracy of the results.)

While it is difficult to describe an econometric model without showing some of the equations of the model, the following examples will give the reader an idea of the need and use of the model, its content, and how to go about developing it.

During the rapid-growth state of color TV, we recognized that economic conditions would probably affect the sales rate significantly. However, the macroanalyses of black-and-white TV data we made in 1965 for the recessions in the late 1940s and early 1950s did not show any substantial economic effects at all; hence we did not have sufficient data to establish good econometric relationships for a color-TV model. (A later investigation did establish that definite losses in color-TV sales in 1967 were due to economic conditions.)

In 1969, Corning decided that a better method than the X-II was definitely needed to predict turning points in retail sales for color TV six to 24 months into the future. Statistical methods and salesmen's estimates cannot spot these turning points far enough in advance to assist decision making; for example, a production manager should have three to six months' warning of such changes if he is to maintain a stable work force.

Adequate data seemed to be available to build an econometric model, and we therefore began analyses to develop such a model for both black-and-white and color-TV sales. Our knowledge of seasonals, trends, and growth for these products formed a natural base for constructing the equations of the models.

Extensive discussions with personnel experienced in the TV business produced the initial framework for the model. This information was incorporated schematically into the system flow chart shown in Figure 2.2, and led next to the determination of what parts of the system would require separate equations (as indicated by the arrows). Economic research had established some relationships in other product areas that were applicable to the TV business, such as the relationship that sales to new owners of a product in the next year are proportional to the amount of stock at the beginning of the year and the difference between the amount of stock at the beginning of the year and the amount of the product the consumer desires to have.

We found that the ultimate penetration level of color TV was a function of the number of households, the hours of color telecasting, and the ratio of prices of TV sets to per capital disposable income. Economic factors that affect penetration (the rate at which the saturation level is being approached) are measures of short-term moves in the economy, such as long-term interest rates (lagged three quarters) and consumption of durables.

We derived separate equations for new sales and replacement sales, with replacement sales dependent on mortality curves as well as some of the factors given above. The total TV econometric model consisted of 15 equations, which were solved simultaneously to obtain forecasts. (Our original formulation of the system would have required 30 equations, but because of the lack of data for several parts of the pipeline, we were forced to reduce the total model to the 15 equations.)

The equations were first established from hypothesized relationships and then statistical methods (primarily regression analyses) were used to determine the coefficients in the equations. Since some of the hypothesized relationships were dynamic, we had to revise the model several times.

Remember that, when we began building this econometric model, color television had not yet reached the steady-state part of its life cycle. Hence revisions to the model were required as the product matured. This is typical of many new products; their sales pattern appears to be somewhat insensitive to the economy during the pre–steady state, but the sensitivity increases in the later stages.

We obtained the economic inputs for the model primarily from information generated by the Wharton Econometric Model, but we also utilized other sources.

Using data extending to 1968, the model did reasonably well in predicting the downturn in the fourth quarter of 1969 and, when 1969 data were also incorporated into the model, it accurately estimated the magnitude of the drop in the first two quarters of 1970. Because of lead-lag relationships and the ready availability of economic forecasts for the factors in the model, the effects of the economy on sales can be estimated as far as two years into the future.

FTC Model-Building Approach. The Federal Trade Commission is using the econometric approach in a quite different way to determine how to set priorities for their lawyers to get the best results from a given enforcement budget. The FTC's problem is to determine, from a backlog of cases, which ones to prosecute, taking into account the costs and benefits of going after a particular company or industry.

The FTC economists have gathered 24 key statistical measures to pinpoint the two FTC concerns of consumer protection and antitrust, with the guides drawing mainly on material collected by other government agencies. Here are the 24 measures.

- Total industry sales
- Growth in sales
- Projected growth
- Profit margins
- Price trends
- Consumer demographics (Who buys the product?)
- Consumer credit outstanding for the products
- Consumer complaints
- Accidents caused by products
- Advertising expenditures
- Research expenditures
- Capital needed for a new plant
- Product differentiation
- Diversification of major producers
- Concentration ratio
- Concentration trends
- Merger activity
- Amount of foreign competition

Here is how *Business Week* has described the way in which the FTC uses these measures.

The current model is an industry-by-industry computation of what economist Paul A. Samuelson calls the "deadweight monopoly loss." A theoretical demand curve would show that the lower the price of a product, the more it will sell. Economists believe that in any industry with relatively few producers, output will be priced at the level where total profits are the greatest; at a lower price, more would be sold but total return would be less.

The difference between the actual output and the amount that would be produced if the goods were sold at cost is lost to society, although a good bit of it shows up as profit for the producers. But some of it "vanishes into thin air," as University of Michigan economist Frederic M. Scherer puts it. It is "captured by neither consumers nor monopolistic producers."

Long is now trying to calculate this loss for all industries, using data on total industry size, concentration, and rates of return, plus a fixed assumption about consumer response to changes in price. He hopes to come up with a matrix ranking all of them by the dollar benefit to society of cutting down the current rate of concentration and of preventing further concentration.

Those two rankings, however, are only the beginning of the FTC project. The harder part is to add in the other measures to provide a reading on what the future would look like with and without enforcement. It is here that such concepts as "barriers to entry" and growth rates come into play.

The third step, and the most subjective of all, is defined by chief economist Mann as "what it's going to cost to win the case." This input will come from the lawyers, not the economists, and will measure not only the man-hours usually spent on a given case but the importance of victory as a precedent setter. The breakup of General Motors Corp., for example, might have the greatest impact on society; but the lawyers might advise first trying to disband the biggest company in a smaller industry. Their reasoning could be that the courts, then under less social and political pressure, might be quicker to accept a new legal theory.[45]

The FTC approach, while different from that taken by the economists who have developed the models described earlier, utilizes the basic concepts of econometric model building.

Econometric and I-O Combination

In the past few years, considerable effort has been expended in combining the input-output technique and econometric models. Input-output tables are first derived from historical data and, unfortunately, are at best several years behind current conditions by the time they are compiled. They basically show product flow from one industry to another and to the consumer.

The United States government is in the process of developing methods for updating the tables to make them more current. However, since several historical I-O tables are now available, there is a foundation for forecasting what future I-O tables will look like—that is, how the flows from one industry to another will change, as well as the total outputs. The research groups making I-O projections rely on statistical techniques and special information which might indicate that past trends will change significantly.

Econometric models produce accurate results for approximately two years into the future, but the accuracy decreases significantly after that time because of (a) the difficulty of forecasting the exogenous variables and (b) the possibility of changes in the functional relationships of the environment. While the economic factors and type of aggregation in econometric models differ from the I-O tables, it is possible to group the

[45] "The FTC Builds A Model Informer," *Business Week*, March 11, 1972, p. 94.

economic factors and I-O industry classifications at higher levels of aggregation to make them compatible.

In this way, the econometric models provide additional data points for the I-O tables so that the longer-term I-O projections might be more accurate. Conversely, the I-O tables provide longer-term inputs for the econometric models so that they can produce economic forecasts of five years or more duration. In short, they give long-term stability to econometric models.

Input-output can be classified as a causal model only in the sense that relationships between industries are expressed in the model and "causal information" about future actions within industries are incorporated into the statistical projections. Otherwise, I-O is more properly considered a statistical technique that has its primary value in tracking and warning, providing signals of industry growth, and suggesting future market opportunities.

When the more detailed data used to compile I-O tables are utilized to obtain lower-level I-O tables in which intra-industry flows are computed, the results can serve as inputs for causal models. However, such efforts are in the early developmental stages, and are more of a technique of the future, as we shall discuss in Chapter 15. The number of industry classifications must increase, and the extrapolation techniques must be improved before I-O will experience widespread applications.

Simulation Models

Because of the increasing understanding of marketing dynamics and the progressive sophistication of the decision-making process, simulation models are now being applied extensively in different areas. The precise definition of a simulation model varies widely among analysts, although most will agree that, as the name implies, it simulates what actually will happen under a given set of assumptions, taking into account the alternative choices or events that can occur within the system and incorporating interrelationships among many factors.

Marketing simulation accounts for a large portion of simulation forecasting models, where they are used to forecast what will happen under varying sets of conditions (e.g. strategies, competitive actions, and consumer trends). Ronald Frank and Paul Green define a simulation model as a representation of some real system or operation (such as the market for a given product) that is sufficiently realistic in its structure and content to be used (a) to determine the effects on the system of a complex set of input conditions, or (b) to make predictions about the phenomenon under study for eventual test outside the simulation.[46]

The simulation model frequently requires the integration of findings from different experimental and nonexperimental studies. One of the main advantages of a simulation model is that it can make maximum use of most computer programming languages (in fact, there are special simulation languages—for example, GPSS and Simscript) in creating models of real systems with quite complicated assumption structures.

Advantages and Disadvantages. H. J. Claycomp and Arnold E. Amstutz have succinctly summarized four advantages of simulation models.[47]

1. The simulation process can be used to explore the implications of management's perceptions about the external environment. Executives, salesmen, agency personnel, researchers, and other members of a company's marketing team can pool their intuitive resources and readily available market data in order to come up with a series of statements about the behavior of consumers, middlemen, and competitors, and the effect of specific marketing actions.

Researchers can translate these statements into mathematical and/or logical analogues, and put them together in the form of a simulation. If the process is done well, the output of the simulation has some claim to representing the implications of the perceptual model inputs. Aberrant results may be traced to errors in the interpretation of manager's statements or, more significantly, to error or inconsistencies in the original formulations themselves.

2. Simulations can be used to integrate and systematize large quantities of information obtained from past market research studies and secondary sources. A model helps to place formerly isolated pieces of data in perspective and often increases the net amount of information that can be obtained from them.

3. A simulation model which has been accepted as a reasonable representation of the real world can be used to guide future research activities. Given confidence in the overall structure of the simulation, the researcher can perform sensitivity analyses with respect to specific parameters or component characteristics.

In addition to gaining knowledge about the system's performance characteristics, these tests help to indicate what kinds of additional empirical or theoretical research will have the greatest impact upon the overall accuracy of the model. Research can then be concentrated in areas where potential results are known to be important.

4. Once a market simulation model has been validated to the satisfaction of both research and management personnel, artificial experimentation can be used to derive forecasts of sales levels, market penetration rates, profits, or other

[46] Ronald Frank and Paul Green, *Quantitative Methods in Marketing,* (Englewood Cliffs, N.J.: Prentice-Hall, Inc. 1967).

[47] *Ibid.,* pp. 89.

criterion variables conditional upon alternative specifications of the elements of the company's marketing mix. As a kind of synthetic test market, the model can be used to screen alternative strategies without incurring the risk or expense of experimentation in the real world.

While some experimentation in the real world may always be desirable to settle crucial policy questions and maintain a continuous check on the validity of the simulation, the ability to screen a large number of test candidates through artificial experimentation is likely to produce both substantial savings and better candidates for experimentation in the real environment.

Pitted against these advantages are four actual and potential disadvantages.

1. Computer simulation is expensive. The combination of methodological and substantive skills required is costly to create, the amount of computer time required can be substantial, and the model may require the conducting of expensive studies to generate raw data.

2. In computer systems, design problems posed by a simulation can be extremely complex. Seemingly trivial differences in the organization of data files and the order in which computations are performed can make the difference between an efficient simulation system and an impractical one.

3. Data-input procedures must be designed with considerable care so that they will not subsequently inhibit the forecaster's ability to use the model for experimental purposes.

4. It is often difficult to develop adequate tests of the validity of the overall simulation model or its components.

Concrete Applications. The following examples present a good cross section of the applications of simulation models.

At Xerox Corporation, simulation has been utilized in many ways. Revenue forecasting is accomplished by (1) forecasting (by a combination of qualitative and quantitative methods) how equipment populations, copy volumes, customer trade-ups and trade-downs, and the like will change, and (2) incorporating these forecasts, along with, for example, equipment populations, pricing plans, and trade matrices, into a simulation model. This simulation model then projects the implications of the forecasts.

A simulation model of tech rep servicing of equipment in the field forecasts the service level (percent of jobs completed within a given time) for different levels of staffing and scheduling rules for the tech reps. Other Xerox simulation models have been developed for long-range planning and for studying manufacturing operations.

One of the most elaborate simulations that has been published to date was developed by Claycamp and Amstutz, and is described as follows by Frank and Green.

The objective of the simulation was to develop a synthetic test market of the prescription-drug field in sufficient detail to enable management to test the effects of alternative marketing strategies without having to invest the time and expense required to conduct comparable studies in its real environment. Management was primarily interested in using the model to:

1. Evaluate the effectiveness of promotional media.
2. Evaluate the effectiveness of the sales force (detail men).
3. Test alternative policies and strategies for marketing particular products to a given market segment.
4. Evaluate the probable success of new products at an early stage of market development.
5. Assess the validity of management's understanding of the dynamics of the prescription-drug marketing system.

It is a forecasting simulation model in the sense that it forecasts what the consequences of future conditions and strategies will be, and can be used both to examine such combinations and to then make forecasts from the chosen strategy and most likely conditions.

Figure 11.8 presents the macro specification for the prescription drug market. This chart presents the flow of product (P), information (I), and others (O) between the various parties represented in the simulation. Though competing firms are not reported in Figure 11.8, they are considered in detail in the actual simulation. To illustrate the logic of the diagram, we shall trace the product flow. Starting in the upper left corner, the product flows from the company to wholesalers and doctors. From the wholesalers it can go to their detail men, doctors, pharmacies, and hospitals, and from each of these parties (with the exception of detail men) to patients.

Based on this configuration of parties, the actual simulation consists of a population of doctors, each of whom is represented by a "file," a magnetic tape that includes such information as his specialization, geographic region, patient load, the probability that he will receive and be exposed to information from various media and companies, as well as the seasonal distribution of each "indication" (e.g., polio or mumps) of interest, etc.

One doctor's behavior is simulated at a time, in the manner described briefly in the following paragraphs. Once the last doctor has been processed, a summary report is written which provides measures of such things as drug usage by company and brand that resulted from the particular configuration of inputs (detail men's activity, advertising, etc.) for each company as well as the configuration of symptoms that occurred during the time period.

DOCTOR FILE INPUT. Each simulated doctor is described by the content of a doctor file record. Doctor files are recorded on tape sequentially by geographic

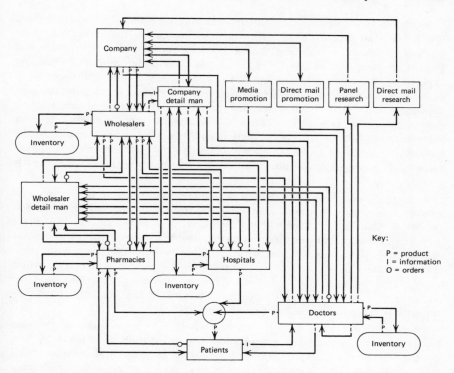

Figure 11.8. Example of macro specifications. (Redrawn from H. J. Claycamp and Arnold E. Amstutz, "Simulation Techniques in the Analysis of Marketing Strategy," a paper presented at Purdue University, July 1966, at a symposium on applications of the sciences in marketing.)

region. A single doctor file is held in (the computer's) core at a given point in time. After simulating the doctor's activity for a specified number of weeks, the file is updated to reflect his experience and written on tape. A new doctor is then read into core, and the procedure is repeated.

THE TIME LOOP. The system is structured so that time is moved past each doctor in turn. This organization of the system is necessitated by the large size of the doctor file record which makes it impractical to move doctors in and out of core or to maintain more than one doctor in core at a given point in time.

During most simulation runs, the time period considered is one simulated year. The time step is one week and the time index (IT) proceeds sequentially from 1 through 52. Events occurring during a particular week are identified by a monotonic data code which, during processing of the simulation, is referenced to the time index (IT).

DOCTOR RESPONSE TO MEDIA PROMOTION.   During each week in simulated time, the publication frequency of each relevant journal is tested to determine whether it is published during the week under consideration. If a particular journal appears, the probability of the doctor then under consideration being exposed to that journal is developed. If, on the basis of this probability it is determined that the doctor will be exposed to the journal, each advertisement appearing in an advertisement schedule table for that journal is examined to determine whether or not the doctor will be exposed to, and assimilate, any new information. When an advertisement is assimilated, the doctor's response to the message is established and his memory updated to take account of information content. This process is continued for all media, messages, and doctors at each point in time.

DIRECT MAIL RESPONSE.   The handling of direct mail response is structured in a manner analogous to media promotion. During each simulated week, a comparison is made to determine whether any direct mail pieces appear. If a direct mail piece is being sent during the week in question, exposure probabilities are developed to determine whether or not the particular doctor then being considered will be exposed to the specified mailing. If exposure occurs, assimilation probabilities are generated and, if on the basis of these probabilities it is determined that the doctor will assimilate portions of the communication, his response is determined and his memory updated.

RESPONSE TO SALESMAN DETAIL.   In developing a representation of the doctor's response to salesman communication, the probability of exposure is first determined on the basis of parameter values in the doctor file record which establish the probability that the doctor will receive a call from a salesman representing any one of the relevant companies. If the doctor is exposed to a salesman from a particular company, the schedule of details (sales messages for a specific drug) presented by that salesman is examined to determine which details are being presented to doctors of the indicated specialty during the week under consideration. If a particular detail is presented and assimilation occurs, the doctor memory is updated. As in the case of all other communication response loops, this procedure continues until all sales messages have been considered.

RESPONSE TO CONVENTION ACTIVITY.   Exposure to presentations at a convention is based on a convention schedule which specifies the probability of a doctor of a particular specialty and residence attending a convention held at a particular time. In keeping with the previously established procedure, the convention schedule is examined once each simulated week to determine whether or not a convention is being held. If a convention is being held, the probability of the doctor then in core attending that convention is determined and, if the doctor is found to attend the convention, procedures similar to those outlined above are used to determine exposure and assimilation of relevant information.

RESPONSE TO WORD-OF-MOUTH COMMUNICATION.   Within the structure of the simulation, messages generated by doctors in a particular region are accumulated along with descriptors of the generating doctor in a table of word-of-mouth messages. Thus, when a particular doctor is in core, messages generated at various points in time by doctors preceding him are available in the word-of-mouth table. This table is referenced in a manner analogous to the schedule and content table discussed for other media. The probability of interaction between the doctor in core and the message-generating doctor who preceded him is established. If the doctor is exposed to the word-of-mouth communication, the probability of assimilation is developed in a manner analogous to other communication functions and the doctor's memory is updated to reflect the word-of-mouth interaction.

TREATMENT OF PATIENTS. The simulated doctor is exposed to patients from an artificial patient population which is supplied as an input to the simulation. An average patient load parameter in each doctor file record determines how many patients will be treated in a given week. In treating a patient the simulated doctor determines what drug or drugs, if any, will be prescribed for the exhibited indication (s) of the patient.

Once treatment has been decided upon the probability that it will achieve desired results is established on the basis of clinical data. If it is determined that the treatment undertaken will not prove effective within a specified period of time, the patient is maintained in a backlog of patients who will return to the doctor at some time in the future. If the outcome of treatment is successful, the patient is for all practical purposes dropped from the model. In either instance, the trial and outcome (including possible side effects) of a particular treatment is noted.

After the first simulated week the doctor has two sources of patients: (1) patients in the population from which his original patient group was drawn; and (2) patients who require continuing treatment. During subsequent time periods the doctor's first source of patients is the returning patient file. After all patients previously treated and scheduled to return have been treated, the doctor considers new patients from the outside population.

GENERATION OF WORD-OF-MOUTH COMMUNICATION. As the doctor considers various drugs in context of the treatment during the simulated week, a record of his attitude toward his experiences is maintained. Following completion of the treatment cycle for a particular simulated week, this record is examined to determine whether the doctor will generate word-of-mouth communication regarding some aspect of his recent treatment experience. If such word-of-mouth communication is generated, communication content is established, dated, and stored in the word-of-mouth communication file for later referencing by other doctors.

FORGETTING. At certain prescribed time intervals, the doctor's memory is examined to determine whether forgetting would have occurred during the lapsed time period. The memory record for each drug is examined and, if forgetting has occurred, the record is reduced.

TIME CYCLE COMBINATION. The basic process described above is repeated for each week in the simulated year for each doctor in the artificial population. Once the final week for a given doctor is completed, an activity report is generated and the doctor file record is updated to reflect his experiences during the simulated year. This record is then written on tape to serve as an input for simulation of future time periods.

Following completion of a given doctor record, another doctor record is read from the tape file and the process described is repeated. After all doctors have been considered for the specified period of simulated time, a final summary report is written and the simulation terminates.

Although this description provides an insight into the logical structure and flow of the drug-market simulation model, it nonetheless is extremely superficial. Extremely elaborate models of doctor behavior are required to make the total simulation perform in a reliable manner.[48]

When we used examples from TV sales earlier, the models were primarily concerned with forecasting consumer demand. In order to forecast demand on Corning Glass Works, we had to construct a simulation model that considered inventory changes at the various levels of the distribution system, the glass losses, imports and exports, and market share. Since each of these have a range of values, the forecast also had a range of values, in the form of a probability distribution.

Terry W. Rothermel has described a chlorine supply-demand model that shows the impact of the growth of all end-uses of each of the key products (chlorine, caustic soda, soda ash, and hydrochloric acid).[49] The supply-demand model and a price-forecasting model were incorporated into an overall forecasting model that also included investment, inventory, competition, and profit sectors.

An approach to simulation that utilizes a special computer simulation language called Dynamo has been developed by Jay W. Forrester of MIT. It has been widely publicized under the names "Industrial Dynamics" and "Urban Dynamics." It essentially assumes that all aspects or factors of a system are one or two types of variables, levels, and rates. Rate variables depend only on levels and level variables are changed only by rates. No rate depends on another rate and no level depends directly on another level—there has to be an intervening rate.[50]

[48] Ronald Frank and Paul Green, Quantitative Methods in Marketing, pp. 90–95. (Englewood Cliffs, N.J.: Prentice-Hall, Inc., 1967)

[49] "Market Simulation Makes a Science Out of Forecasting," Chemical Engineering, March 24, 1969, p. 157.

[50] This is explained more fully in Jay W. Forrester, Industrial Dynamics (Cambridge, Mass.: The MIT Press, 1961).

Forrester's approach has been applied in several areas, such as in studying social systems—for example, entire municipalities—to determine the effects of changes in policies and other strategies and in evaluating the implications on corporate performance of alternative organizational and functional structures. Again, while the main objective is to understand how the systems function and to determine the implications of changes, the simulation models are in fact used for forecasting.

Simulation expresses, in a complex network of relationships, the best understanding of a system, derived from experimental and nonexperimental research and the knowledge of experts functioning in that system. As in econometric models, simulation models must be finely tuned and continually revised to reflect the latest understanding of the system. They will provide both a method for evaluating the effects of change and for forecasting.

IN SUMMARY

Causal models are easily the most comprehensive of the forecasting techniques. They can be developed only when there are sufficient data and there has been enough analysis to understand why things happen the way they do. They not only provide accurate forecasts, but increase knowledge about the system under study so that those involved in decision making for the system will better understand the environment in which they are operating. Causal models are an important and almost essential method for functioning in an increasingly sophisticated environment.

Chapter XII

The Phasing-out Stage

In the early 1960s, Mattel was just a little California toy stock selling over the counter, with a history not too different from other toy manufacturers. Then, with the introduction of the Barbie doll, and later her friends, Ken, Francie, Christie, and Brad, Mattel became the glamour stock of the toy industry. The Hot Wheels racing car and other fast-selling product lines helped Mattel to maintain that position into 1971, when the bottom seemed to drop out. Sales for the Barbie line fell off considerably, and the Hot Wheels sales fell to $40 million for the car, as against $90 million the year before.

Mattel suddenly experienced a 70% drop in market price, producing a paper loss for its investors, many of them supposedly well-informed institutions, of over $500 million. Neither the investors, nor apparently Mattel, had been able to identify in sufficient time the entrance of its major product lines into the phasing-out stage.[51]

The analyst must be able to forecast not only when the rapid growth and steady-state stages are to be reached and how the sales levels will change during those stages of the product life cycle, but also when the product will leave the steady-state stage, begin the phasing-out stage, and ultimately leave the market. The phasing-out stage can extend over a long period of time (e.g., for major appliances) or it can be very short (e.g., for cereals, clothing, fad toys).

The decisions that are made can involve significant amounts of money, and they can also have an impact on future company growth, since it may be necessary to divert resources to new product development in order to

[51] See "Love Story," *Forbes,* September 15, 1972, p. 37.

meet long-range corporate objectives. Here are some of the decisions that must be made during the steady-state stage with respect to the phasing-out stage, and during the phasing-out stage itself.

- Should resources be expended to continue to develop the product and the market, or should the business employ a "milk-cow" strategy?
- What should the production quantities be and what inventory levels should be maintained?
- How can the production facilities be scheduled so that the excess facilities can be converted for manufacturing other products? Also, if facilities are leased, should the lease be renewed and for how long?
- How soon should personnel be transferred to other businesses?

REASONS FOR PHASING OUT

These and other decisions rely on accurate forecasts of the beginning of the phasing-out stage, how long it will last, and the sales rates throughout the entire final stage of the product life cycle. The technique that can best provide these forecasts depends on the reason for a product, technology, or the business phasing out. Consider these factors.

- A new product or technology has replaced or obsoleted existing ones.
- The market has become saturated, and there is little or no replacement (because of long life).
- The product life has increased over time, reducing overall demand.
- Legislation has made the product illegal, or it requires major modifications.
- There have been changes in consumer preference, either over a long period of time or shortly after introduction (a fad item).
- Competition or imports have reduced the available market so that sales are rapidly declining.

Examples for each of these types of phasing out are given in the remainder of this chapter, along with the techniques that are most suitable for forecasting when phasing out will occur and its extent.

Before doing so, however, we shall first discuss the application of statistical techniques in determining whether downward turns in the sales rate are actually an indication that the product is in the phasing-out stage, or if such a downward turn is a false signal. To interpret correctly the implications of a decline in the sales rate, the analyst must study historical patterns of the sales rate to learn if there has been any consistent cycling and what the causes of previous decreases in the sales rate have been. Such an analysis can be effectively accomplished by the Census Bureau X-11 technique described in Chapter 10, where the first difference or change in the sales rate is plotted over time.

Consider the example in Figure 12.1, where the trend-cycle (deseasonalized and smoothed data) for a time series for the sales of a component that is ultimately sold as a consumer product is shown, having been obtained from an X-11 analysis. At the present time (the latest data point) the sales trend is downward, and the indications are that the product has possibly entered its phasing-out stage.

Because of several levels in the distribution system between the component part and the end product (e.g., ophthalmic glass blanks that are made into prescription eye glasses), there is the possibility of cycling, particularly if there is some pattern of inventory adjustments that occur at regular intervals over time. Another reason for cycling might be that there is a repetitive pattern in the economy or some other factor that is related to sales of the product.

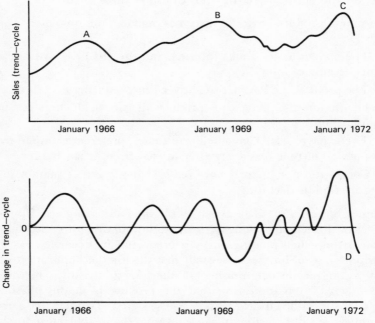

Figure 12.1.   Examples of the trend-cycle for a component part.

On studying the sales rate in Figure 12.1, we might conclude for points in time A, B, or C that the downward slope is a signal of the phasing-out stage. However, a closer examination of the data indicates a long-term upward trend, with a cycle of three years' duration. The deep decline of long-term duration between points B and C appears to show more than normal cycling; it could have been due to the recession and changes in field inventories (tracking the pipeline for component parts and consumer products that have multilevel distribution is critical at this stage). Although the change in the sales rate is negative at point D, it appears that this could be a result of a regular cycling, and there is not yet evidence that the decline will be a long-term one.

A similar situation occurred at Corning Glass Works for clear white ophthalmic sales. A long-term cycle was definitely spotted in the data through time-series analysis, and in mid-1972, there was a deep concern that there would be a significant long-term decrease in the sales rate because of the enthusiastic market reception of photochromic (Sunsensor™) lenses that turn dark in the sunlight or whenever they are exposed to ultraviolet rays.

Market surveys had indicated that photochromic sales did not and would not have a large effect on clear white lens sales, but the decline in clear lens sales, in absolute figures and in the trend-cycle, raised considerable doubt about the market findings. Shortly thereafter, the clear white lens sales turned upward and have remained strong since then.

While it was not possible to state positively that the clear lens had entered the phasing-out stage, there was also no evidence that clear white lens sales had then (mid-1972) resumed a growth situation. It was necessary to continue close tracking of sales for several months thereafter.

The trend-cycle, such as that shown in Figure 12.1, should be followed closely, and considered in the light of significant changes in the environment, where the impact of previous events can be measured and used as a basis for forecasting sales. Since tracking-and-warning techniques are an important part of forecasting, we shall discuss them more fully in Chapter 13. Statistical techniques should serve in a supplementary role to the techniques we will next describe. They indicate what can be done in forecasting for the phasing-out stage under varying sets of conditions (i.e., reasons for phasing out).

New Replacement Product or Technology

The primary methods for forecasting when introduction of a new product or technology will replace, render obsolete, or reduce the sales of existing products are technological forecasting and tracking of signals (e.g., comments at professional meetings, patent applications). Experts should first be queried about what products or technology are most likely to replace existing ones, and estimates should then be obtained for the most likely time and associated probabilities. If it is possible, the milestones or tasks (if any are required) necessary for the breakthrough should be identified and tracked. Here are four examples of this type of phasing out and the important events needed for them to occur.

1. Glass commercial lighting panels, replaced by acrylic panels. In this instance, the key event was the manufacturing process for the acrylic panels, where the costs had to be low enough to compete with glass.

2. Electronic mini or pocket calculators, replacing slide rules and mechanical calculators. Two things were necessary here: the development of low-cost integrated circuits and research involving disaggregation of the market to determine what portion of slide rules' and mechanical desk calculators' market would be affected by the electronic calculators.

3. Supermarkets and chain stores forcing out neighborhood grocery stores. No major technological inventions were needed—only public acceptance of this new form of shopping, the setup of distribution centers, and available financing.

4. Hybrid circuitry replacing tubed circuitry, which is in turn being replaced by solid state. Consider the history of the number used in color sets, as shown in Table 12.1.

The phasing out of resistors and capacitors by integrated circuits did not take place as forecasted by "experts" because of new electronic applications to absorb most of the production of integrated circuits and the types of markets (products) utilizing resistors and capacitors.

Table 12.1   Color-Television Sets Produced in the United States

Year	Number of Tubed	Number of Hybrid (Transistorized IF Functions)	All Solid-State	Total
1967	5040	500	50	5590
1968	3707	1700	150	5557
1969	2796	2400	300	5496
1970	1080	2965	260	4305
1971	900	4476	600	5976
1972	520	4470	2460	7450
1973	80	3970	4050	8100

According to *Business Week*, Magnavox made a decision that has since come back to haunt it.[52] While other television manufacturers were rushing to convert from electronic tubes to all-solid-state sets, Magnavox decided to move more gradually toward this objective. Management did not think the solid-state sets would catch on quickly with consumers, and also wanted to wait until a brighter picture tube was available in 1973 before making a full-scale switch to the new devices.

But to management's surprise, it found that consumers had been eagerly scrambling to buy 100% solid-state TV sets because of their greater reliability and ease of servicing. In 1972, the industry's output boomed to a record 8.8 million color sets (up 21.6% over 1971), and 8.2 million monochrome sets (up 7.8%).

Belatedly, Magnavox introduced a limited line of 25-inch consoles that were 100% solid-state. But it was too little and too late. While the competition was scoring solid gains with full lines of the new models, Magnavox's television sales—representing one-third of the company's total volume—were dragging; they fell to $226 million in 1972 (down 2.6% from 1971 and 36% below the 1968 peak).

To perk up earnings and regain lost market share, Magnavox introduced a full line of solid-state sets in May 1973, at a special showing for dealers in Las Vegas. The question is whether Magnavox will be able to make up for lost time.

Another article in the same issue of *Business Week* discussed the impact of radial tires on the United States tire companies' profits.[53] Figure 12.2 shows the impact of radial tires on the "Big Four" companies' sales and margins. The better mileage—40,000 miles for the radial, compared with 22,000 miles for the bias-belted and 17,000 miles for the cross-ply tire—along with higher prices for textile-belted radials (80% higher than the cross-ply and steel-belted radials, and 100% higher than the cross-ply) has helped the tire companies in this growth.

No technological breakthrough was needed (radial tires have been sold in Europe for years); the major question was the United States market's readiness to accept the product. Although the overall number of units sold has been reduced because of longer tire life, the proportionately higher selling price has enhanced the sales dollar.

The second type of phasing-out solution is a variation of the tire-life problem, where a market has become saturated and there is low mortality so that replacement sales will not offset the loss of new consumer sales.

[52] See "Magnavox Tries for a TV Comeback," *Business Week*, April 14, 1973, p. 49.
[53] See "Radials Put a Spin on Akron's Profits," *Business Week*, April 14, 1973, p. 66.

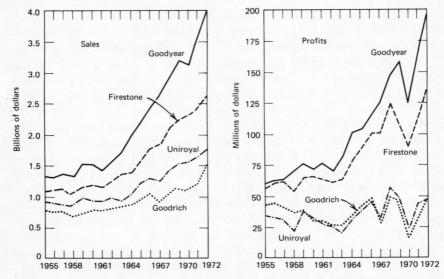

Figure 12.2. Sales and profits of Big Four rubber companies. (Data: Commerce Department.)

Saturated Market—Low Mortality

While product comparisons may have provided a basis for initial estimates of penetration levels, market research involving consumer psychology should follow these estimates to establish more positively what the penetration levels will be. The possibility of multiple ownership within a family must be considered. The likelihood of the product failing or of the consumer seeking to find a replacement for the product should it fail must also be taken into account.

Two examples of products that achieved rapid market penetration in early years and then had significant declines in sales are electric slicing knives and electric toothbrushes. The sales for these items started falling off in about the third or fourth year after introduction, as shown in Table 12.2. (Replacement sales have been quite low, suggesting that these were somewhat fad products.)

The use of market surveys can reveal which factors are most important in predicting repeat buying behavior when the original product needs replacement. Such surveys provide information about product utilization which, along with product design and experimental-life test data, should

Table 12.2 **Rapid Rise and Decline of Two Consumer Products (sales in million units)**

Year	Electric Toothbrush	Electric Slicing Knife
1963	2.2	0.0
1964	3.1	2.7
1965	3.3	5.9
1966	3.0	5.0
1967	2.6	3.8
1968	2.4	2.5
1969	2.5	2.6
1970	1.8	2.1
1971	1.3	2.1

yield enough data to estimate the time between replacement and therefore the replacement rate. The difference between the total sales and replacement sales provides an estimate of new-owner sales and its rate. An estimate of repeat purchases is especially important for nondurable goods, and market research techniques are extremely useful for forecasting their replacement sales.

Increased Product Life

Because of competitive factors, manufacturers may be forced to increase product life, which can substantially reduce the total available market, even though the total market utilizing a product is increasing. Mortality, however, is not always a function of life, but of changes in consumer attitudes and preferences (e.g., tableware, where the housewife may be bored with her dinnerware pattern).

The primary method here is data collection on product failure and statistical analysis to determine whether there have been any changes in product life (life curves such as the Weibull curve are of particular value). Tire life (new and replacement tires) and engine life (diesel and gasoline engines) depend not only on the product quality, but also on the way the product is used and maintained. Furthermore, economic factors (such as labor for rebuild) may cause changes in product life, which can be revealed by market research and statistical analysis.

Legislation Makes Product Illegal

Tracking of signals (e.g., public sentiment, legislative "issues," manufacturer influence on legislation) are the best means for predicting when legislation will drive a product from the marketplace. This is a "sudden" type of phasing out, and pipeline inventories should take into account the imminence of such action. Consider Phisohex® detergent soap, cyclamates, and thalomide—products that were under heavy criticism prior to actually being taken out of the market.

Changes in Consumer Preference

This type of phasing out is the most common and requires close tracking of signals and extensive market research. The phasing out can be long term, as in the case of trading stamps; or it may be short term, as illustrated by fad toys such as hoola-hoops and click-clacks, and by clothes, certain foods, and other items. Even within a product class, the life curves may not all be the same shape, nor have comparable lives.

Figure 12.3 shows how the product sales for some selected automobile makes have declined after generally reaching peak sales in the second or third year after introduction. In the case of consumer preferences, these sometimes run in cycles and may reverse over time. Consider the compact versus the large car, where the penetration of the compact reached a plateau after a very large initial sales impact.

Special events have affected the trading stamp penetration of food sales, as demonstrated in Figure 12.4. Customer games, which initially appeared to be a threat to trading stamps, have rapidly fallen after a brief surge. To predict the future distribution of stamps and use of games by supermarkets, it is necessary to: (1) understand the conditions that favored the adoption of these tools; (2) analyze the primary stages in the diffusion of stamps and games; and (3) interpret the present market and competitive environments that will have an important bearing on the future of these tools.

In an analysis of supermarkets, Fred C. Allvine studied hundreds of trade press reports, compiled a weekly time-series index of the food industry's use of customer games of chance, and interviewed 50 supermarket executives concerning their views on the future of trading stamps and games.[54]

[54] "The Future for Trading Stamps and Games," *Journal of Marketing*, January 1969, pp. 45–52.

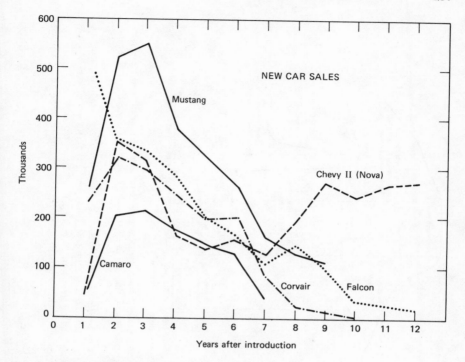

Figure 12.3. Product life curves for selected automobiles.

For the shorter-life products (e.g., cereals, clothes), the slope-characteristic method (described below) is particularly effective. Many of these products have life curves that are of the same family, and early sales will help establish the parameters that provide the basis for phasing-out estimates.

Competition or Imports Reduce Available Market

Tracking of critical events, legislation, and new competitor products is essential here. For color TV, the import duties and relative monetary exchange rates were the critical events. The sales data for black-and-white TV sales given in Table 12.3 show that imports cut severely into the total market up to 1971. The United States dollar devaluation caused this trend to level off in 1973. To understand the overall trends, it is important to disaggregate total sales into those sets larger than 13 inches

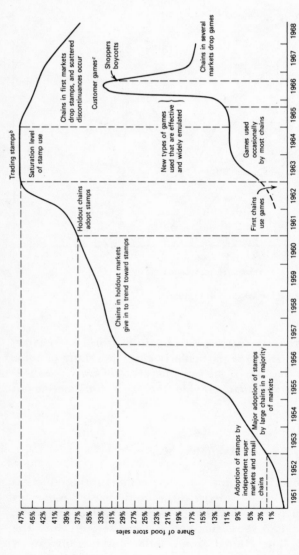

Figure 12.4. Share of food store sales by stamp-giving and game-using supermarket chains.[a]

[a] Food store sales include both sales of speciality food stores and grocery stores. Grocery store sales as a percent of food store sales were 80.9% in 1948, 86.5% in 1954, 89.1% in 1958, and 92.1% in 1963. Source. Bureau of the Census. *Census of Business, Retail Trade, Summary Statistics*, 1954, 1958, and 1963.

[b] National Commission on Food Marketing, *Organization and Competition in Food Retailing—Technical Study No. 7* (Washington, D.C.: U.S. Government Printing Office, June 1966), p. 439, through 1963. Data for 1964 to 1968 (first quarter) from a weekly time-series index maintained by the author of supermarket chains using trading stamps in 52 major United States markets.

[c] A weekly time-series index maintained by the author of supermarket chains using customer games of chance in 52 major United States markets.

Source: "The Future for Trading Stamps and Games," Fred C. Allvine.

diagonally and those sets below the 13-inch size, where the trend is to smaller sets, sales for which are dominated by imports.

Table 12.3 Black-and-White Television Sales to the Public

Year	United States Produced	United States Brand Imports	Foreign Brand Imports	Total
1967	4820	780	570	6170
1968	4680	770	1180	6630
1969	3840	1120	1860	6820
1970	3100	1350	2100	6550
1971	3300	1300	2550	7150

Textiles have had a similar problem, where imports have made increasing penetration into markets supplied by domestic products. Again, tariffs and monetary exchange rates are the important factors.

SLOPE-CHARACTERISTIC METHOD

This analytical technique pertains to saturation levels and hence is applicable to forecasting phasing out, once the parameters for the curve have been determined. The cumulative market penetration and total annual sales curves are shown in Figure 12.5. There are mathematical ways for estimating total penetration (saturation) from early sales, which will determine the annual sales.

The approach is very similar to technological forecasting, and requires good market research and knowledge of the market. The main hazard in using the slope-characteristic method is that, if the product has a long life cycle, many extraneous factors (e.g., the economy, market) may change quite dramatically, causing the saturation level and the growth rate to that level also to change.

The slope-characteristic method cannot adequately handle that type of problem. However, if enough data exist, the sales rate can be forecasted by regression analysis or econometric models via dynamic models in which the regression parameters themselves are made functions of the economy and competitive marketing variables.

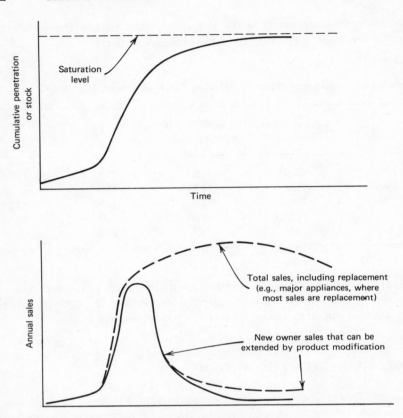

Figure 12.5.   Examples of slope-characteristic method.

IN SUMMARY

The most commonly used methods for forecasting for the phasing-out stage are market research and tracking of signals. Statistical techniques have some value; but, with the exception of the slope-characteristic method, which will at best generally identify the turning points as they occur, such techniques do not signal changes soon enough for effective decision making. The major decision at this stage is "if and when" to divert resources to other products. Since future growth is dependent on this decision, the expenditures for good forecasting can be easily justified.

Chapter XIII

Tracking and Warning

A current statute in the State of New York states that anyone who purports to be able to predict the future is subject to a fine of $250 and six months in jail.

We trust that by this time the reader has deduced that the forecaster does not purport to predict the future precisely, but to use the best techniques and information available to him in preparing his forecast. We have indicated that the objective of forecasting is to make the best use of the information available at that time to obtain estimates of future sales and profits, for example, and to indicate the accuracy of these estimates. The decision utilizing the forecast will take into account the measure of accuracy, which in some instances may be a relatively wide range about the forecast.

Furthermore, no forecast is likely to remain the same as when prepared earlier if three or more months have passed since the forecast was first made, because of economic factors, competitive factors, or internal delays. Forecasting in a systematic way forces a discipline and thus helps to improve decision making. This same discipline enables the analyst to do tracking and updating in the shortest possible time and in a more effective way.

As more information becomes available, it will be possible to reduce the range of error and to consider whether a new strategy or tactic should be followed in light of the revised forecast. For example, a decision might be made to build additional capacity, fully recognizing that there is a high probability that the additional capacity will not be needed, but that the trade-offs between potential loss of market share, the cost of additional capacity, and the effects on overall unit cost favor the economics of an expansion.

When the decision is dependent on an accurate forecast, tracking the assumptions, trends, and relationships that have been built into the forecast and making any required revisions can affect profitability as much or more than the initial forecast. Two of the major reasons for tracking are (1) to avoid severe mistakes from being made because of incorrect assumptions, and (2) to identify opportunities in sufficient time to capitalize on them.

Most of the techniques described earlier can be utilized for tracking and warning in much the same way that they are used for preparing forecasts, except that they may now incorporate new factors that had not previously been identified and included in the analysis. Since tracking and warning are to be performed at all stages of the product life cycle, it will therefore affect virtually all decisions made after those relating to the initial forecast.

We shall not attempt to list the decisions that might be affected by tracking and warning. In one sense, therefore, this chapter can be viewed as a summary or overview of the techniques described earlier. In some instances, we shall refer to examples given earlier. For convenience, we have split the tracking-and-warning techniques into two groups, qualitative and quantitative.

QUALITATIVE TRACKING TECHNIQUES

The three major types of qualitative tracking techniques are internal development signals, technological signals, and competitive signals. A qualitative signal is generally associated with some event occurring or not occurring, although it may involve a change in attitude. The signals usually relate to assumptions that have been made in preparing the forecast, and they may include the conditions (e.g., timing, sequence) under which the event occurs.

Internal Development Signals

These can best be tracked by the use of some event-timing-resources flow chart, such as the Tasks, Goals, Resources, Integration Program (TGRIP) described earlier. This is an effective method of coordinating information for tracking when an event takes place. Since information can be gathered routinely at less cost than if collected irregularly, TGRIP provides a basis for resource allocation to identify and accelerate certain tasks that are critical.

If events do not occur when planned, there should be a downward revision in previous forecasts. Revision is essential, since it is quite likely that there will be a slippage in timing, and possibly a loss of market share or a decrease in the total market. These results may be caused by an unanticipated delay in product development, building of a distribution system, development of the manufacturing process, ability to reduce price, and similar factors.

In the case of automobile emissions, the concession the government has made in delaying the requirement of meeting specific antipollution standards has not only changed the competitive situation for several component suppliers, but it has also enhanced the potential market share for companies working on developments that have been lagging technologically. In addition, the delay has favored the stratified charge engine, which may reduce the total revenue to be derived from antipollution devices.

Sales and profit forecasting are often dependent on the rate at which physical expansion can be accomplished. Computerized project-control systems help manage corporate physical expansion in several different industries. Consider the electric utility industry, for example, where the demand for electricity doubles every 10 years. The utility companies must provide the additional facilities needed to meet the demand while achieving new levels of operating efficiency.

In the case of Northern States Power (NSP), which serves Minnesota and three adjoining states, there are several thousand construction projects active at any given time.[55] NSP utilizes a computerized project-management system to standardize construction design for both labor and material. This system has increased project-designer productivity by 25%, while maximizing manpower, materials, and money resources. Project designers input details of proposed projects into the computer each day. The following morning the system provides them with cost estimates and comprehensive breakdowns of labor and material requirements, as well as showing exactly what materials are needed for each working crew and location.

The system furnishes management with both short- and long-range forecasts of construction requirements, thereby improving resource management. It schedules and tracks the progress of all active projects, originates accounting records, and generates exception reports when there will be delays or costs exceeding limits. Forecasts of revenues and profits are dependent on the completion dates and costs of each project.

[55] See *The Wall Street Journal*, March 29, 1973, p. 15.

Technological and Competitive Signals

These can usually be tracked without a formal system such as TGRIP or the one just described. Three of these techniques are (1) questionnaires and surveys, (2) telephone and personal interviews, and (3) indirect methods of deduction.

For example, on the one hand, the success of the self-cleaning oven has given the flat-top cooking supporters the confidence that the housewife is willing to pay premium prices for genuine improvements in appliances. On the other hand, a new product such as a windshield that provides better protection against lacerations may not penetrate the automotive market because the auto companies are placing a higher priority on other safety devices that are more effective in saving lives for the amount of money spent.

In the color-TV industry, in 1965, the major networks found they could not afford to ignore an audience that was growing so rapidly that it developed viewing tastes often at variance with what the ratings showed. An American Research Bureau (ARB) study revealed that color-set owners had a strong tendency to view color programs, even when a show on another channel was more popular with most black-and-white viewers.[56]

The ARB study showed that 51% of black-and-white TV viewers tuned in Jackie Gleason on Saturday nights. Mr. Magoo, a show on at the same time, but in color, was watched by only 25%. In contrast, in color-set homes, Mr. Magoo outdrew Gleason 45 to 39%.

Tied in with forecasts of color-set sales (based on signals such as total color programming hours), such findings provide the basis for forecasting viewing audiences and determining how advertising resources will be allocated.

The demand for CGW's Photogray®—a photochromic glass that darkens in sunlight—accelerated so rapidly in 1970 that the lens manufacturers (Corning's customers) began to believe the eyeglass wearers were purchasing Photogray instead of white crown and fix-tinted sunglasses. The lens manufacturers concluded that the demand for the latter would diminish as Photogray penetrated the ophthalmic market. The statistics of the shipments of sunglasses for the 1970-1971 gave further credence to the conclusion that standard glass demand was decreasing as photochromic increased.

However, after the first few months of 1972, the standard product lines returned to a historical upward trend for the remainder of the year. The

---

[56] See "TV Advertisers Rush to Color Commercials as Sales of Sets Soar," *The Wall Street Journal*, September 28, 1965, p. 1.

shipment rate quickly surpassed all previous sales records for the non-photochromic lens blanks. Three major factors in the marketplace, which had an impact on this trend reversal, were (1) an increase of the diameter of the blanks required by the lens manufacturers, (2) an increase in the thickness of the blanks to meet FDA ball-drop requirements, and (3) the expansion of the safety-lens market brought about by FDA and the occupational Safety and Health Act (OSHA) requirements.

It is extremely important in tracking and warning that we pay attention not only to the present data, but to the events taking place that could change their direction in the long term. If an effective tracking-and-warning system is developed for tracking the variables and events, the chances of a false alarm can be minimized.

Marketing Information Systems

These will help track numerical data as well as attitudes. Since marketing is fundamentally the effort expended to influence sales by changing stimulus conditions—such as the content and mix of advertisements, package prices, products, and type of media—the success of marketing is measured by the extent to which sales change in response to these stimuli.

However, the market researcher faces a dilemma; he normally cannot identify which stimulus is reponsible for a sales fluctuation. There is simply too much noise most of the time to permit the researcher to identify a particular activity as the cause of a change in sales, even when only one stimulus is changed at a time.

Therefore, in order to draw any conclusions from tests, the market researcher needs a more immediate measure that not only reflects the immediate effect a stimulus has on a customer, but which also predicts his subsequent purchase behavior. Statistical techniques, combined with designed (planned) market and consumer surveys, are important tracking-and-warning tools.

Joel Axelrod has published a study made while he was at Lever Brothers, where statistical analyses were performed to determine which intermediate criteria are most effective in forecasting switching behavior and repeat purchasing.[57] The study indicated that brand awareness is clearly the best predictor of switching behavior, while a Constant Sum Scale is best for repeat purchasing (i.e., where the person questioned can indicate, for a given number of points, how likely—in terms of some portion of these points—he or she is to buy each of several different brands).

[57] Attitude Measures that Predict," *Journal of Advertising Research*, Vol. 8, No. 1, p. 3.

This study was based on premium brands and focused on verbal behavior without manipulating stimulus conditions such as ad exposures, packages, or product experience.

Conrad Berenson provides some insights into the value of marketing information systems for tracking market developments, discussing the benefits, organizational needs, structural requirements, and general limitations of such systems.[58] He cites the change in product life cycles (becoming far shorter), and increasing differences between market segments as reasons for having a marketing information system.

The speed with which business decisions are made today requires timely marketing information and techniques for identifying turning points. Since such information systems can provide both quantitative and qualitative information, with perhaps more emphasis on the quantitative types, we shall now turn our attention to that area.

QUANTITATIVE TRACKING METHODS

These techniques range from arithmetic manipulation (i.e., studying the numbers to see if they suggest anything) or simple cross-tabulations to sophisticated statistical analyses. For example, the percent of people watching Mr. Magoo versus Jackie Gleason might be considered a quantitative rather than a qualitative method. We shall discuss the more formal quantitative tracking techniques in the remainder of this chapter.

As we have discussed in several of the earlier chapters, the statistical techniques do the important job of determining what is happening to the sales rate at the present time. Here are the four most common techniques.

1. The Census Bureau X-11 Routine for evaluating performance (actual versus budget)—by using deseasonalized trend-cycles of orders versus sales as a leading indicator, tracking inventory levels, and tracking margins.

2. The slope-characteristic method for tracking the performance of new products when relatively little data are available (for a new product).

3. Various time-series analysis techniques for spotting turning points in sales rates.

4. Time-series analysis and regression analysis, in which economic indicators are related to sales.

[58] "Marketing Information Systems," *Journal of Marketing*, October 1969, p. 16.

Specific Applications

Rather than elaborate on the technical aspects of the quantitative methods, we shall consider specific applications. The first relates to the situation described at the beginning of Chapter 10 and then later shown in Figure 10.2, where the sales rate for a business in a dynamic industry had doubled over the previous year, but was in a no-growth state when a forecast was to be made (at the end of the first quarter of 1968). Time-series analysis, and the Census Bureau X-11 routine in particular, can be used to identify the time when changes in trend first occur.

In Figure 10.2, we saw that the growth rate (change in the sales rates) actually peaked early in the fourth quarter of 1967, even though there was still small growth during the first quarter of 1968.

The downturn (or upturn) in the growth rate is the first warning of a decrease (or increase) in the sales-rate trend, and the data should therefore be tracked to identify as early as possible when the downturn occurs. (We have found, by studying patterns in the data, that we can signal the peaks or valleys as they occur and quite frequently anticipate when they are about to occur.)

After a change in direction of the growth curve has been spotted, the next job is to estimate the slope and length (time) of the downturn (or upturn). One way of doing this is to study previous patterns, relating them to special events whenever possible. The magnitude of the change in direction, as well as the turning point, can often be determined by studying a time-series analysis of the order rate. If there is a lead-lag relationship of orders and sales, the turning points can be identified as far in advance as the degree of lead-lag.

In the example cited, orders were a good lead-indicator of sales, with the signal of trend changes being provided three months ahead of subsequent changes in sales. This relationship became particularly valuable in mid and late 1969, when there was a very sharp decline in the order rate and a subsequent drop in the sales rate. The orders also provided a good measure of the severity of the decline and when it would "bottom-out."

The relationship of orders and sales has been treated in a slightly different way by Robert L. McLaughlin and James J. Boyle, with a method called a pressure index.[59] They state that when two series such as orders and sales have a time lag between them, it is useful to develop pressure indices showing their relationship. If orders received in March are 1100 units and sales billed in that month total 1000, then the "pres-

[59] *Short Term Forecasting*, American Marketing Association Booklet, 1968, p. 32.

sure" of orders on sales in March can be depicted as an index of 110. If orders are lower than sales, the pressure is below 100.

These pressure indices can then be examined in conjunction with time-series analyses for orders and sales. Such a comparison is shown in Figure 13.1, where the trend-cycles, changes in trend-cycles (expressed as a percent), and the pressure indices for orders and sales are shown.

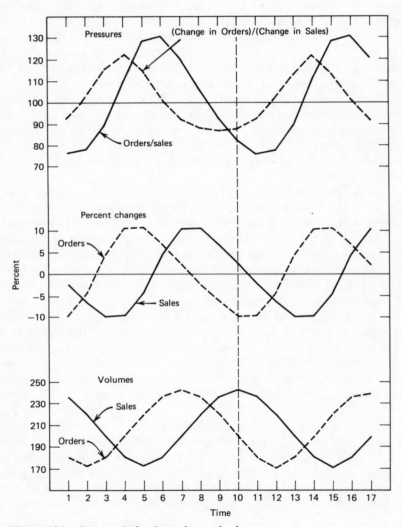

Figure 13.1. Pressure index for orders and sales.

If you look at the bottom line of Figure 13.1 (representing sales billed) at the point where the vertical dashed line passes through, you can see how the system is used to signal an impending turning point. The sales-billed line is still rising at that point, but this is not so for the other five lines.

Given that these are two identical lead-lag series with perfectly oscillating cycles, the identification of the turning point can be made visually. An example of this is given in Figure 13.2, where a peaking situation for the brass industry is shown along with one for durable goods' orders and shipments.

A similar type of analysis can be done for tracking inventories to determine when they are getting out of control. To do this, a time-series analysis is first made of inventory turns to obtain the seasonal factors. The deseasonalized inventory turns for an actual situation are shown in Figure 13.3. An analysis of this graph suggests that there are three (steady-state) levels for the deseasonalized turns for the 1968-71 period, as indicated by the horizontal lines. A trend-cycle plot would show how these turns reached the steady-state levels.

Because it is apparent that there is noise in the data, a cumulative-sum approach is taken, where the cumulative deviations from the target inventory turns (in this case, six turns per year) are plotted. Usually, changes in inventory levels can be spotted quickly by visually observing a cum-sum graph, such as the one given in Figure 13.4, for the example contained in Figure 13.3. When there is a high degree of randomness, statistical confidence limits can be used to determine when a significant change has occurred. If the inventory turns are about six per year, the cum sum should oscillate randomly about the zero level.

The cumulative sum of forecasting errors is also very useful for tracking the performance of a forecasting model. It should signal when the forecasts are becoming biased, thereby signaling a needed modification of the model, its assumptions, or its inputs.

Market Research

Another type of tracking involving quantitative methods is the use of statistical techniques in analyzing the results of market surveys. Forecasts almost always assume, either implicitly or explicitly, the types of consumers that will buy a product and the product characteristics that will be most acceptable to the consumer. As the product is introduced, either nationally or in test areas, comprehensive data should be collected to verify these assumptions.

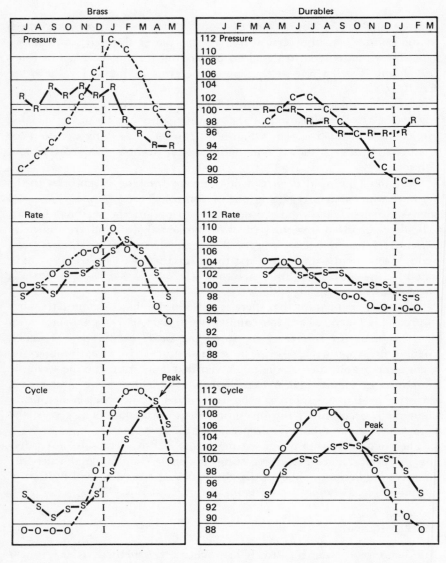

Figure 13.2. Pressure indices and time-series for brass industry and durable goods. O = orders; S = sales; C = orders/sales; R = (change in orders)/(change in sales).

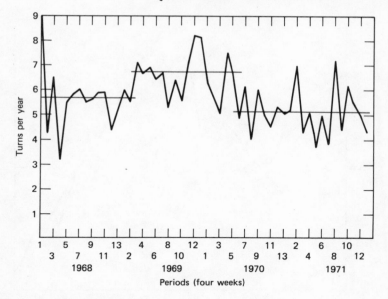

Figure 13.3.   Deseasonalized inventory turns per year.

When Corning introduced a tableware product several years ago, for example, a market research study was conducted to determine if the assumptions made in an earlier forecast (on which initial decisions were based) were valid. Some of the factors considered in the test and subsequent statistical analysis (made with the AID routine described in Appendix B) were: price; customer material preferences, decorations, and patterns; type of consumers who most preferred the product; and various demographic factors. Customer trade-off choices and the effects of the factors on market share were the major questions considered.

Changes in Proven Theories

Since we are living in a dynamic and changing world, even previously proven theories must be regularly tracked. The so-called Phillips curve (an economic theory relating inflation and unemployment) is a good example of where a well-accepted theory appears to be changing. In the 1970 recession, we had a low unemployment rate with high inflation, but in 1972-1973, there was high inflation with a relatively high unemployment rate. The relationship of low inflation to low unemployment seems

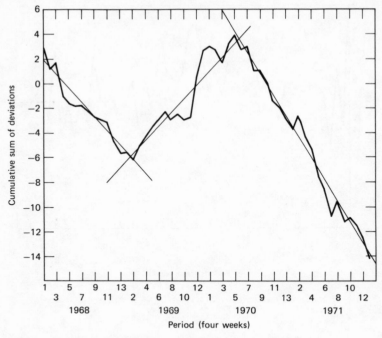

Figure 13.4.   Deviation of inventory turns from transient levels.

to have markedly changed since 1967, as indicated by the numbers in Table 13.1.

Input-Output

While I-O methodology serves a useful purpose for some companies in making long-term projections (five to 10 years out), it is of more value in tracking and warning, where changes in overall market growth might be signaled. Past statistical relationships may be invalid because of changes in the industries interacting with the one under consideration. Also, input-output can be used as a check on forecasts derived by other techniques, since I-O enables us to see how the pieces fit together when all of the individual segments are added—for example, when independent industry forecasts are made, they must add consistently to a realistic GNP forecast.

However, there are problems associated with I-O that must be resolved. I-O methodology relies heavily on future technological changes, and the

Table 13.1   Inflation and Unemployment Rate Data

Year	Inflation Rate	Previous Year's Unemployment Rate	Sum of Inflation Rate, plus Previous Year's Unemployment
1955	1.5	5.6	7.1
1956	3.4	4.4	7.8
1957	3.7	4.1	7.8
1958	2.6	4.3	6.9
1959	1.6	6.8	8.4
1960	1.7	5.5	7.2
1961	1.3	5.5	6.8
1962	1.1	6.7	7.8
1963	1.3	5.6	6.9
1964	1.5	5.6	7.1
1965	1.9	5.2	7.1
1967	3.2	3.8	7.0
1968	4.0	3.8	7.8
1969	4.8	3.5	8.4
1970	5.5	3.5	9.0
1971	4.7	4.0	9.7
1972	3.0	6.0	9.0
1973	3.6	5.6	9.2

changes that are kept secret will therefore not be incorporated into the I-O tables. The impact of a new invention not made yet—such as was true with Xerox copiers, electronic computers, and Polaroid cameras—could have an important bearing on the future projections of some industries. The quality of I-O as a long-range forecasting technique depends on the interaction of economic analysts with technical and marketing experts.

Because of this situation, the I-O forecasts made by well-known economic groups can vary significantly. For example, the I-O models developed by Arthur D. Little, Inc., University of Maryland, and Battelle do not agree in their ranking of various industry segments. As shown in Table 13.2, among the top 30 industries, not one growth industry is included on all three lists. Consider that within the top 10 industries, there are three that are common to two lists:

1. Computers and related machinery (ADL and University of Maryland).

Table 13.2 Top 30 Long-Term Growth Areas

Arthur D. Little	University of Maryland	Battelle
1 Computing and related machinery	1 Computer rental	1 Scrap and secondhand goods
2 Semiconductors and integrated circuits	2 Pulp mills	2 Transportation services
3 Fabricated plastic products	3 X-ray, electronic equipment	3 Material handling machinery
4 Air Transportation	4 Computers and related machinery	4 Paving and asphalt products
5 Surgical and medical instruments	5 Electrical measuring instruments	5 Pipelines
6 Electric utility services	6 Cycles, transportation equipment	6 Clay and cement products
7 Plastics materials and resins	7 Chemical fertilizer mining	7 Organic manmade fibers
8 Noncellulosic organic fibers	8 Other primary nonferrous metals	8 Industry controls
9 Typewriters, scales, and balances	9 Special industrial machinery	9 Radio and television broadcasting
10 Duplicating and other office machines	10 Motor vehicles	10 Manufactured plastic products
11 Manifold business forms and blank books	11 Watches and clocks	11 Oil field machinery
12 Other agricultural chemicals	12 Other office machinery	12 Lighting fixtures and devices
13 Telephone and telegraph equipment	13 Aircraft	13 Advertising
14 Optical, photocopying and photographic equipment	14 Banks, credit agencies, brokers	14 Iron and ferroalloys
15 Vending machines and air conditioners	15 Lumber and wood products	15 Motor freight
16 Watches, clocks and parts	16 Airlines	16 Scientific instruments
17 Cyclic intermediates and crudes	17 Railroad equipment	17 Nonelectrical heating equipment
18 Industrial gases	18 Jewelry and silverware	18 Electric lamps
19 Household refrigerators and freezers	19 Metal stampings	19 Other rubber products
20 Radio and television communication equipment	20 Pumps, compressors, blowers	20 Plastics materials and resins
21 Noncompetitive imports	21 Apparel	21 Miscellaneous chemical products
22 Pharmaceutical preparations	22 Power transmission equipment	22 Medical and surgical equipment
23 Household vacuum cleaners	23 Forestry and fishery products	23 Service industry machinery
24 Orthopedic and surgical appliances	24 Aluminum	24 Education
25 Dental equipment and supplies	25 Truck, bus, trail bodies	25 Telecommunications
26 Industrial organic chemicals	26 Canned and frozen foods	26 Primary aluminum
27 Engines and turbines	27 Copper ore	27 Electrical motors and generators
28 Radio and television receiving sets	28 Mechanical measuring devices	28 Electrical measuring instruments
29 Mobile homes and campers	29 Machinery tools, metal cutting	29 Construction machinery
30 Communication services	30 Other nonferrous ores	30 Agriculture chemicals, except fertilizer

256

2. Organic manmade fibers (ADL and Battelle).
3. Fabricated plastic products (ADL and Battele).

By adding 10 more industries, we increase the common list by four.

4. Watches and clocks (ADL and University of Maryland).
5. Air transportation (ADL and University of Maryland).
6. Typewriters, duplicating, office machinery (ADL and University of Maryland).
7. Plastic materials and resins (ADL and Battelle).

Finally, by adding the last 10 industries, we increase the common list by another four.

8. Medical and surgical equipment (ADL and Battelle).
9. Communication services (ADL and Battelle).
10. Aluminum (University of Maryland and Battelle).
11. Electrical measuring instruments (University of Maryland and Battelle).

Hence, out of the 30 industries, only 11 are agreed on by any two of the three organizations as belonging somewhere on the list of the top 30 industries. From the point of view of the decision maker wishing to utilize I-O for long-range planning, this lack of agreement seems to cast doubt either on the state of the art of I-O analysis, or on the quality of one or more of the I-O practitioners.

For the reader who wishes to know more about how I-O tables are constructed and how they can be used, we have included a description of I-O in an appendix at the end of this chapter, along with some other applications.

Only a handful of United States corporations have developed I-O tables for their own companies that tie in with those developed by the government. Other companies utilizing I-O have either viewed it primarily as a checkpoint, or have used regression analysis to get simple relationships between company and industry sales, which provide a rough measure of future sales.

Leading Indicators

These indices can be of value in both the preparation and tracking of a forecast. In most instances, they are used primarily as visual qualitative indicators, such as those released by the United States government and which are meant to be a predictor of changes in the economy.

This approach, developed by the National Bureau of Economic Research, basically consists of (a) analyzing the behavior of many economic time series that extend over several business cycles, (b) determining the dates of the turning points for these cycles, and (c) then deciding whether this indicator is leading, coincident, or lagging, depending on whether it leads, moves coincidentally, or lags cyclical movements of aggregate economic activity (such as the FRB index).

The better known of the leading indicators is the one developed by Julius Shiskin of the Census Bureau, which is a composite index consisting of 12 economic factors. This index has proven to be reasonably accurate since its introduction, but has only been available for a little more than five years.

Michael Evans has discussed the accuracy of leading indicators under various conditions in considerable detail.[60] Often, either the lead time is too short or too erratic, and false recessions are signaled. Evans discusses leading indicators only as they relate to the overall economy; very little has been published about the accuracy of leading indicators for business forecasting and tracking.

We have found that single factors provide little accuracy for most businesses (because they are only a small segment of any single economic sector), with the best relationship accounting for less than 30% of the variation in sales (after removing seasonality). However, when we developed a special composite leading indicator for a total consumer-products business, it performed quite well. We obtained this by analyzing which economic factors were most significant for each part of the total business, and weighting them according to their significance and the contribution of the business segment to the total.

The reader should bear in mind that it is not an easy task to select the correct factors and related weights; therefore, special cycle analysis is necessary.

Anticipatory Data

The Survey Research Center (SRC) at the University of Michigan has an index that contains information about consumer sentiment (what the consumer thinks about the economy) and buying plans. Several studies, some conducted at SRC and others at Wharton, concluded that an index based on attitudes rather than buying plans was most relevant for pre-

---

[60] *Macroeconomic Activity, Theory, Forecasting and Control* (New York: Harper and Row, Publishers, Inc., 1969), pp. 445–455.

diction. Furthermore, attitudes were most useful in predicting purchases of automobiles rather than other durables.

Recently, even using an attitude or sentiment index for this purpose has been questioned, since consumer attitudes consist of many diverse economic and noneconomic phenomena that are reflected in the compiled index. Most of the questions asked consumers deal with how individuals feel about the future state of the economy. Since the average individual is probably not a very good forecaster, his own view of the future state of the economy is probably closely related to the present state.

Studies have shown that consumer attitudes did not add to the predictability of car purchases in the 1957–1962 period. In the 1963–1965 period, the performance was not better. For example, the attitudes predicted a decrease in car sales in mid–1963 that did not occur; and they have also had several other minor fluctuations that cannot easily be related to movements in car purchases.

Furthermore, consumer attitudes underestimated the growth in car purchases that occurred during the 1963–1965 period. In the period 1952–1962, a 1% increase in the sentiment index was associated with a 1.8% increase in car purchases. However, in the period 1963–1965, the attitude index increased less than 9%, while actual car purchases increased almost 30%.

Another problem with "sentiment" indices is that consumer dynamics change. A *Wall Street Journal* article, in quoting a recent study of consumer attitudes by the SRC at the University of Michigan, stated: "Despite widespread complaints about past price increases, and greatly increased pessimism about the personal financial situation and about the economy, a greatly increased proportion of people said that it is a good time to buy . . . before prices go up further."[61]

This, the report stressed, signified a troubling departure from most past inflationary periods when disappointment and uncertainty induced consumers to reduce their spending and increase their savings. The Research Center concluded: "The present approval of buying in advance suggests that confidence in the dollar has been badly shaken in recent months."

We have had little success in relating any businesses to this index on an empirical (regression-analysis) basis. However, we have found that the information collected along with the index is quite useful in explaining the short-run surge or decline in color-television sales.

For example, the SRC survey conducted in February and March 1973 detected an increase in the proportion of the people surveyed who be-

---

[61] "Appraisal of Current Trends in Business and Finance," May 14, 1973, p. 1.

lieved it was a good time to purchase "big ticket" items—such as autos, large household durables, and homes—before prices rose further. The survey reported that this prebuying psychology is expected to sustain a high level of durable goods sales in the immediate future.

The quarterly econometric models are not sensitive enough to pick up such changes; thus information from these surveys is useful in massaging the econometric forecasts to improve short-term (one to four months) accuracy.

Arthur Okun argues, however, that "the investment anticipations reported in the Commerce-SEC survey have an impressive record of predictive accuracy. I know of no naive mode (and no causal explanation resting on predetermined variables) which rivals the anticipations data in accuracy."[62] Other economists question the accuracy of anticipatory data.

We shall not further discuss the merit of anticipatory data, but will leave it to the analyst to determine the value of such a factor for the businesses in his company.

IN SUMMARY

Tracking is an important and essential part of forecasting. It will help verify or suggest revisions to prior assumptions and possibly identify new relationships not previously considered. Many of the techniques used in preparing a forecast are applicable to tracking. In one sense, tracking is a prelude to preparing forecasts for later points in the life cycle.

Also, it should be noted that we have not attempted to discuss all of the tracking-and-warning techniques available (especially the statistical ones), but only to indicate some of the more important ones.

APPENDIX: THE I-O TECHNIQUE[63]

Input-Output (I-O) is founded on the simple propostion that what goes *into* the production process must also come *out* and eventually find its way to final consumers or demanders. Thus one can define an industry's purchases (including materials), services, labor, capital and construction costs, as well as indirect costs such as taxes and profits, as equal to the sales of that industry (e.g., input is equal to output).

[62] See *The Predictive Value of Surveys of Business Intentions,* American Economic Review Papers and Procedings, May 1962, Vol. 52, No. 2, p. 221.

[63] This appendix is based on I-O material prepared by Arthur D. Little, Inc., Cambridge, Massachusetts.

The I-O accounting scheme is a systematic organization of each industry's purchases from and sales to every other industry, plus its sales to domestic and foreign consumers, governments, and investment and construction markets. Every sale by the selling industry is a purchase from the point of view of the purchasing industry. Hence each output from one industry can be viewed as a purchase by another.

Business transactions among industries are organized in the analytical framework into a square "interindustry" or "flow" matrix, in which sales of each industry are shown along a horizontal row and purchases by each industry are found by reading down a column.

Changes in the size of markets for each industry, and ultimately the growth rate of the industry, are related to two basic elements of the model:

1. Growth and shifts in general purchase patterns of households, government, new construction, foreign trade, and capital equipment buyers and inventory. These are known as *final demand* sectors or *ultimate users* of products in our society. (Changes in usage by these sectors are projected partly by the model and partly outside of the model.)

2. Changes in technology employed by industries. (The relationships are recorded in an I-O table and are referred to as the *interindustry demand* and *coefficient matrix*. Each year the coefficient matrix changes to reflect the changing technological relationships.) This element is of greater importance to the forecasts for the decade of the 1970s than for the forecasts made for 1973.

ELEMENTS OF INPUT-OUTPUT ANALYSIS

I-O analysis permits the systematic investigation of the interrelationships of producing and consuming industries to final markets and primary inputs; thus it is particularly useful for analyzing problems of the industries that primarily sell their output to other industries, and it permits the tracking of direct and indirect effects on total demand of changes in final goods markets. There are three essential elements of input-output analysis: (1) the analytical technique, (2) the analytical components, and (3) the technological change analysis.

1. The Analytical Technique

Table 13.3 provides an understanding of the fundamentals of an I-O model by depicting an oversimplified I-O analysis involving an economy

Table 13.3   Illustration of Changes in Technology (totals may not add because of rounding)

Panel 1   Before Technological Change

	Consuming Sectors			Total Intermediate Output	Final Demand	Total Gross Output
	1	2	3			
Producing sectors:						
1	161.6	56.9	74.2	292.7	200.0	492.7
	1.561	0.334	0.254			
	0.328	0.150	0.114			
2			29.3	29.3	350.0	379.3
	0.018	1.028	0.064			
			0.045			
3	95.6	148.7	156.1	400.6	250.0	650.6
	0.409	0.616	1.415			
	0.194	0.392	0.240			
Intermediate Inputs	257.2	205.6	259.8	GNP	GNP → 800.0	
	0.522	0.542	0.399			
Primary inputs (Value added)	235.5	173.7	391.0			
	0.478	0.458	0.601			
Total gross inputs	492.7	379.3	650.6			
	1.000	1.000	1.000			

Panel 2   After Technological Change

	Consuming Sectors			Total Intermediate Output	Final Demand	Total Gross Output
	1	2	3			
Producing Sectors:						
1	173.1	78.5	72.8	324.4	200.0	524.5
	1.574	0.414	0.259			
	0.330	0.207	0.112			
2	2.1		27.3	29.4	350.0	379.3
	0.025	1.026	0.061			
	0.004		0.042			
3	108.0	130.1	161.8	399.9	250.0	649.8
	0.443	0.582	1.430			
	0.206	0.343	0.249			
Intermediate Inputs	283.2	208.7	261.9	GNP	GNP → 800.0	
	0.540	0.550	0.403			
Primary inputs (Value added)	241.3	170.7	387.9			
	0.460	0.450	0.597			
Total gross inputs	524.5	379.3	649.8			
	1.000	1.000	1.000			

262

with three major industry sectors. The I-O framework depicts an economy in matrix form. Panel 1 of Table 13.3 shows a hypothetical three-sector matrix with an $800 GNP before technological change is introduced. Each row represents a producing sector. Each column represents a consuming sector.

In our example, we may imagine Sector 1 to be Agriculture, Sector 2 to be Services, and Sector 3 to be Manufacturing Industry. We can insert in each cell of the matrix, in monetary units, the transaction between a producing sector and a consuming sector. Thus, for example, we may record that Producing Sector 1 sells $161.6 of its output to Consumer Sector 1, $56.9 to Sector 2, and $74.2 to Sector 3.

In addition to producing for intermediate consumption industrial markets, each sector produces for final markets: consumer, investment, and government, represented in Panel 1 as a final-demand column. Thus Sector 1 has a total intermediate output of $292.7 and an output of final consumption of $200.0, for a gross output of $492.7. Similarly, Sector 2 has a total gross output of $379.3, and Sector 3, $650.6.

To produce the total output, each sector purchases or consumes goods and services provided by other sectors. For example, Consuming Sector 3 purchases $74.2 worth of goods and services from Sector 1, $29.3 from Sector 2, and $156.1 from Sector 3. In addition to purchasing from "intermediate inputs" (i.e., consuming goods and services provided by other sectors), each sector consumes primary inputs such as labor and capital, and pays taxes and profits. This additional consumption is shown as in the "value-added" row.

Consequently, Sector 3, in order to produce $650.6 worth of total output, purchases $259.8 worth of goods and services from its suppliers and $391.0 from primary inputs. Thus total output equals total inputs for each industry—a balancing condition that is the chief characteristic of the I-O framework.

The flows shown in Panel 1 are the direct purchases of industries and represent the amounts required directly from each sector to support the output of any given sector. The consumption patterns or proportions of the direct contribution by each sector to each other sector's output, called *technical coefficients,* are shown on the lower left side of each cell in the matrix. Thus for Sector 3, the $74.2 input from Sector 1 required to support the $650.6 output of Sector 3 represents a portion of 0.114 or 11.4% of Sector 3's output. Similarly, Sector 3 contributes to Sector 2. In addition, 45.8% of the output is paid to labor, depreciation, taxes, and profit.

These are also called *structural* or *technological* coefficients, since they represent the particular "structure" and production technology of an economy. Given a specific structure, any final demand pattern can be applied to find the output levels of each sector.

The so-called *inverse coefficients* are derived from the technical coefficients through a mathematical process called *matrix inversion*. In our example, they are shown on the lower right side of each cell. Called *the total requirements per dollar of delivery to final demand*, these represent the total (direct plus indirect) load on the row sector generated as a result of one unit's of delivery to the final demand of the column sector. In our example, $1 of delivery to final demand by Sector 1 (the column sector) generates $0.409 worth of output from Sector 3 (the row industry) in total. Thus the contribution of Sector 1 to Sector 3's total output is $200 × 0.409 = $81.8.

2. The Analytical Components

The two areas of interest to the analyst in investigating cause and effect are: (1) final demand and (2) structure.

The components of *final demand* are:

- Personal consumption, investment (including construction), government expenditures, and foreign trade.
- Variables (e.g., government policy decisions, investment levels, disposable income, changes in consumer tastes) that affect final demand patterns.

The components of *structure* are:

- Technical coefficients.
- Price changes.
- Product-mix changes or material input.
- Production-process changes.

3. The Technological Change Analysis

Consider, for example, Sector 2 in Figure 13.3. Most of this sector's output is delivered to final demand. Sector 2's only industrial customer is Sector 3, but Sector 2 is the smallest supplier to Sector 3. Changing production patterns in Sector 3 may eliminate any industrial market for Sector 2.

From the supply side, Sector 2 consumes 15% of its input in purchases from Sector 1, and 39.2% in purchases from Sector 3.

Let us consider a case in which substantial technological changes occur in the input and output distribution of industrial consumption and produce. Imagine these conditions:

• Sector 1 has had approximately an 11% increase in total shipments to industry (intermediate output).

• There is a shift in the *production mix* of Sector 2, to the extent that Sector 1 will now supply 38% *more* to Sector 2, and Sector 3 will supply 12.5% *less* to Sector 2. The change in all other sectors and primary inputs is "small."

• These stated changes will alter the structure of the economy, causing different input and output distributions.

The application of the final demand used in our example to a technologically changed I-O matrix is presented in Panel 2 of Figure 13.3. The same definitions used previously apply here. In analyzing the results, we readily see that even though there is no change in GNP and in final-demand patterns, the industrial input and output distribution was changed and so was the total gross output. The gross output of Sector 1 changed from $492.7 to $524.5, or about 6.5%.

Interestingly, the outputs of Sectors 2 and 3 hardly changed in the total sense, but showed a market distribution change. Below is the distribution of the markets of the two sectors before and after the technological changes.

Markets	Before Change				After Change			
	Sector 1		Sector 3		Sector 1		Sector 3	
Sector 1	161.6	32.8%	95.6	14.7%	173.1	33.0%	108.0	16.6%
Sector 2	56.9	11.5%	148.7	23.8%	78.5	15.0%	130.1	20.0%
Sector 3	74.2	16.0%	156.1	24.2%	72.8	13.9%	161.8	25.0%
F.D.	200.0	40.7%	250.0	38.3%	200.0	38.1%	250.0	38.4%
		100.0%		100.0%		100.0%		100.0%

In this illustration, we have kept the final-demand (F.D.) area constant, varying only the processing side. Shifts in consumer, government, export, and investment patterns will alter the final-demand distribution. There are a vast number of interrelationships among expenditure categories, durable, nondurable, and services relationships, disposable income, taxation, and government expenditures. Such variables would also change the final-demand structure, which—when combined with a new technological structure—will again cause completely different output levels.

The reader may want to refer to Arthur D. Little, Inc., *Prospectus for the Long- and Short-Term Growth Patterns of U.S. Industries and Markets* (Arthur D. Little, Cambridge, Massachusetts). Another reference is *A Businessman's Introduction to Input-Output* released by the Battelle-Columbus Laboratories of Columbus, Ohio.

Chapter XIV

Inventions, Innovations, and Forecasting

Considerable attention has been devoted in recent years to the fact that several hundreds of the largest United States corporations have been steadily expanding their share of the nation's production. As the economy grows, it appears to become the domain of the giants. But much of the potential of free enterprise, innovation, and social progress resides elsewhere—namely, in the group of entrepreneurs who launch new ventures in high technology areas.

These businessmen perceive a human need and seek to make it profitable by mobilizing management, capital, and technology. Often, they are themselves scientists or engineers who have emerged from major corporations, where they found an environment or a management unwilling or unable to pursue their ideas with sufficient vigor. In their ventures, which are small in scale but great in ambition, they encounter and are willing to take special risks. As they push out the boundaries of technology, even the best financed among them work nearer to financial uncertainty than their contemporaries in large companies. A misjudgment about the market could bring them to ruin; but the rewards of success can be as bountiful as their imaginations.

The type of contribution an analyst can make to situations that depend on inventions or innovations is different from that described in the previous chapters. For companies that are willing to take the risks associated with inventions, such as a Polaroid, Corning Glass, or Xerox, the approach to forecasting must be more concerned with providing tools for determining the implications of the cost of inventions, the risks, the rewards, and the timing than with forecasting the most likely outcome.

The approach to exploring technology, which centers about tracking signals, is applicable to some extent, since there are milestones or events that must occur for the invention or innovation to become a successful venture. However, the main "forecasting" need for inventions is to have analyses performed by a seasoned analyst who has a good understanding of the inventive mind. He must be able to take the conceptual logic of the inventor and translate it so that some type of quantitative analyses can be employed, perhaps putting relevant information into the form of a decision tree, making factor comparisons on a rating-ranking scale, or through structured questions eliciting the underlying primary assumptions.

The following case example, drawn from the pharmaceutical industry, illustrates why the forecasting techniques and approaches described earlier are typically not applicable in forecasting for inventions and innovations.

ALZA CORPORATION APPROACH

The major pharmaceutical companies have been so successful in compounding powerful new medicines and protecting their inventions with patents that there would appear to be little opportunity for an individual enterpreneur in the drug business these days.

But that has not deterred Alejandro Zaffaroni, Uruguayan-born biochemist and businessman who is building an extraordinary company in Palo Alto, California.[64] Though his Alza Corporation has yet to sell a single product, Zaffaroni has raised the phenomenal sum of $37 million, mainly from institutional investors and wealthy men eager to finance his ideas. He has assembled as unlikely a team of scientists and engineers as any drug company has ever seen—polymer chemists, mechanical engineers, physicists, and other professionals who are not normally encountered in the drug business. And he is trying to introduce an entirely new scientific approach to the ancient art of administering drugs—an approach so radical that his success depends on revolutionizing medical practice itself.

Zaffaroni's idea is to seize an opening left by a strange anomaly in the development of medicine. Over the years, especially since the discovery of the so-called wonder drugs, the pharmaceutical companies have developed increasingly powerful potions to fight disease. Yet the methods used to deliver these drugs to affected organs in the body have not kept pace; we still depend predominantly on pills, which were being used by the Egyptians as long ago as the fifteenth century B.C.

[64] "Visionary on a Golden Shoestring," *Fortune*, June 1973, p. 150.

The gap has become dangerous. A pill must contain thousands, even millions, of times more medication than is needed at the target organ. The drug contained in a pill must survive the attack of the digestive enzymes, penetrate the stomach and intestine walls, and pass through that efficient filtering plant, the liver. It diffuses through 60,000 miles of arteries, capillaries, and other tubing, reaching all sorts of organs to which it is not directed and often causing undesirable side effects. The approach is about as sensible as flooding a skyscraper to douse a fire in a waste-basket. Small wonder that ailments started by drugs intended as cures are responsible for an increased number of hospital admissions.

Zaffaroni believes that society needs not more powerful drugs but better ways of delivering those already in existence. His goal is to develop novel devices that can administer minute amounts of medication as directly as possible to the affected organ, cutting down on the dangerous side effects and greatly increasing the efficiency and convenience of therapy. Now, after five years of work, Zaffaroni hopes Alza will win regulatory approval to begin selling its first products abroad in late 1973, in the United States in 1974.

One of these products is a tiny oval reservoir called an Ocusert, which contains an antiglaucoma drug; a patient can wear it under his lower eyelid. A single Ocusert lasts a week and it controls glaucoma by admin-istering, in a steady flow, about one-tenth the amount of drug normally taken as eyedrops four times a day. The quantity is tailored to a patient's need.

Another product is a birth-control device, a kind of successor to the pill. It is inserted into the uterus, where for an entire year it steadily re-leases amounts of progesterone so minute that they equal the medication contained in just three of the daily birth-control pills. Since the proges-terone is not circulating in the body, the side effects associated with the pill appear to be eliminated.

THE INVENTION PROCESS

We believe that an inventor goes through a structured approach. How-ever, it is not easy for everyone to comprehend his thinking. An inventor has to be handled with great care and patience; and the potential risks or rewards of his work have to be carefully assessed. This will often re-quire considerable probing with the inventor and learning the process that he hopes will lead to an invention.

Inventor Jim Giffen of Corning Glass Works was once asked the question: "How do you conceive a new idea for an invention and what is your approach?" The following is an excerpt of his reply.

I think my answer to this would be—you see a human need for an article, process, machine, or whatever—and then progress from that point.

At first, it is only a vision or idea in the inventor's mind, much like a seed in a field. In this field, there are many seeds, and if all are allowed to germinate and grow, it will become a brush lot with nothing of any value. As time goes on, the inventor must cultivate the most promising trees that have the most value from an economic and practical standpoint. Does this idea tree solve mechanical or human problems that exist? Has it real value to our society? Will this be a useful tool to mankind? Has it basic values that others do not have?

Now as the roots of the tree reach out, they pick up needed bits of information, just from daily observation or from other inventions. Probably new inventions will have to be made to feed the main tree. Now this tree is only a vision and, like a tree, it can only grow in one field. It cannot be pruned or fertilized by others or it may shrivel and die. Finally, in due season it will mature, blossom, and be ready to bear fruit and, like all trees, it will produce seed for many more inventions.

The inventor is now confronted with selling his vision to others. Now it is easy to sell a going machine or working process, but try to sell a vision that no one has seen but you! The more revolutionary and outstanding the invention, the more difficulty one encounters in selling it to others. People naturally resist change and it is not possible for them to visualize deeply into (to them) the unknown.

Selling his idea and training others in the use of it has always been the inventor's most difficult problem.[65]

Inventing a New Glass

In his speech, Giffen continued by giving an example of how this process works.

Now let us apply the tree analogy to my recent invention—stratified glass. For a number of years, I have watched others trying to make articles of glass. The biggest problem they encountered was that glass would break; it was a fragile, weak material. I know well that glass, when properly handled, is one of our stronger materials. Glass, being nonductile and having very little elasticity, its apparent weakness is caused by the propagation of cracks. Once a crack is started in this type material, a slight force puts tremendous tension at the apex of this crack and it will propagate through the entire body.

[65] From a speech given by J. W. Giffen at the occasion of Honorary Doctor of Science Degree presentation to him by Alfred University, June 3, 1973.

It was rationalized that if we could stop this crack propagation, glass would be much stronger and useful for many, many applications. My thoughts were: Why not stratify or laminate two or more glasses or glass-ceramics of different coefficients of expansion together so as to have thin layers of highly compressed glass and much heavier layers of relatively low tension glass? A crack started in this type matrix will propagate only until it reaches a highly compressed layer and it will be inhibited at that point. This was the seed in the field of thought, and, as this type of glass would have many applications, this seed was cultivated.

We constructed an orifice of suitable material, flowed these glasses together in the molten state, and formed them into a sheet, which proved to have the desirable characteristics—a working strength of about 8 to 10 times that of annealed glass.

As only sheet, tubing, or cane could be made by this process, the roots of the tree reached farther for more information. A method had to be invented to form sheet glass into useful articles: Why not a vacuum forming machine using the still molten sheet for the forming of articles? This would be a fast, economical operation. This process, now known as the "hub machine," was necessary for this tree to produce fruit and the tree roots had to reach for much needed information— that is, suitable orifices; molds had to be invented, and so forth.

Other companies were developing tools that were useful in the process and the roots quickly seized onto them: (1) electrical discharge machining—Elox Corporation; (2) methods for applying metal oxides to metal surfaces—Kaman Nuclear Corporation; (3) mechanized hard face welding—Union Carbide Plasma Jet Process; and (4) electron beam welding—United Aircraft Corporation.

While the process could have been developed without these four tools, they made the process easier to mechanize and provided greater economy of operation. This illustrates how one invention feeds on others. Many more ideas had to be developed and will be developed in the future to make the whole system more universal, efficient, and profitable.

Today, the fruits of this tree are Corelle Livingware and Hercules Resistors; and many, many more items will be developed. The seeds of this tree will take root in other minds and produce new trees for the future.

IN SUMMARY

The four critical elements of an invention process are costs, risks, rewards, and timing. While the rewards can be considerable, as was true for stratified glass, there are many more failures than successes. The techniques described in this book will be of little value for assessing what the most likely outcome of an invention will be. The analyst must be able to assist the inventor in estimating the costs, risks, rewards, and importance of timing, and in bringing these factors together in a logical, consistent way so that the desirability of continuing research can be evaluated. The approach to be taken in probing the inventor's mind will depend on the way in which his thinking is disciplined.

We shall not attempt to elaborate further, other than to caution that forecasting for inventions and innovations is not particularly meaningful. The analyst can better spend his time working with the inventor-innovator in quantifying his knowledge and invention process.

Chapter XV

Forecast Management

In many companies, people are selected to direct particular functions primarily because of their ability to manage. Consideration of how knowledgeable they are about the area that is to be managed is of secondary importance—if given much attention at all. The assumption is that they will be able to develop measures of performance about the function for which they are responsible so that they can properly evaluate it.

In many functional areas, this is not difficult. For example, in a sales function, total sales is an obvious criterion; in manufacturing, the criteria are the units produced and unit manufacturing cost. However, in most staff activities, the criteria are not nearly so obvious.

With respect to evaluating a forecasting activity, one might immediately think of the primary criterion as the accuracy of the forecasts that have been prepared; and, since most persons are results-oriented, this could be considered adequate. On the other hand, it is possible that the analysts making the forecasts were fortunate in the time period considered and that over the long run they would produce inaccurate forecasts.

The manager must therefore ascertain whether the methods used in deriving the forecasts are sound and whether the performance achieved during the recent period of time can be replicated.

In this chapter, we shall consider two aspects of forecast management: (1) measurements of the overall output or activity of the forecasting section; and (2) how to evaluate individual analysts or forecasters.

In effect, we can consider this chapter as a summary of much of the preceding material, since the principles that are employed in performing these two management functions have been stated throughout the book.

273

MEASURING THE OUTPUT

In one sense, those in forecast management can evaluate the work of their function in much the same way as the consumer of a forecast evaluates the work presented to him. However, the ultimate means by which forecasting must be evaluated is whether the forecast is accurate and whether the forecast has been used in decision making. Both of these elements are absolutely necessary; otherwise the effort expended on the forecasting has not been effective. In speaking of accuracy, we are concerned with whether the factor being forecast—sales or whatever—has fallen within the range of the forecast (i.e., the forecast plus or minus the forecast error).

For example, the recent pressures for companies to make public their earning forecasts (and the Securities and Exchange Commission not only allowing it, but also encouraging the issuing of such forecasts) will place increased emphasis on having a competent forecaster. Rather than making a single forecast, the analyst will have to indicate the variability of his model forecasts so that the company will not be accused of releasing incorrect information.

An example of how this can be done is shown in the approach taken by the North Carolina National Bank. Its technique of putting probabilities on various economic scenarios is a realistic representation of the true situation. The bank made its forecasts available to security analysts in June 1973 in the following manner.

Assumption A	Assumption B	Assumption C
• Restrictive monetary environment	• Restrictive monetary environment	• Expansive monetary environment
• Severe margin squeeze	• Moderate margin squeeze	• Normal margins
5% probability	85% probability	5% probability
Estimated earnings per share:		
$1.52 to 1.58	$1.59 to 1.67	$1.68 to 1.74

There is a 5% probability that earnings will be less than $1.52 or greater than $1.74.

This forecast was made with the help of a computerized "earnings simulation model" that relates the effects of such critical economic and regulatory variables as GNP, money supply, and the prime lending rate on the

firm's earning and balance sheet. There is always the possibility of cata-
strophic but unforeseen events, such as a devastating hurricane in North
Carolina National Bank's operating area, which might make the earnings
lower than $1.52 per share.

A good forecaster will consider the critical factors and spell them out
clearly to other people. Since the objective of forecasting is to aid in a
decision process, the ultimate aim must be to have the forecast incorporated into the decision process. This means not only the forecast but
also the estimate of the forecast error, since the best decision may not be
the one which relies on the forecast itself but on a range of the forecast.
If the range of the forecast is relatively large, then the decision will generally be made so that the results or actual sales can be tracked and the
strategy revised should the actual sales be significantly different from the
estimate.

Associated with the value of the forecast to the decision is the timeli-
ness of the forecast. Was it prepared on time? Or did the decision have
to be delayed until the forecast was available? The latter might have
caused a poor decision to be made because it could not have been as
timely.

The manager of the forecasting activity should keep a record of the
percent of forecast requests that have been submitted to the requester at
the proper time. The ability to meet deadlines for forecasting services is
just as important as for any other type of staff activity.

A related problem is the situation where the client has also requested
other groups to prepare forecasts. In this case, the manager of the forecasting activity will want to compare the output of his group with that
of the other groups, as well as how the client used each of the forecasts in
arriving at a decision.

A good discussion of this type of situation appeared in "What Do You
Do With 35 Conflicting Forecasts?"[66] The article described a problem
confronting the Committee on Interior and Insular Affairs of the U.S.
House of Representatives. In preparation for a series of hearings on fuel
and energy resources, the Committee staff collected 35 different forecasts
of energy utilization in the United States. These forecasts, which were
prepared between 1960 and 1971 by corporations, private research organizations, associations, and government agencies, covered varying periods of
time, with many going out to the year 2000.

Although virtually all of these forecasts utilized some form of trend
extrapolation, there were significant differences among them. The Com-

[66] *The Futurist*, June 1973, p. 134.

mittee staff set about to examine the forecasts in more detail, to determine why the differences arose, and what conclusions, if any, could be drawn from the set of differing forecasts. The resulting document, "Energy Demand Studies: An Analysis and Appraisal," is an excellent example of the art of analyzing forecasts and should serve as a model for those with similar problems.

Six-Phase Analysis

While we are not advocating a rigorous "phased" approach to forecasting, it is of value to break the forecast into specific segments (phases) and to ask questions continually on whether each segment has been performed for each forecast. In general, these phases are sequential, although it is often possible to perform two or more of the phases concurrently. Here are the six phases of a forecast study and some of the questions involved in performing them.

1. FORMULATING THE FORECASTING PROBLEM.   What is the decision to which the forecast applies? How will the decision be affected by various forecasts—that is, what types of decisions are most likely to be made and within what range of estimates will each decision fall? How firm is the decision—that is, can it be overridden later or can the strategy to which the decision applies be revised as the forecast is tracked and is found to be inaccurate? What is the value of the decision—that is, how many dollars are involved in the alternative strategies or decisions? (This will enable the forecaster to determine the cost benefits and hence the cost effectiveness of the forecast study.)

What data are available or can be obtained? How soon will the decision be made and what are the effects of a delay in the decision? How well does the decision maker understand the environment pertaining to the decision? Does he have a good understanding of the relevant factors or will it be necessary to obtain better and more meaningful relationships? How much previous market research or analyses have been done in the area under study?

2. *Structuring the Forecast.*   After the dynamics of the environment to which the forecast applies have been identified, they should be put in a flow-chart form so that the analyst can study them and choose the one or more techniques most appropriate. The flow chart will include not only the various elements of the system and the way they relate to each other and the different parts of the pipeline, but it will also indicate in some way where data are available or how readily they can be obtained.

In structuring the forecast situation, the extent to which relationships are known—and the degree to which these relationships have been established—will determine how much research is necessary. It is at this point that the assumptions pertaining to the forecast must be explicitly stated. The importance or effect that each assumption has on the forecast must be estimated. What assumptions will delay or could prevent the major turning points in the S-shape to occur? Which assumptions will make the forecast come true and which will cause significant forecasting errors?

Success requires the balancing of technology, values, and customer wants. If these factors are all highly dependent on each other or are out of the control of the company for which the forecast is being prepared, the analyst will not be able to derive a forecast with a small error range.

At the conclusion of this phase, the analyst will select the techniques that will be initially used to derive the forecast. We say initially, since he may find that the techniques do not produce the desired accuracy. However, the techniques he chooses are the ones that are most likely to give him the type of accuracy that is required.

3. COLLECTING THE DATA. The first two phases will have identified how well the system is understood and (a) whether the relationships are not well known and must be established through detailed market analysis, or (b) whether the main job is getting data to estimate trends and getting coefficients for previously determined relationships.

Since market research can be very expensive, the research must be well designed. Much market research is performed and conducted such that it is very difficult, if possible at all, to draw inferences from the data collected. Hypotheses must be established in advance and the experiment designed so that inferences can be made. The hypotheses will be based on opinions of the persons available who are most knowledgeable about how the market functions. The analyst must anticipate what the decision will be for various results and hence for various relationships that are found in the marketplace.

It is of value, if it is possible to do so, to construct what we call a decision table, where the decisions are listed along one axis and the range of the forecasts along another. The table is then filled in to show which decisions will be made for the various ranges of the forecast.

In designing market research, the analyst must work with persons with marketing expertise so that the correct questions are asked. For example, in the case of products such as appliances, the question may be: What brand will they buy and at what cost?

4. ANALYZING THE DATA AND CONSTRUCTING THE MODEL. Analyses will often include the use of a variety of statistical techniques, such as analysis

of variance and regression analysis, to identify relationships and incorporate them into the forecast model. The data will then be used to establish the model parameters.

As we have previously stated, the data should not be run through a variety of statistical techniques to attempt to establish relationships, but rather to test hypotheses to see if they are true. If the most likely relationships are not found to be statistically significant, new hypotheses must be tested. The analyst should try to identify the next most likely set of hypotheses and to design the data collection so that these hypotheses also can be tested.

The final model will provide not only a method for preparing the forecast, but it will also provide the capability for estimating the accuracy of the forecast.

5. PREPARING THE FORECAST. The model will then be used to prepare the forecast and the degree or measure of variability. (Hopefully, by this time, any previous biases have been eliminated so that the forecast is completely objective.)

In the early stages of the forecast, the analyst will have determined the range of the "reasonable" forecast, and he will now check to see if the forecast falls within this range. If it does not, he must be prepared to defend it, since the forecast will most likely be questioned.

The forecasting manager should keep a record of how often the forecast model conforms to expert opinion and how often it is different. If the forecast-model relationships are always the same as expert opinion, he should become concerned, since he should quite often discover anomalies in the environment that have not previously been determined and that will significantly revise his perception of the system.

It is at this point that the forecasting manager should closely examine the range or estimate of variability of the forecast. If the range is proportionately large in comparison with the forecast, the manager should determine whether sufficient analyses have been performed.

6. TRACKING THE FORECAST. Are the assumptions being tracked—that is, are data being obtained to ascertain what assumptions are valid and are other data being collected to determine whether relationships are remaining constant or changing? Are the models being updated as new data are collected?

Is the tracking being done on a timely basis? The answer to this question will depend on the checkpoints or the times at which strategy can be effectively revised. Data should be collected and new forecasts prepared prior to these points in time.

The manager of forecasting should develop measures to evaluate the level of completeness to which each of these phases of forecasting are performed. These may be quite simple measures, such as whether documents exist to show work has been done or whether some rating method is required to establish how well the activities have been performed. Again, for an accurate forecast, the measurement of output can be done with a simple arithmetic comparison of to what extent new relationships and better understanding of the system under study have been established.

BUDGETING FOR FORECASTING ACTIVITIES

In a sense, we might call budgeting a forecasting effort. Some form of a forecasting model is needed here, just as in the cases of the preparation of other forecasts. It is not sufficient to merely do time-series analysis or trend projection. This is because the demand for forecasts are very much a function of the types of businesses currently undertaken by the company and the number of new studies that are initiated.

For example, in one year, many new products may be in the development and introduction stages, and forecasts must be prepared for them. The manager should therefore keep sufficient records to indicate the amount of forecasting effort required for new products versus established products.

(In general, more effort will be required during the testing and early introduction stages than after more complete data are available, although —as we have indicated—the amount or intensity of analysis will depend on the value of decision.)

Hence the manager should examine the plans for the year to determine what types of decisions must be made and when they will be made. There may be a serious problem concerning the distribution of effort required for the forecasts, since many of the decisions may fall within the same time period. In this case, there is little difference between the scheduling for forecasting and scheduling for production. If there are several major forecasting projects, it is of value to use PERT or some similar technique for scheduling the overall forecasting effort.

EVALUATING THE FORECASTER

The criteria here are very similar to those used by the manager to evaluate the overall forecasting activity. He will want to know how well each forecaster is accomplishing the various phases of the forecasting project. Therefore, the manager will request data to be collected so that it can be used to evaluate individual forecasters as well.

There are also other ways in which the manager can evaluate the forecasters. One of these is the number of requests for an individual forecaster, when the consumer requests a specific service from the forecasting activity. The manager can deduce that a request for a specific analyst's services indicates satisfaction with the latter's previous work. On the opposite end, how many complaints or indications of dissatisfaction has the manager received about an analyst's work? Obviously, the manager should keep records on the accuracy of forecasts, the ratio of forecasting errors to forecasts, and other similar statistics for his own use in comparing or seeing differences among individual forecasters.

There are four other important factors that the manager should consider in evaluating a particular forecaster.

1. THE CHANGING ENVIRONMENT.   Has the forecaster accumulated sufficient knowledge to comprehend the changing business climate? Does he consider information about changing life-styles, values, and consumer wants? Has he considered the demographic trends that are available from the Department of Commerce's Bureau of Census or Bureau of Labor Statistics? Has he considered the energy and balance-of-payments problems facing our nation?

Has he studied, for example, the implications of the serious inflation trend? (The Economic Forecasting Institute, Inc., is predicting an inflation rate of 10 to 12% in the early 1980s.) The forecaster must be ready and willing to incorporate the impact of inflation and other economic factors into his forecasts.

How well does he understand the role of government and other consumer crusaders? Product development business strategies must take these kinds of pressures into account in setting future strategies.

How does the trend of multinationalism and the way other nations are competing with the United States affect his forecast? Japan and Western Europe are now exceedingly strong competitors to the United States. Where relevant, foreign competition should be reflected in product forecasts.

What consideration has the forecaster given to the availability of resources? Many nations are only now realizing the potential value of their resources.

2. THE CLIENT'S SATISFACTION.   Does the client feel that the forecaster has reflected his thinking and understanding into the forecast? If not, is

the client satisfied that the analyst has explained or shown why he has not?

This consideration will be reflected in the influence that the forecast has on the decision, so that it may not be necessary to ask these questions. Obviously, if the forecast is not used, the manager should attempt to ascertain why the client has not used it.

3. THE FORECASTER'S FAMILIARITY WITH VARIOUS TECHNIQUES.   Does he limit himself to only one or two favorites or does he select from a wide range of techniques? Does he modify them as necessary to the situation at hand? It often happens that a forecaster is biased and thus tends to force all problems to be formulated so that his pet techniques are appropriate. The manager should continually assess whether the analyst is technique- or problem-oriented.

4. THE FORECASTER'S WORKING RELATIONSHIPS.   To what extent has the analyst been able to get the client and those working with him involved in the preparation of the forecast? Has there been a good working relationship with considerable interaction or has the analyst prepared the forecast primarily in isolation? As in most staff activities, it is important to have a cooperative effort in the forecasting process.

While the manager may not feel that some of these considerations are necessary, forecasting is the type of staff activity where an analyst can be fortunate (you might call him lucky) over a short period of time and hence provide accurate forecasts. Nevertheless, he may not be following the steps that should be taken for consistency over time. Consider some of the nationally known economic forecasters who do quite will when the economy is relatively stable but when there are significant changes do not do nearly so well as other forecasters. Experience shows that the forecasters who do a consistently good job are those who follow most of the principles that we have described in this book. The same is true for other types of forecasting.

As in any discipline, the ability to be continually effective depends on adherence to the principles related to the discipline. It is not sufficient to have only a few measures of forecasting effectiveness, such as accuracy and direct incorporation of the forecast into the decision. Over the long term, several forecasting principles should be followed to ensure continued effectiveness in a forecasting area. Although there are always exceptional persons who can do outstanding work without following previously proven principles, most forecasters who are successful over the long run follow the specific principles outlined here and in the other chapters.

IN SUMMARY

The manager of a forecasting group should be aware of the steps good analysts take in preparing their forecasts; and he should assess the people who work for him according to how thoroughly and effectively each analyst performs those steps. The effective forecaster will consider all important factors (sorting out the important factors), often discovering new relationships that will be of value in other decisions as well as the one to which his forecast applies.

Chapter XVI

Forecasting Techniques of the Future

In conclusion, it is appropriate that we make a prediction about the techniques that will be used in the short- and long-term future. Although this at first appears to be a very formidable task, it is in reality rather easy, especially with respect to the next five years; it is not too difficult to forecast the immediate future, since long-term trends do not change overnight.

We might use the analogy we heard some years ago in a management meeting, where there was considerable concern and discussion about the future profit situation. The president of the company had described how the current and projected profit statistics indicated lower earnings, and he had raised the question about what might be done to correct the situation. After many suggestions had been submitted about possible new courses of action, one of the vice-presidents indicated that he did not think any new actions were required. In his words, the managers weren't "dancing as well as they knew how to."

Similarly, we do not believe that any significantly new or different forecasting techniques are needed in great demand or will emerge in the next 10 years. Instead, we think that those previously described in this book will not only be applied in greater and more diverse decision situations but also with increased proficiency. The proportion of situations in which a particular technique is used will change, and more accurate forecasts will be derived from the same technique than previously. We shall therefore describe how we believe the techniques will be applied in the future and the intensity of their use.

LOWER COMPUTATIONAL COSTS

The cost of using forecasting techniques, and particularly the more sophisticated and comprehensive ones, will be reduced significantly, which will enhance their implementation. We expect computer time-sharing companies to offer access at nominal cost to input-output data banks, broken down into more business segments than are available today. Such services are now offered by a few consulting companies at an annual software "rental fee" of $5000 to $20,000 plus costs of computer time. Experience shows that the availability of such a service, once it has been purchased, leads to considerable computer usage. Accordingly, many companies will prefer to purchase such services for in-house usage, rather than to have them on time sharing.

The continuing declining trend in computer cost per computation, along with computational simplifications, will make techniques such as the Box-Jenkins method economically feasible, even for some inventory-control applications (high-cost parts). Computer software packages for the Box-Jenkins technique, other statistical techniques, and some general models will become available at a nominal cost (e.g., the University of Wisconsin sells the Box-Jenkins computer program for $50.)

Virtually all of the time-series analysis techniques are now offered by various time-sharing services. The ease of performing analyses in an interactive mode will accelerate considerably the acceptance and routine use of these techniques. APL (which stands for *A Programming Language*) is rapidly becoming accepted as a time-sharing language that can be both quickly learned by noncomputer-trained persons and effectively utilized for analytical purposes and planning information systems. One APL service (Scientific Time Sharing) offers a forecasting package developed by Robert G. Brown, who has been responsible for much of the developmental work in exponential smoothing and adaptive forecasting. All of the large computer companies provide some form of forecasting software.

With the rapid and relatively low-cost availability of forecasting techniques, there will be a tendency to overuse them—that is, to apply them in situations where forecasts are not really needed. To help the manager detect such situations, Brown has prepared the following list of questions and comments to ascertain whether the decision maker can truly profit from computer-aided forecasting.

● Do you carry stocks of material to meet demand? If you can buy or build to order, you don't need much of a forecast.

- Are there a great many different items in stock?
- If you only stock half a dozen or so items, you can keep track of the market in your head.
- Are there many different customers for most stocked material?
- If you are a captive supplier to one large customer, get an estimate of requirements from him.
- Do you carry similar merchandise over several selling seasons?
- Even if the particular items change from time to time, you can forecast the market for a functional need.
- Is your market growing and shifting under competitive and economic pressures?
- If you have the only drug store in a remote village, who cares about services?
- If you have to anticipate demand for many items sold to a broad market base and need to provide good service, modern techniques of statistical forecasting can markedly improve your performance.

At the present time, most short-term forecasting uses only statistical methods, with little qualitative information being considered. Since qualitative information is only used in an external way, it is not directly incorporated into the computational routine.

We predict a change to total forecasting systems, where several techniques are tied together, such as exponential smoothing and the Census Bureau X-11, along with a systematic handling of qualitative information. Some companies, which have manual override features in their statistical models (e.g., to change the seasonals or trends), will take the next logical step of putting in "qualitative" statements (such as "sales promotions are now in June instead of March") and letting the computer then make the necessary adjustments. Statistical-analysis routines (e.g. analysis of variance, spectral-density analysis) will in some instances become integral parts of the forecasting models.

ECONOMETRIC MODELS

These will be utilized more extensively in the next five years, with most large companies developing and refining econometric models of their major businesses. This is already being done to some extent, since with large economic data bases and econometric model-building statistical routines now available on time sharing, it is economically feasible to do such work. (Most companies have found it too costly to establish and maintain their own data bases, and to develop or modify their statistical routines.)

Econometric models of the United States economy are now available for corporate economists to generate forecasts based on their own set of assumptions (General Electric and other companies are already doing this).

The Economic Forecasting Unit at Wharton is engaged in a large-scale project with other countries that will lead to a world econometric model (however, continually changing economic relationships will make this difficult). Input from such a world model will make corporate international-investment models more accurate.

The Box-Jenkins technique permits the forecaster not only to design his own model, but also to incorporate special information and relationships with other variables. Accordingly, it is not difficult to see how the Box-Jenkins technique will be "merged" with econometric models to provide forecasts for lower volume items, so that the forecasts will not be purely statistical. Information from the econometric models, which will provide estimates of the effects of the United States economy on larger product classes, will be applied to the items within that product class.

Econometric models are presently revised "manually" as new information becomes available. (We say manually because the effects of the new data are first analyzed, and then the model is updated as necessary.) Econometric models will become more adaptive, since the parameters will automatically change as new data are obtained and put into the data bank supporting the model. (That is, the parameters will be stochastic, and new values will be taken on as additional data are inserted.)

We shall not attempt to further discuss the future of econometric models, since this has been ably done by a number of persons. An article by Otto Eckstein and Donald L. McLagan provides one such example, where they describe how corporate information is combined with national economic data to enable managers and investors to model a firm's future more accurately.[67]

We discussed in Chapter 11 how econometric models and input-output models are merged to complement each other, with the econometric models supplying inputs to I-O for the next two years and the I-O models providing inputs to the econometric models for longer-range economic forecasts. In addition, we see more extensive use of I-O in the next 10 years.

[67] See "National Economic Models Help Business to Focus on the Future," *Computer Decisions*, October 1971, p. 12.

INPUT-OUTPUT MODELS

We have previously attempted to describe both current and future I-O applications. However, there are several considerations (and dangers) to take into account in using I-O.

1. Even though the I-O models and services provided by consulting companies are very similar, the outputs or forecasts are quite different. One reason is due to the inputs, which depend on information available to the persons preparing the I-O forecast, their assessment or interpretation of the information, and the subsequent assumptions on which the forecast is based (e.g., trends, turning points, new technologies). Most of the companies have different sources of information and different methods of analyzing it.

2. I-O models start with gross numbers (high levels of aggregation) obtained from the government and then break down the data into smaller industrial and economic sectors. Generally, the information for this disaggregation is not available from companies, and it is necessary to make "educated guesses." We have found instances where such estimates are significantly in error (in situations where we had access to confidential industry data).

Moreover, it is necessary to make forecasts of the technological coefficients, which require technological forecasting. The various consulting companies use different "experts," which can lead to different technological forecasts. The assumptions of the long-term growth rate in real GNP can account for some of the variation in I-O. For the three major I-O models, the estimates of GNP growth rate were: Arthur D. Little, 4.5%; University of Maryland, 4.1%; and Battelle Institute, 3.3%.

Hence it is not surprising that, of the top 30 long-term growth industry forecasts for these companies, there was little consistency. Not one industry was on all three lists of the 30 companies; and, of the top 10 for each model, only three industries appeared on any two of the lists. Continuing this comparison, we found that only 11 industries appeared on any two of the listings.

3. As companies attempt to develop their own I-O models, they often have to rely on outside data sources. Several of these MIS services have sprung up, such as Predicast, Economic Information Systems, and Dun and Bradstreet. What some of these services have done is to reproduce government and other data that may be three or four years old. They then apply some form of an update method.

Whether using a commercially available MIS or a national I-O model service, the reader should investigate how the data are obtained, how they are analyzed, what the method of projection was, where they got the data from, and whether it involved getting proprietary data that companies usually do not release.

For example, the I-O data from Dun and Bradstreet, which has approximately 11,000 persons collecting data on public companies, have generally been proven reliable.

We expect the consulting services to develop better methods for filtering data and making projections. As these take place, there will be increasing use of I-O. The major applications will be in identifying market opportunities, in using the I-O tables as guides to industry trends, and in studying product and material flows (which will serve as inputs into product-decision models).

SIMULATION MODELS

Over the longer term, consumer simulation models will become commonplace. The models will predict the behavior of the consumer and forecast his or her reactions to various marketing strategies such as pricing, promotions, new product introductions, and competitive actions. It will take several years of development for these models to provide sufficient accuracy. Considerable market research will be necessary to establish the needed relationships.

In one sense, the simulation models will supply the direction for a total coordinated market research program. As special studies are performed to obtain information for an imminent decision, the studies will be designed also to provide inputs for the simulation model.

Conceptual models will first be developed to determine the sensitivity of the model to the assumed relationships and individual factors, and market experiments will be conducted to validate or change the most critical parameters. In this way, there will be tracking systems for continually updating and improving the models until they yield the desired accuracy. Heuristic programming will be a vehicle for refining simulation and other large causal models.

Although only a few such simulation models have thus far been developed, others are currently in process. We believe consumer simulation models will be a necessity in the highly competitive markets. The byproduct of the market research—better understanding of the consumer—will easily be worth the cost of the model development. Most of the techniques needed for good market research exist, and the primary attention will be given to better methods for relating consumer responses to subsequent market decisions.

Also, we anticipate improvement first in the design of market surveys and other methods for signaling changes in social trends and consumer preferences, and then in their application to planning and other decision-making situations, where turning points must be identified well ahead of when they will occur. As we have indicated, statistical techniques at best will signal turning points as they occur. Hence more extensive tracking systems, similar to those described in Chapter 13, will be utilized.

In an article describing the activities of The Institute for the Future, reference was made to research on computers involving the collection and organization of the opinions of large numbers of people.[68] This research will make it possible to focus a greater collective wisdom on social problems, and it should also be applicable to many other forecasting and tracking problems.

This article also discussed how the Institute for the Future uses pre-modeling, which is the determination of the significant variables in a futures or forecasting inquiry, and a description of their interrelationships and interactions prior to detailed modeling. Premodeling is of value because many future's studies start at the point at which the general area for focus is yet to be selected, the decision to be made is yet to be defined, or the information to be collected is yet to be determined. Premodeling of some kind must be done to describe interrelationships and interactions among forecasts generated independently (e.g., social, economic, technological).

Here, more effective methods must be found for linking forecasts in one area to conditional statements used as the basis for forecasts in other areas. The tools that are presently employed for doing this—cross-impact analysis, scenario writing, and gaming simulations—are even less well-defined than those for forecasting. We expect these methods to be developed, which will enhance the application of the technological, economic, and sociological forecasting techniques.

MAN-MACHINE SYSTEMS

The announcement in June 1973 by F. W. Dodge Division of McGraw-Hill Information Systems Company of its "Dodge Product Potentials" is

[68] See "The Institute for the Future: Its Evolving Role," *The Futurist*, June 1973, p. 123.

an example of new services that will be made available in the next few years. This computerized service combines Dodge's current new-construction data with "product use" factors by building type, and with shipment "timing factors" by building size. This produces information and forecasts of the different kinds of products that will be needed within the next four calendar quarters by 28 different kinds of structures, throughout the 50 states, subdivided further by various sales territories in terms of dollar value, tons, and barrels, for example.

Data Resources, Inc., has built a very useful time-sharing economic data bank that, along with accessibility to various statistical techniques on time sharing, makes the job of model-building less cumbersome. We have already realized greater time savings in building models with the aid of these time-sharing services. The data bank will be expanded soon to include economic data for many countries throughout the world, which is extremely important for a multinational corporation.

The exploitation of time sharing for forecasting has been discussed earlier. Within five years, we shall see extensive use of man-machine systems, where statistical, causal, and econometric models are programmed on computers, with man interacting frequently. As we gain confidence in such systems, so that there is less exception reporting, human intervention will decrease.

Basically, computerized models will do the sophisticated computations, and man will serve more as a generator of ideas and a developer of systems. For example, man will study market dynamics and establish more complex relationships between the factor being forecast and those of the forecasting system.

Finally, the application of sophisticated forecasting techniques will extend to areas beyond sales, such as personnel requirements, capital expenditures, unit manufacturing costs, R&D expenditures, and other important factors. In many cases, these factors at best are given superficial treatment, with only the simplest forecasting methods and principles being applied. The attitude is that the biggest unknown is sales, and all other factors are simple to forecast compared with sales.

However, we are finding that the "simple" relationships between these factors and sales are becoming more complex and are requiring forecasting models. As these applications are made, and forecasting for established and stable product businesses is fully computerized, the forecaster will be freed to spend most of his time forecasting sales and profits of new products.

Doubtless, new analytical techniques will be developed for new-product forecasting, but there will be a continuing problem for at least 10 to 20 years and probably longer in accurately forecasting various new-product factors, such as sales profitability and length of life cycle. While we see the accuracy of the forecasts and the scientific discipline improving, we still feel that forecasting will remain an art in the immediate future.

IN SUMMARY

The techniques now available and described in this book are the ones that will be more extensively and expertly applied in the next 10 to 20 years. Not only will the analysts become more expert in their use, but managers will become more comfortable "in accepting them," and using them in their decision making. We shall learn to "dance as well as we know how" before looking for new and better techniques.

Appendix A

Bibliography for Forecasting and Market Research Techniques

The literature included in this bibliography is not exhaustive. A brief description provides the reader with some idea of the content of the book or article. We have included the publications that we feel are the best sources for describing the techniques at the elementary or intermediate levels. In a few instances, we have given complete lists of references for a specific subject. Within each category (technique), the literature is listed in sequence of increasing difficulty. More advanced books are included only if they are the only or best source known to the authors on a particular subject.

Moving Averages, Exponential Smoothing, and Trend Projections

1. Brown, R. G., see reference 1 under section entitled "Miscellaneous."
2. Imperial Chemical Industries, *Techniques of Production Control* (Princeton, N.J.: D. Van Nostrand Co., Inc., 1964). The book is divided into three sections: (1) *Mathematical Trend Curves: An Aid to Forecasting*, which is primarily concerned with the slope-characteristic technique; (2) *Short-Term Forecasting*—an elementary treatment on exponential smoothing emphasizing Winter's method; and (3) *Cumulative Sum Techniques*, which are very useful for tracking and warning.
3. Brown, R. G., *Statistical Forecasting for Inventory Control* (New York:, McGraw-Hill Book Company, 1959). A very good discussion on the application of exponential smoothing techniques in production planning and inventory control. It has the unusual characteristic of containing mathematically oriented models and still being an easy book to read.

4. Dudman, R. S., *Forecasting with Three-Factor Adaptive Smoothing*, presented at the 13th International Meeting of TIMS (Philadelphia: The Institute of Management Sciences, 1966). An interesting article on the use of Holt's method for forecasting and how long-term stability can be built into these forecasts.

5. Hadley, G., *Introduction to Business Statistics* (San Francisco, Holden-Day, Inc., 1968). This is an excellent book on basic statistics. It contains a very good treatment of both regression analysis and time-series analysis (in particular, seasonality and moving averages), and requires only a good working knowledge of algebra.

6. Harrison, P. J. "Short-Term Sales Forecasting," *Applied Statistics*, Vol. 14, Nos. 2 and 3, 1965, p. 102-139. This is a critical review of various short-term forecasting techniques. Also included are the author's suggested modifications to these techniques, using Fourier analysis in the estimation of seasonal factors. A hybridized version of his suggestions was found to provide good results in applications at the Corning Glass Works.

7. Johnson, N. L., and F. C. Leone, *Cumulative Sum Control Charts*, June, July, and August, 1962, Milwaukee, Industrial Quality Control. The best source available on the underlying statistical theory for cumulative-sum techniques. These articles are statistically advanced but are complete.

8. Kendall, M. G., *The Advanced Theory of Statistics*, Vol. 3 (New York: Hafner Publishing Company, Inc., 1966). A mathematically focused book well worth reading for the advanced analyst. The first part of the book is concerned with experimental designs and multivariate techniques. More important, however, the last part of the book discusses time-series analysis. It is the best treatment on moving averages available, describing how they may be designed for a particular application.

Regression Analysis and Econometrics

1. Bennion, E. G., see reference 1 under "Miscellaneous."

2. Spencer, M. H., C. G. Clark, and P. W. Hoguet, *Business and Economic Forecasting* (Homewood: Richard D. Irwin, Inc., 1961). Although we disagree with their statistical approaches to estimating the parameters of a predicting equation (stagewise regression analysis), the book is very instructive in how to build such a model. It is full of interesting examples and hints about how to form hypotheses to be tested in econometrics and perform preliminary analyses. It is a very readable book, requiring little mathematical background.

3. Elliott-James, M. F., *Economic Forecasting and Corporate Planning* (New York: The Conference Board, 1973). An excellent discussion on the use of regression analysis and econometrics in forecasting. It contains an example of how economic theory is merged with regression analysis (econometrics).

4. Clelland, R. C., J. S. DeCani, F. E. Brown, J. P. Bursh, and D. S. Murray, *Basic Statistics with Business Applications* (New York: John Wiley and Sons, Inc., 1966). This book includes chapters on the analysis of economic time series, index numbers, regresssion analysis, and econometric models. It does require a knowledge of elementary calculus; nevertheless, it is a very readable book.

5. Harberger, A. C., editor, *The Demand for Durable Goods* (Chicago: University of Chicago Press, 1967) . This book consists of several econometric studies of durable

goods demand (e.g., refrigerators, automobiles). It contains some classic studies by such noted economists as Gregory C. Chow.

6. Chow, Gregory C., "Technological Change and the Demand for Computers," *The American Economic Review*, December 1966. A good discussion on how to use the Gompertz and Logistic growth curves when building econometric models for products that have not reached the steady state of their life cycle.

7. Houthaker, H. S., and L. D. Taylor, "Consumer Demand in the United States," *Analyses and Projections with Applications to Other Countries* (Cambridge, Mass.: Harvard University Press, 1970). This comprehensive analytical study of the composition and magnitude of consumer expenditures for over 80 commodities in the United States is quite interesting for those attempting for the first time to build an econometric model of their consumption sector.

8. Draper, N. R., and H. Smith, *Applied Regression Analysis* (New York: John Wiley and Sons, Inc., 1967). An excellent introduction to regression analysis. Probably the best introductory text in print from the user's standpoint. It covers many of the more subtle aspects necessary for the intelligent use of regression analysis. The use of matrix algebra is introduced and developed.

9. Christ, C. F., *Econometric Models and Methods* (New York: John Wiley and Sons, Inc., 1966). A very good introductory text on the subject of econometrics. The more advanced aspects of statistics and mathematics necessary for the study of econometrics are covered as necessary. There are many illustrations.

10. Klein, L. R., editor, *Studies in Quantitative Econometrics*, Vols. II, III, IV and V (Philadelphia: University of Pennsylvania, 1969). Volume II is entitled *The Wharton Econometric Forecasting Model* and gives good insight into the nature and equations of a macroeconometric model. Volumes III to V are *Essays in Industrial Econometrics:* each has complete and comprehensive examples of econometric models at the industry level. They are very instructive in showing how such models are built and the systematic hypothesizing that goes into them.

11. Evans, M. K., *Macroeconomic Activity, Theory, Forecasting, and Control* (New York: Harper and Row, Publishers, 1969). An econometric approach to macroeconomic theory. It has an especially good critique of forecasting with leading indicators and anticipatory data, and of econometric models at the macro level. The book requires the reader to be conversant with mathematics.

12. Pyatt, Graham F., *Priority Patterns and the Demand for Household Durable Goods* (London: Cambridge University Press, 1964). A very mathematical discussion of household priority patterns, and of the way in which the demand for durable goods will vary as family budgets change.

13. Davis, B. E., G. J. Caccappolo, and M. A. Chaudry, "An Econometric Planning Model for American Telephone and Telegraph Company," *The Bell Journal of Economics and Management Science*, Vol. 4, No. 1, Spring 1973.

Market Research Statistical Techniques

1. Shainin, D., see reference 1 in "Miscellaneous."

2. Moroney, M.J.,*Facts from Figures*, Third Edition (Baltimore: Penguin Books, Inc., 1963). This is a well-written book on basic statistics that reads like a novel.

It requires no strong mathematical background and covers the subject in an interesting way.

3. Ferber, Robert, editor, *Determinants of Investment Behavior* (National Bureau of Economic Research, New York: Columbia University Press, 1967). The section entitled "Consumer Expenditures for Durable Goods" by M. Snowbarger and D. B. Suits, pp. 333-354, has many good illustrations on the use of the AID technique in the analysis of cross-sectional data.

4. Sonquist, J. A., *Multivariate Model Building: The Validation of a Search Strategy* (Ann Arbor: University of Michigan, 1970). This is the best book available on the intelligent application and interpretation of the AID (Automatic Interaction Detector) technique. It also provides validation of this sequential data-analysis procedure. It is written in a sociological context and is mostly nonmathematical.

5. Harman, H. H., *Modern Factor Analysis* (Chicago: University of Chicago, 1960). This is an in-depth study into the mathematics and use of factor analysis. The examples are taken from the field of psychology. The book is missing some of the newer extensions of factor analysis; nevertheless is "must" reading for the serious students of multivariate techniques.

6. Tintner, G., *Econometrics* (New York: John Wiley and Sons, Inc., 1965). This book is different from other books on econometrics. It gives an introduction to econometrics, multivariate analysis, and time-series analysis. It is rich with examples and "puts the pieces together." It does require, however, a fair mathematical background, but the examples can still be read to show some of the many applications of multivariate techniques.

7. Morrison, D. F. *Multivariate Statistical Methods* (New York: McGraw-Hill Book Company, 1967). An elementary treatment of multivariate statistics, requiring a good background in calculus and elementary mathematical statistics. It is fairly complete, but the examples are taken mainly from the behavioral sciences.

Input-Output Models

1. Leontief, W., *Input-Output Economics* (New York: Oxford University Press, 1966). A very readable first course in input-output economics. The book progresses from the simple to the complex, with the latter part of the book discussing some of the mathematical aspects of I-O theory.

Time-Series Analysis and Box-Jenkins Technique

1. McLaughlin, R. L., *Time Series Forecasting*, Marketing Research Techniques Series No. 6, American Marketing Association, 1962. The best, if not the only, nontechnical description, tableau by tableau, of the Census Method II (X-11) deseasonalizing computer program.

2. Box, G. E. P., and G. M. Jenkins, *Time-Series Analysis Forecasting and Control* (San Francisco: Holden-Day, Inc., 1970). This is the authoritative book on the Box-Jenkins forecasting and control technique and also contains very good material on time-series analysis. It belongs in every serious analysts' library. It requires a strong mathematical and statistical background.

3. Granger, C. W. J., *Spectral Analysis of Economic Time Series* (Princeton: Princeton University Press, 1964). It is a mathematically advanced treatment of spectral techniques. It shows the results of spectral analyses of the National Bureau of Economic Research's leading, coincident, and lagging indicators of the economy. Spectral analysis theory is covered, together with some discussion of moving average theory.

Qualitative Techniques

1. Kiefer, David M., "The Futures Business," *Chemical and Engineering Journal*, August 11, 1969. This article describes how long-range forecasting is spreading from the think tanks into the executive suite as more companies and government agencies, in planning their operations, try to assess the future or several futures— beyond tomorrow. Various pioneering applications, including their success with these techniques, are discussed.

2. Martino, Joseph P., *Technological Forecasting for Decision-making* (New York: American Elsevier Publishing Company, Inc., 1972). A handbook on forecasting that can serve both the practitioner and the person seriously interested in using technological forecasting.

3. Bright, James R., *A Brief Introduction to Technology Forecasting: Concepts and Exercises* (Austin, Texas: Permaquid Press, 1972). A workbook designed for use in technology forecasting courses.

4. Martino, Joseph P., *An Introduction to Technological Forecasting* (New York: Gordon and Breach, Science Publishers, Inc., 1972). A selection of articles by experts in the field of technology forecasting.

Miscellaneous

1. Bursk, E. C., and J. F. Chapman, editors, *New Decision-Making Tools for Managers* (New York: Mentor Executive Library Books, The New American Library, Inc., 1963). This collection of articles previously published in the *Harvard Business Review*. Here are some of the articles pertinent to forecasting and well worth reading.
   - Miller, R. W., "How to Plan and Control With PERT."
   - Bennion, E. G., "Econometrics for Management."
   - Lipstein, B., "Tests for Test Marketing."
   - Brown, R. G., "Less Risk in Inventory Estimates."
   - Busch, G. A., "Prudent-Manager Forecasting."
   - Shainin, D., "The Statistically Designed Experiment."

2. King, J. R., *Probability Charts for Decision Making* (New York: Industrial Press, Inc., 1971). A unique and comprehensive coverage of the use and interpretation of various probability papers. The analysis of failure data is thoroughly covered together with a good discussion of binomial paper and how it may be used in new product forecasting.

Appendix B

Market Research Statistical Techniques

Multivariate Statistics

The importance and role of good market research in forecasting have been mentioned frequently throughout this book. We shall describe here the statistical techniques most frequently used by the market researcher, and refer to the dependent and independent variables, which are, respectively, the variables to be explained (effect) and the explanatory (causal) variables.

For example, if one is attempting to explain sales as determined by advertising expenditures, disposable income, and geographical location, sales is called the dependent variable and the other factors are called the independent variables.

All of the techniques we shall describe belong to the general classification called multivariate statistics. Broadly defined, this is the branch of statistics that simultaneously considers the effects that two or more independent variables have on one or more dependent variables, or that determines the latent structure of many independent variables. We consider multivariate statistics to be the main technique in the analysis of market research data, since they are the most appropriate in the multivariate, interdependent world in which we live.

All of these techniques require the use of a computer. The software needed is usually available at most computer centers. The data entry and computer cost to perform a typical analysis would vary from about $5 for a regression analysis to about $30 for an AID analysis. (These costs do not include the data collection effort.)

CLUSTER ANALYSIS. This technique is concerned with grouping entities into homogenous groups, based on several pertinent factors (or inde-

297

pendent variables) relating to these entities. In determining the effect of price on the sales of a product, cities may be classified into homogenous groups with respect to such characteristics as average income, unemployment rate, number of department stores, relative proportions of various ethnic groups, and similar factors.

For example, if five different cities are found to be statistically equivalent with respect to these variables, one city may be used as a control, with the product offered for sale at a given price, and each of the remaining four cities may offer the product for sale at four different prices. Since the cities are implicitly assumed to be similar with respect to the independent variables, the only difference in the relative sales rate would be attributed to the price level.

DISCRIMINANT ANALYSIS.   Like cluster analysis, discriminant analysis is also a classification technique. However, unlike cluster analysis, it is intended to predict the likelihood of an entity belonging to a *given* population, based on several predictor variables or characteristics of the entity. Discriminant analysis is appropriate when the dependent variable is nonmetric, in the sense that it may be dichotomous (male-female), trichotomous (high-medium-low), or multichotomous, if it is desired to classify an entity into one of these mutually exclusive and exhaustive groups.

Discriminant analysis has been used to predict whether a person is a good or bad credit risk based on his socioeconomic and demographic profile, to distinguish innovators from imitators by their psychological and socioeconomic profiles, and to separate private label buyers from national brand buyers by discriminating according to purchasing and socioeconomic factors.

MULTIPLE REGRESSION.   This is commonly called least squares, which we briefly described earlier. It is an appropriate method of analysis when the researcher has a single dependent variable that is hypothesized to be a function of one or more independent or predictor variables.

For example, sales might be predicted from previously determined past relationships with marketing efforts and disposable income. Market share has been found in several instances to be a function of retail structure and advertising and promotion.

Multiple regression does a good job when (a) the data are in relatively good shape (i.e., no missing observations for any of the variables), (b) the data are at least partially designed, (c) there is some idea of the important variables, and (d) the user has some preconceived notion of the structure of the data.

In short, multiple regression is used for determining and estimating how the variation in a dependent variable is related to one or more predictor variables via the least-squares methodology.

AUTOMATIC INTERACTION DETECTOR (AID) is a technique with the objective, when there is one dependent variable (e.g., sales, market share), generally being to identify the variables that most likely affect the value of the dependent variable. When the five conditions we just saw for multiple regression do not exist, AID is a very effective technique for establishing the relative importance and functional relationships of the independent variables to the dependent variable. As its name implies, however, AID is primarily concerned with identifying the interactions between the independent variables.

In a study to determine the important factors in the purchase of a refrigerator, the "tree" shown in Figure B.1 resulted. On the average, only 4% of the people bought refrigerators. Of the people who intended to buy a refrigerator, 27% did buy, and of those people 49% have disposable incomes of $4000 to $6000 and $7500 to $10,000. Of the people who did not expect to buy, 3% did in fact buy. Of the people who indicated during the initial interview that they did not know what their

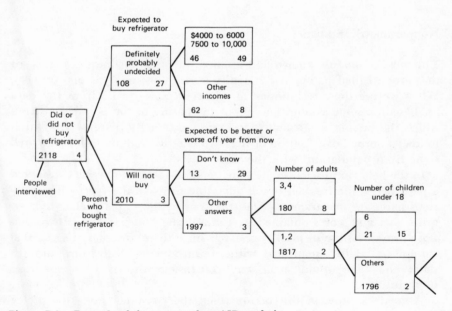

Figure B.1. Example of the output of an AID analysis.

situation would be a year from then but did not expect to buy, 29% did buy, and so forth.

The AID technique has been constructed so that no other combination of variables ("tree") will explain more variation in the dependent variable (in the example just cited, whether they did or did not buy) than the "tree" shown. Of course, this does not guarantee that all of the combinations are causal. It is especially valuable in analyzing questionnaires and other cross-section data, since it tells the user analyst what is in the data.

FACTOR ANALYSIS. This technique is primarily concerned with understanding the interdependence of several factors or independent variables. It attempts to find the variation that these factors have in common with each other. Factor analysis is based on the proposition that, if there is a systematic interdependence among a set of observed variables, this commonality must be a result of a more fundamental quality. Factor analysis is an excellent tool for reducing many independent variables to fewer, more conceptually basic, new variables or factors that are easier to understand from the marketing standpoint. An illustration of the use of factor analysis appears in Chapter 8. It is important to note that factor analysis does not utilize a dependent variable.

Nonparametric Statistics

The most commonly known and applied statistical techniques belong to that group called parametric statistics (e.g., t-tests, analysis of variance). When we use these techniques, any inferences we make from the data are based on some assumptions about the nature of the population from which the sample was drawn: for example, that the parent population follows a normal distribution or that two samples that are to be compared come from populations with the same variance.

In the behavioral sciences, of which market research may be considered a part, it is quite frequently not advisable to make the types of assumptions necessary in parametric statistics. Furthermore, parametric tests require that any scores obtained in a sample be numerical. Again, this is not always possible in market research since there are many factors that cannot be readily quantified without introducing distortions into the data, and that would make any conclusions drawn from the data doubtful.

A good example of this occurs when the consumer gives his preferences for several brands of the same product. Although he can rank the brands according to his likes and dislikes, he cannot accurately say, for example, that Brand A has a rating of 95.2 and Brand B a rating of 30.0, and then be able to add that he likes Brand A more than three times better than Brand B. In other word, he cannot accurately quantify his preferences; they are very subjective.

These kinds of problems led to the development of the branch of statistics called nonparametric statistics, which has these advantages.

1. They make no assumptions about the population being sampled.

2. They can be used on data that are measured on nominal, ordinal, or interval scales. A nominal scale is no more than classification of objects or persons (males vs. female; smoker vs. nonsmoker); an ordinal scale is the same as ranking; an interval scale is an ordinal scale with the additional condition that the "distances" between any two numbers on the scale are of known size.

Nonparametric statistics is a very large subject and includes many techniques. We shall not attempt to be comprehensive but shall describe the techniques only in general terms. The particular technique used depends on the number of samples being compared and whether the data are nominal, ordinal or interval scaled (these will be abbreviated, N. O, and I, respectively).

1. ONE-SAMPLE CASE. This kind of test tells us whether the particular sample could have come from some specified probability distribution.

    a. Binominal test (N)
    b. Chi-squared test (N)
    c. Kolmogorov-Smirnov test (O)
    d. Runs test (O)

2. TWO-SAMPLE CASE. This is used when it is desired to establish whether two treatments (e.g. two prices of a product) are different, or whether one treatment is "better" another. These are divided into two groups, for related or independent samples. An example of a related sample is that situation where a subject is used as his own control and is exposed to two different products at different times. If a different group of people is selected for the second product, this is called an independent sample.

Related samples
    a. McNemar test (N)
    b. Sign test (O)
    c. Wilcoxon matched-pairs signed-ranks test (O)
    d. Walsh test (I)
    e. Randomization test for matched pairs (I)

Independent samples
a. Fisher exact probability test (N)
b. Chi-Square (χ^2) test (N)
c. Median test (O)
d. Mann-Whitney U test (O)
e. Kolmogorov-Smirnov test (O)
f. Wald-Walfowitz test (O)
g. Moses test of extreme reactions (O)
h. Randomization test (I)

3. K-SAMPLE CASE. This is a generalization of the two sample case where we are now comparing more than two treatments.

Related samples
a. Cochran Q test (N)
b. Friedman two-way analysis of variance (O)

Independent samples
a. Chi-Square (χ^2) test (N)
b. Extension of the median test (O)
c. Kruskal-Wallis one-way analysis of variance (O)

4. NONPARAMETRIC MEASURES OF CORRELATION.
a. Contingency coefficient (N)
b. Rank correlation coefficients: Kendall and Spearman (O)
c. Kendall coefficient of concordance (O)

We hope that this summary of the major multivariate and nonparametric statistical techniques does not give the reader the impression that these techniques are "ends in themselves." That is, even the best techniques will not be of value if the data are not good; the "garbage in-garbage out" expression is most appropriate here.[69]

It often happens that the market researcher has little or no control over the levels of the variables that he observes and, in that situation, he has to do the best he can with what is available. On the other hand, the researcher frequently does have control over the levels of the variables that he observes. Therefore, he should select those variables, the levels of each variable, and the combinations of the levels of the variables that will give him the most information for his money and effort. This is what the subject called "the design of experiments" is all about.

[69] All of these techniques are well explained with easy-to-understand examples in Sidney Siegel, *Nonparametric Statistics for the Behavioral Sciences* (New York: McGraw-Hill Book Company, 1956). It is a very readable book and only requires an elementary statistical background.

In talking about processes, D. Shainin said:

"The essential feature of the most up-to-date statistically designed experiment is the simultaneous consideration of a large number (sometimes all) of the possible causes for a product or process problem. It can categorically rule out most of the possible causes after a limited number of experiments. This means that the major source of trouble can be more and more closely pinned down until it is finally isolated.

The approach often makes use of, but never depends on, hunches and guesses in problem diagnosis. If the initial hunches happen to be right, the time for the experiment may be cut down; yet, if the hunches are wrong, as only too often happens, the experimenters' efforts are not held up until new hypotheses can be formulated. Because statistical design can impartially evaluate most or all of the causes of a problem, it is a completely objective device.

Finally, acceptance or rejection of hypotheses and consideration of alternatives can be evaluated in terms of known confidence levels. The risk of wrong decision can be reduced, for all practical purposes, almost to zero.[70]

These same remarks apply equally to market research. The analyst must combine a sound knowledge of statistical techniques with a well-disciplined approach to experimental design if he is to obtain the relationships that will lead to good forecasting.

[70] "The Statistically Designed Experiment" in E. C. Bursk and J. F. Chapmen, editors, *New Decision Making Tools for Managers* (New York: Mentor Executive Library Books, The New American Library, 1963).

Index

DATE DUE

DATE DUE			
APR 29 '80			
NOV 27 '84			
DEC 3 '85			
DEC 20 '85			
AP 01 '88			
AP 29 '88			
DEC 06 1996			